The World Crisis
Its Economic and Social Impact on the Underdeveloped Countries

Fidel Castro

Maroon Publishing House, Morant Bay, Jamaica

Zed Books Ltd., 57 Caledonian Road, London N1 9BU

IN DE KNIPSCHEER HAARLEM

The World Crisis was published in 1984.

In the United Kingdom
Zed Books Ltd.
57 Caledonian Road, London N1 9BU

In the West Indies
Maroon Publishing House
Morant Bay P.O., St. Thomas, Jamaica.

In the Netherlands
In de Knipscheer, PO Box 6107, 2001 HC Haarlem

Originally published in a limited edition by the Oficina de
Publicaciones del Consejo de Estado, Havana, in 1983
under the title: *The World Economic and Social Crisis: Its
Impact on the Underdeveloped Countries, Its Somber
Prospects and the Need to Struggle if we are to Survive — a
Report to the Seventh Summit Conference of Non-Aligned
Countries.*

Cover design by Magenta Design
Printed by Cox and Wyman Ltd.

British Library Cataloguing in Publication Data

Castro, Fidel
   The World Crisis.
   1. Developing countries — Economic conditions
   I. Title
330.9172'4   HC59.7

ISBN 0-86232-250-2
ISBN 0-86232-251-0 Pbk

NL ISBN
90 6265 169 0

US Distributor
Biblio Distribution Center, 81 Adams Drive, Totowa,
New Jersey, 07512.

Distinguished Heads of State,
Government Leaders,
Political Leaders and Statesmen in general, and especially of
the Third World:

The report we put before you is not the fruit of my personal effort alone. It stems from concerns, thoughts and ideas I have expressed over the last few years at various international meetings, the United Nations included. However, they have now been developed and elaborated in greater depth with the necessary and decisive cooperation of a group of young economists from the World Economic Research Center, set up in our country a few years ago, and the International Economic Research Center of the School of Economics of the University of Havana.

It was necessary to gather, arrange and analyze thousands of dispersed data in publications put out by the most prestigious international agencies and specialized journals on each of the subjects taken up. This may well be the first time core questions of crucial importance to our countries have been compiled in a single document, from the world economic perspective outlined by the Movement of Non-Aligned Countries at successive Summit Conferences.

Hard work has been done for its preparation, but circumstances have been pressing and time short for such an ambitious endeavor. There has been some inevitable reiteration on certain questions in order to examine each problem carefully. This is because of the inseparable relationship between certain phenomena and the various topics taken up in each chapter.

We thought it would be of interest to provide the Heads of State or Government and political leaders in general – especially those of the Third World – with official data that are beyond suspicion of bias and demonstrate the tragedy of our peoples. We have sought to do so with an economy of data and explanation, since we know that those of us with public responsibilities have little time in the midst of weighty problems. It is written, moreover, in simple, straightforward language. While we derive great experience from the exercise of our functions as Heads of State or Government, we do not have the privilege of being – nor could we be – specialists in all economic and social spheres. We are basically politicians – in itself one of the most difficult tasks in today's world – and above all we must be responsible ones.

We know, moreover, and have borne this in mind, that as public figures we are as a rule reluctant to use very abstract language and highly technical terms. I, at least, feel this way, and I never try to explain – I could not – that which is not perfectly clear to me.

I am convinced that it is utterly impossible to situate ourselves in the reality of today's world if the panorama presented by the facts and problems set forth here is not made readily available to statesmen for their daily use and profound meditation.

This is why we attempted to compile the data leading to a diagnosis that is familiar to us all, but which we have not always been able to back with the hard statistics as such.

Many will find in this book an exact portrait of the distressing difficulties they each face today.

I am aware that our world – I refer especially to the Third World – takes in an enormous variety of widely differing concepts, ideologies, beliefs and perceptions. We have, however, one thing in common, even with those who are part of the developed world: our responsibility to mankind. But, in the underdeveloped countries, we particularly have in common our national economic interests; the overwhelming problems of accumulated poverty and backwardness; an immense external debt that the vast majority cannot pay; an increasingly brutal inequality that hangs over peoples and is combined with the squandering of enormous sums on an absurd arms race in the midst of the dreadful exploitation that weighs on our nations in the most diverse forms; and the horrendous historical heritage of centuries of colonialist and neo-colonialist plunder in each of our countries, right up until the present situation, in which the exploitation is that much more refined, that much more merciless, that much crueler than ever before in history. We also share the bitter feeling of impotence that many governments have in the face of such problems and the concern of all statesmen for the political instability to which these problems give rise.

So gloomy are the realities and prospects for the future viewed as a whole that they could generate pessimism and discouragement if we were not sure of our aims. They are inevitably a bitter pill to swallow, but if we are to face up to the realities we have first to become aware of them.

We do not have, nor do we think anyone has, magic remedies for such difficult, complex and apparently insoluble problems. History shows, however, that no problem has ever been solved until it has become a tangible reality of which everyone is aware. Today, we are faced with the most universally serious and anguishing situations ever known to mankind. In short, for the first time we are faced with the question of whether or not we are to survive. But, no matter how enormous the difficulties, no matter how complex the task, there can be no room for pessimism. This would be to renounce all hope and resign ourselves to the final defeat. We have no alternative but to struggle, trusting in the great moral and intellectual capacity of the human race and in its instinct for self-preservation, if we wish to harbor any hope for survival.

Only with a tremendous effort and the moral and intellectual support of all can we face a future that objectively appears desperate and somber, especially for the peoples of the Third World.

We hope that our modest effort may help create this necessary awareness, which is why we will be deeply grateful to colleagues who are kind and patient enough to look through this report, especially if they excuse its shortcomings and deficiencies.

Contents

1
Introduction

The world is undergoing one of the worst economic crises in it's history.

It is a crisis that has its origins in the major capitalist powers but has most brutally affected the underdeveloped countries, which are now experiencing the sharpest economic deterioration in the whole post-war period.

The initial symptoms of depression became evident by the end of 1979, at the time of the Sixth Summit Conference of Non-Aligned Countries. The situation has swiftly continued to worsen, however, and now, at the time of the Seventh Summit Conference, it is at a calamitous juncture. Even so, it would not seem to have reached rock bottom, casting a somber shadow of uncertainty over short – and even medium-term international economic prospects.

Although this Report covers a period of just over three years (1979-82/83) between the two Summit Conferences, the complexity of the situation is such that there will be occasion to examine some of the antecedents. It is hoped that this will be of help to Heads of State or Government in deciding, on the basis of solid data, the strategic lines of action such dramatic circumstances demand.

Overall assessment of the present situation

The growth in world Gross Domestic Product, which – despite obvious fluctuations – had averaged about 4 per cent in the '70s, fell to 3.8 per cent in 1979 and to just over 2 per cent in 1980, only to drop to 1.2 per cent in 1981 and, in the best of cases, to a similar level in 1982.

This decline in economic activities consequently extended to world trade, whose average annual growth fell from about 7 per cent in 1976-78 to 6 per cent in 1979, 1.5 per cent in 1980, 0 per cent in 1981; and the general estimate for 1982 is that the situation of virtual stagnation continued.

Monetary and financial events complicated the crisis. The US dollar's strong appreciation at the end of 1980 resulted in the depreciation of almost all currencies of the leading market-economy countries. The unprecedented rise in US interest rates, beginning in late 1979, produced great fluctuations in exchange rates, pushed up interest rates in other countries and spread to capital markets. All this heightened economic uncertainty and further hampered the chances of cyclical recovery.

Moreover, between 1979 and 1982, there were continued serious disruptions in the current account balance of payments from the previous period but with great recent changes in the positions of groups of countries: the largest capitalist powers tended to equilibrium; the small but developed market-economy countries maintained significant deficits; big oil-exporting countries experienced a sharp reduction in their surpluses; and the non-oil underdeveloped countries' deficits increased to such unbearable levels that many were forced to reschedule their external debt.

In the context of the foregoing analysis, it should also be noted that this crisis is taking place at a time when the world population is over 4 billion. It occurs at a time when the internationalization of economic life has reached a point whereby changes in one or a few highly developed countries can, through the closely-knit and sensitive network of dependence links existing today, transmit their own boom or depression to dozens and dozens of countries – indeed, practically to the whole world. And it is taking place against the backdrop of a widening and deepening of the notorious gap that today separates the large group of underdeveloped countries from the smaller group of industrialized powers. The impact of a depressive course originating in those market economies plunges hundreds of millions of people and entire regions into greater backwardness, abject poverty and want.

Under such circumstances, it would probably not be an overstatement to say that this crisis may have far more devastating effects than mankind has ever experienced before.

The crisis in the developed capitalist countries

During 1979-82, the adverse economic situation extended to practically all countries of the world.

Even the developed socialist countries – which with their centralized economic planning had not experienced for decades the cyclical fluctuations typical of the market economies – experienced a marked deceleration in their growth rates during that period due to a complex set of domestic and external factors.

The origins of the crisis and its effects on the rest of the world can be clearly found in the developed capitalist countries, especially in the group formed by the seven major powers and more specifically in the United States (35 per cent of this area's GNP). Moreover, it is also evident who has been most seriously hit. In this connection, the UN has pointed out that:

> The recession in Western industrialized countries has been the main reason for the poor results in the world economy. The reduction in economic activity produced both a great increase in unemployment – which in turn depressed salaries – and a weakening of commodities.[1]

The outbreak of the crisis in 1979-80 was reflected in a sharp drop in the growth rates of the Gross National Product of OECD countries. In the seven major countries – the United States, Japan, West Germany, France, the United Kingdom, Italy and Canada – there was a drop to 3.7 per cent in 1979, slightly over 1 per cent in 1980 and 1981, and -0.5 per cent in 1982. Similar trends can be observed for the remaining seventeen countries of the organization.[2]

Contraction in investments persists due to the poor outlook for a deeply depressed market, which is also affected by inflation and unemployment, high interest rates and the failure of restrictionist government policies. The underutilization of installed industrial capacity continues at an unprecedented level, while the wave of bankruptcy occasionally rises, spectacularly, as in the case of the United States. Unemployment – particularly among the young and, in certain countries, among ethnic minorities – has reached figures that, in absolute terms, can only be compared to those during the Great Depression of the 1930's. In fact, initial forecasts in this respect for the OECD area – 8 per cent of the labor force, i.e. 28 million unemployed – were surpassed by far. By the end of 1982, in the United States alone, where up to 9 per cent unemployment was expected, the figure was nearly 11 per cent – over 12 million unemployed – according to what is usually considered an official underestimate.

The crisis in the underdeveloped countries

The Movement of Non-Aligned Countries is particularly interested in the effects of the crisis in the underdeveloped countries under the present conditions of dependence and through the well-known commercial and monetary-financial mechanisms. The impact is indeed felt in a tragically magnified way. This is due to the fact that it occurs in a socio-economic environment where it is estimated that, chronically, the number of the unemployed and underemployed totals 400 to 500 million people (one third to half of the labor force), per caput income is 7 to 40 times lower than in the developed capitalist countries, and dire poverty – physical hunger, deplorable housing, and almost non-existent medical care and education – affects over one billion human beings.

The underdeveloped countries had attained growth rates of about 5-6 per cent in the '60s and '70s. According to the goals set for the UN Third Decade of the International Development Strategy, they had hoped to reach a 7 per cent rate during the '80s. But, if present trends persist, there is not the slightest possibility of attaining that goal.

The real evolution, until now, has been as follows:

The growth rates of the underdeveloped countries as a whole dropped – averaging data from various sources to reach an approximate estimate – from 4.8 per cent in 1979 to 2.8 per cent in 1980 and to about 1 per cent in 1981. When this Report was in preparation, 1982 figures were not available, yet it may be foreseen that performance during that year, far from improving, was probably worse.

The crisis affected different groups of countries to varying degrees.

It seems that during the period under examination, only a dozen net oil-exporting countries were able to maintain positive growth rates, some even relatively high (6 per cent). The large oil-exporting countries experienced negative growth rates since 1980 and the net importers experienced a vertical drop in their growth rates: from 4 per cent in 1980 to 1.5 per cent in 1981 – the lowest in the post-war era – and it will probably drop further in 1982.

This sudden economic deterioration – undoubtedly worsened by the acknowledged inadequacy of the internal structures, typical in most underdeveloped countries – clearly originated in the crisis unleashed in the most important capitalist centers. Even when there is direct government action by those countries – restrictive fiscal, credit and monetary policies – it is frequently due to the need to counter pressures resulting from serious imbalances from outside.

The decline in the volume of exports and in the prices of the main commodities exported by underdeveloped countries has been the worst in recent decades. It is estimated that when compared with 1980 values, the 1981-82 accumulated losses amount to some $29 billion. The drop in prices has been particularly dramatic. According to the UNCTAD Monthly Price Bulletin published last November, the combined index of commodity prices – excluding oil, in terms of current dollars and on a basis of 1980 = 100 – dropped to 84 in 1981 and to 71 during the first ten months of 1982. In real terms, it declined steeply from almost 100 by the end of 1980, to less than 70 by late 1982. But actually, as stated in a working paper of the Group of 77 recently examined in UNCTAD:

The terms of trade for commodities from non-oil-exporting developing countries has notably deteriorated since 1978 and present data indicate a further deterioration on the terms of trade for commodities in 1982.

On the other hand, in its 1982 Annual Report, the IMF acknowledged: that in the case of the net oil-importing underdeveloped countries, the cumulative deterioration of the terms of trade from 1977 to 1981 was over 15 per cent – that is, the equivalent of some $45 to 50 billion.

The corresponding impact of these developments, on the balance of trade and, therefore, on the current accounts balance of payments, caused the impressive acceleration of the increased external debt of oil-importing underdeveloped countries. On the other hand, this evolution has led to a situation *wherein the appearance of a new trait in the traditional monopolist exaction procedures in the underdeveloped world has also become prominent: now, it is not only performed through unequal trade and foreign private investments, but also through typically financial means, that is, through external debt.*

The problem of the underdeveloped countries' external imbalances has thus sharpened recently. The flows of official development assistance in concessionary terms have been decreasing, both in nominal and in real terms, and do not even reach half the required minimum 0.7 per cent of the developed countries' GDP. The IMF lacks sufficient resources; its quota system – and, therefore, voting system – besides its asymmetric distribution, restrains the amount of the credits that, on the other hand, are granted under a set of conditions which disregards the underdeveloped countries' economic and social needs, the structural and long-term nature of their external imbalances and the present features of the world economic juncture. The attempts made as of 1978 at lending greater flexibility to the practices of that institution proved unsuccessful. And the new financial facilities introduced in the '70s have far from solved the serious payment imbalances that, due to external reasons beyond their control, the underdeveloped countries are experiencing.

On the other hand, the role played by private sources of capital – namely transnational banks – has also failed to solve the problem. The fact is – as has been pointed out by the Group of 24 in the IMF and the Group of 77 in UNCTAD – that "privatization" of international monetary and financial relations has increased even more in recent times. Transnational banks – particularly active in the Euromarket – are decisive in the growth and decline of international liquidity; their huge speculative capital movements are also decisive in the variations of exchange rates and have reflected – and sharpened – the increase in interest rates. These sources of private funding are only available to a number of underdeveloped countries at high costs and have furthermore showed a restrictive trend. As a matter of fact – as both the Group of 24 and the Group of 77 have stated – they are equally incapable of solving the problems of supporting balance of payments deficits and meeting funding requirements for development in the underdeveloped countries.

Capitalist economic developments in the post-war period: background factors to the present crisis

It would be of little help in understanding the present economic problems to confine their examination to the framework of a cyclical process, even if due note is taken of its aggravated complication owing to concomitant phenomena of chronic stagnation, inflation and unemployment – feature of the so-called stagflation – in addition to policies, life daily proves inadequate. The present capitalist juncture forms part of a more protracted historical evolution – covering at least several decades – in which complex processes have taken place, thus hindering its medium- and long-term growth possibilities, creating deep and seemingly unsolvable imbalances and provoking the emergence of critical situations in decisive areas of economic activity.

A series of new and, occasionally, far-reaching phenomena occurred in the developed capitalist world during the past post-war period.

Some of these important events were associated with an upsurge in the concentration of power, capital and production and, after a given moment, with the extraterritorialization of those processes by the emergence of transnational corporations. Today, these conglomerates control 40 to 50 per cent of world trade, and market 80 to 90 per cent of the main commodities exported by underdeveloped countries. The effects of this phenomenon in international economic life have been sufficiently examined so as to currently constitute one of the most extensive bibliographies of our times. It has become tradition among the Non-Aligned Countries, particularly since the Fourth Summit Conference in Algiers, to examine, diagnose and denounce this phenomenon.

This increasingly concentrated monopolization process – or oligopolization, to use a more technical term – was undoubtedly one of the decisive factors in the changes in the balance of forces among capitalist powers during the post-war period. The almost unquestionable US hegemony in that part of the developed world at the end of the war began changing in the '50s with the recovery and growth provided by big industrial consortia to the economies of Western Europe (particularly West Germany) and Japan. In the '60s, the process continued to sharpen, and in the '70s it led to the virtual establishment of three large centers of capitalist power in the world: the United States – preeminent –, the European Economic Community and Japan; they were allies in the struggle against socialism and united against the vindicatory movements of the underdeveloped nations, yet rivals in the fight for energy sources, the use of cheap labor and raw materials and the sale of their products in international markets.

The upsurge of monopolization, on the other hand, took place under circumstances concomitant with the role of the State in the economies. This evolution, that in the past would only become evident in times of war, could be quantitatively confirmed and illustrated by the fact that government spending, as a percentage of the Domestic Product in the OECD area, went from about 28 per cent in 1960 to some 40 per cent by the late '70s. However, official action in developed market economies goes beyond the role played by government spending. In many countries the State is the owner or co-owner of big corporations and even of total branches of economy. In others, it attempts telling macro-economic planning. And in

16

all, by manipulating the monetary and fiscal levers, it influences – at times decisively but not always successfully – the course of the cycle.

Today, the ever closer ties between the interests of the big economic power groups and the policies of the top echelons of State power – another important development of the post-war period – is unchallenged by any authority on this subject, or even by a mere observer of these phenomena. But in this connection, underdeveloped countries can offer convincing evidence whenever they have sought to negotiate a just, vindicatory demand in international fora. The secret of the "lack of political will" on the part of developed capitalist powers in such cases lies precisely in this very fact.

This interrelationship is evidenced in the development of one of the most genuinely far-reaching events of our times: the *scientific and technological revolution*, a process that would have been rendered completely impossible without an active, joint monopoly-State participation.

Indeed, the scientific and technological revolution could never have taken place without State backing – financial and otherwise – to research and development activities (R&D). This revolution is an integral fusion of extraordinary scientific accomplishments and formidable achievements in the ability to apply those accomplishments to technology and production. In other words, the resulting science-production system is such that ideas generating in the former are spread to and may be applied in the latter, thus becoming, in an incredibly short period, material realities (goods and services).

From the theory of relativity to that of the quantum theory – passing through nuclear physics, polymer chemistry, cybernetics and molecular biology – many of the findings that under other circumstances would not have gone beyond the scientific abstractions of a researcher or the color in the test tubes in some small laboratory, today become inspiring sources of projects which swiftly move from drawing board to production plant and then to market. Thus, a decisive change has occurred in the historical development of the productive forces of society that, in terms of investment processes or net capital formation at unprecedented scales and diversity, today appear in the form of new products, lines and even branches of production which only two or three decades ago would have been figments beyond the scope of the richest imagination.

But the tragically paradoxical essence of these events cannot but move the most insensitive soul.

The unquestionable links between this scientific and technological revolution and the developments in the destructive capabilities of the modern military arms build-up machinery – which keeps the world on the brink of a thermonuclear holocaust – stand in contrast with the possibilities that same revolution would offer if devoted to efforts aimed at improving mankind's well-being. The enormous production of goods – at times both superfluous and sophisticated – facilitated by this very scientific and technological revolution in consumer societies, stands in contrast with the lack of the essential goods that plagues hundreds of millions of people living on the various continents. And the prodigious leap of the productive forces resulting from this very same revolution stands in contrast with the similarly phenomenal scientific, technological and material backwardness of entire peoples for whom the concept of civilization is, at best, but a rather remote hope. In short, paradoxes of a society like that of our times which has mastered the techniques for surrounding us with artificial satellites, for placing men on the Moon and investigating the rings around Saturn; but which seems equally incapable of mitigating the hunger that day after day strikes down one fourth of the inhabitants of its own planet and of agreeing upon an efficient system to prevent disaster in the prices of the underdeveloped countries' commodities.

During the last post-war period and somewhat linked to the aforementioned events, various important changes took place in the internal structures of the economies of the industrialized countries, to which reference should be made due to their influence – mainly negative – in underdeveloped countries.

The role of agriculture in those advanced economies, for instance, continued diminishing to the extent that by the end of the '70s it only contributed 3-4 per cent to the Gross Domestic Product and absorbed as a source of employment only about 3 per cent (in the United States) and 12 per cent (in Japan) of the labor force. On the other hand, about that time, industry accounted for one fourth (United States) and one third (Japan) of that GDP and, in general, about 30 per cent of employment. Actually, the sector that grew faster was services which also by late '70s, contributed 52 per cent (Japan and Western Europe) and 63 per cent (United States) to the GDP, with similar employment ratios.

Significant changes also occurred in the industrial sector: the so-called traditional branches lagged behind in relative terms, and others showed a dynamic upsurge, mainly electromechanics and chemistry. In addition, processes evolved in the industrial sector – some related to the scientific and technological revolution – that very directly affected the underdeveloped countries, such as raw material-saving technological innovations and the replacement of natural raw materials by synthetic products.

But more important from the point of view of the underdeveloped world's interests were the world-wide scale changes, partly related to the aforementioned.

The post-war period indeed witnessed an important upsurge in the phenomena related to the internationalization of economic life. There was a significant increase – even in real terms – in the capital flow between countries and trade grew at unprecedented and sustained rates. Deep changes occurred in the distribution of trade in different geographical areas and sectors and new international division of labor schemes began emerging. In the framework of the latter, some underdeveloped countries became – within certain limits – exporters of manufactured goods thus increasing their share in the total exports of the non-oil-exporting underdeveloped countries from 30 per cent in 1950 to 40 percent in 1979-80.

But the changes that had the greatest and, to a certain extent, demolishing impact on underdeveloped countries were those in the distribution of world investments and trade in different geographical regions and sectors.

As known, the main investment trends of the developed capitalist countries before World War II was directed to the then colonial, semi-colonial and dependent world. Since the end of that war, a new phenomenon started to develop: *international capital flows showed a tendency to move mainly within the developed capitalist countries*. In 1946, for instance, Latin America absorbed 43 per cent of all direct US investments abroad and Western Europe barely 19 per cent. By the mid-'70s, Latin America received only 17 per cent of these investments while Western Europe was already receiving over 37 per cent.

In addition, by the early '70s another process began: *private capital, representing then only a little over 40 per cent of total financial flows to underdeveloped countries, some ten years later absorbed over 65 per cent.* On the other hand, another unprecedented process occurred in the '70s: of all private capital flows to underdeveloped countries, direct investments decreased (from 56 per cent in 1970 to only 28 per cent – exactly half – in 1979), *while the financial flows of the transnational commercial banks (loans and credits), practically non-existent in statistical terms in 1970, increased to the point of absorbing 44 per cent of total private flows in 1979.* That is why in 1979, according to UNCTAD, underdeveloped countries were paying, on account of the interest on their fabulous external debt, an amount three times the earnings from direct foreign private investments.

The other decisive evolution took place in the sphere of world trade.

Before the war, most of world trade was between the developed capitalist countries (the metropolises) and the underdeveloped world (colonies, semi-colonies and dependent countries at the time). But that structure started changing totally in the post-war period, to the extent that *the accelerated growth world trade experienced in the past decades took place mainly among developed nations*, clearly displacing underdeveloped countries (excluding the large oil exporters since 1974).

This phenomenon is closely related both to the structural changes and expansion experienced by developed market economies during the first quarter of the century after the war, and the effects of these developments in the volume and branch and geographic composition of world trade. Thus, the volume of food, beverages and raw materials, constituting the main export items of the underdeveloped countries in world trade decreased from some 40 per cent in 1955 to only 25 per cent by the end of the '60s; this process sharpened further in subsequent years.[3] The result is quite obvious: the non-oil underdeveloped countries' share in total world exports dropped from almost 25 per cent in 1955 to an average of slightly over 11 per cent in 1970-1980.[4] That is to say, those underdeveloped countries, representing most of the population and of the world territory, only participate in – and are forced to live with – just over one-tenth of the world trade.

Other aspects of the situation

The study of the problems faced by the underdeveloped countries today, notoriously worsened in the past three or four years, is not limited to the impact that the negative cyclical evolution of the world economy has had on them. There are other aspects that affect them severely and to which we must at least make reference to in this introduction, subject to a more detailed and separate analysis. The arms race is one such problem.

In 1979-1982, the amount spent on the arms build-up has continued increasing, especially by the great powers. Between 1979 and 1981 military expenditures averaged $505 billion a year. It was higher in 1982. The United States and other developed capitalist countries, and the Soviet Union and the European socialist countries, accounted for over 70 per cent of all military expenditures.

Recently, the contrast between the underdeveloped countries' financial requirements and the potentially suicidal squandering of world resources on the arms build-up has been even more paradoxically highlighted by the fact that such squandering has yearly equalled, and even surpassed, the total external debt of the countries of Asia, Africa and Latin America, a debt that has forced them to cut back – if not cancel – their development programs and introduce restrictions that have severely affected their people's income, employment and living standards.

At various Summit Conferences, the Non-Aligned Countries have repeatedly stressed the potential danger the absurdity of the arms race implies for the survival of mankind, and they have called, again and again, for peaceful and constructive alternatives particularly that of a possible linkage between disarmament and development financing.

The world food problem is another matter that requires close examination. It is estimated that more than a billion people in the underdeveloped world suffer from malnutrition, of whom over 500 million are starving. Although this situation affects all the underdeveloped countries to a greater or lesser degree, the most severely affected areas are sub-Saharan Africa and Southern Asia, where serious food shortages coincide more explicitly with insufficient agricultural production as compared to population growth. These regions also account for an important part of the projected cereal shortfall estimated at $24 billion (at 1975 prices) by the year 2000.

The worsening world food problem is a post-war phenomenon that coincides with the upsurge of neo-colonialism. On an overall world scale, this problem tends to appear, not as a discrepancy between production and consumption but rather as a sum of inequalities in the structure of distribution. The aforementioned $24 billion cereal deficit, for example, stands in contrast with a $32 billion surplus in the developed countries.[5] At regional, sub-regional and national levels, food deficits are generally due to inadequate agrarian structures (latifundia, minifundia, etc.); and technical backwardness – sometimes at a primitive level – in land usage. In any case, these situations also influence other environmental problems such as degradation of soils, exhaustion of forestry resources, and desertification, the most extreme expression of generalized deterioration of the ecosystem.

Another matter to be considered is the so-called energy crisis. The 1973-74 oil price rise by the Organization of Petroleum Exporting Countries (OPEC) was generally supported by Third World countries as a fair demand, in principle, in the hopes that the oil countries' newly-acquired power and the abundant resources consequently available to them could be used to defend fair prices for commodities and for Third World economic development aid.

But that step severely affected the economies of the underdeveloped countries and in some years – particularly 1974, 1976 and from 1980 on – it became a heavy burden on their balance of payments. Those countries were thus confronted with a new unequal exchange, this time related to oil, which affects them not only in terms of the oil they import but also in terms of the products they buy from the developed capitalist countries, where price increases surpassed oil cost. This enormous expense is compounded by the investments aimed at solving their future energy needs according to their possibilities.

The capitalist crises, the crisis of neo-colonialism and the Movement of Non-Aligned Countries

From the economic point of view, the 25 years immediately following World War II were the richest in developments, structural changes and in the emergence of new trends in all the history of capitalism. This evolution, however, unleashed contradictions, imbalances and tensions theretofore unknown by the system.

Capitalist powers and, in general, all the developed market economies are now facing problems whose depth and gravity were inconceivable just 10 or 15 years ago. One such problem is the *alterations in the cycle's performance* now featuring ever shorter, weaker and hesitant recovery phases alongside the persistent and seemingly concomitant phenomena of *high inflation and unemployment rates.* But still, other problems – all inter-related, equally serious and allegedly without a solution – could be added, namely, *the low medium-and long-term trend growth rates, chronic processes of monetary and financial instability, the energy crisis, the ecological crisis, and the already evident crisis of the entire neo-colonial system.* This last phenomenon is of particular interest to the Non-Aligned Countries.

It is a well-known fact that the imperialist colonial system collapsed after World War II. This process, however, dovetailed with the development of neo-colonialism, a new and more subtle form of the metropolitan policies of the past. Neo-colonialism, while representing an unavoidable tolerance for the formal political independence of the former colonies and semi-colonies, sought to consolidate their economic dependence based both on direct imperialist exploitation in every country and on an inequitable system of international economic relations. *But now the history-making news is that, according to massive and uncontestable data, neo-colonialism, as was the case of colonialism in the past, has also gone into crisis.*

It has come into crisis, first of all, because of the contradictions with the underdeveloped world that the aforementioned capitalist developments have provoked.

For example, in diverting a substantial share of the trade and investment flow from the underdeveloped to the developed countries, the former's structural problems particularly sharpened and development possibilities were checked inasmuch as these countries were forced into a fully marginal position in the midst of the accelerated growth in the flows of capital and goods that have characterized world trade in recent decades.

The very flow of capital to the underdeveloped countries in the form of private direct investments – for ages an expression of exploitation, malformation and economic dependence – has tended to ebb in recent times, but, as noted previously, merely to be supplanted by onerous flows of bank loans which have led to gigantic debts, whose servicing has created a crisis not only for Third World economies but for imperialism's own financial system. The mechanism of unequal exchange, aggravated to the utmost by inflation, oil prices, and, on top of it all, by the present crisis, has decisively contributed not only to an increased debt, but also led to a chronic deficit in the balance of trade with the consequent impact on the balance of payments which, due to structural reasons as well as to economic prospects, *simply cannot be solved within the framework of the neo-colonialist regime characteristic of current trade relations between the developed capitalist countries and the underdeveloped world.*

The crisis of neo-colonialism is also evidenced through developments such as the oil price demands by OPEC in 1973-1974 and the launching then of the program for the New International Economic Order at the initiative of the Non-Aligned Countries. Now, on the 10th anniversary of this historical initiative at the Fourth Summit Conference in Algiers, its results might seem disheartening at first glance. Little progress has been made in achieving its most essential and just economic demands. On the contrary, the capitalist powers succeeded in stifling, one by one, the most constructive and important projects set forth in that inspiring program, projects such as the Integrated Commodities Program, the Global Negotiations and the implementation of the set of principles materialized – only to vanish afterwards – during the Tokyo Round of the Multilateral Trade Negotiations. Nevertheless, these disappointments should not lead to defeatism. They are part – episodes – of the process of a system in crisis and of the failure of a regime of international economic relations, both doomed by history, to whose gradual development the vigorous Movement of Non-Aligned Countries has greatly contributed, precisely by increasing its capacity to defy the most adverse circumstances.

Assessment of the efforts made in establishing a New International Economic Order

During 1979-1982, the Non-Aligned Countries and the developing countries as a whole steadfastly upheld their banners in defense of a New International Economic Order. Unfortunately, the assessment of their efforts was as negative as the one dating back to May 1974, when Resolutions 3201 and 3202, containing both its Declaration and Action Program were adopted by the Sixth Special Session of the UN General Assembly. Consequently, during the Seventh Summit Conference, the Heads of State or Government may reaffirm the views expressed at the Havana Summit Conference – were the situation not to require a more forceful language – as it truly seems to require at present:

The Heads of State or Government reaffirmed their deep conviction that a lasting solution to the problems of the developing countries can only be achieved by a constant and fundamental restructuring of international economic relations through the establishment of the New International Economic Order. However, five years after the adoption of Resolutions 3201 (S-VI) and 3202 (S-VI) of the United Nations General Assembly [...] the economic situation faced by the developing countries continues its pervasive deterioration, aggravated and accelerated by the effects of the world economic crisis [...] The Heads of State or Government deeply deplore the intransigency of most of the developed countries and their refusal to engage in serious negotiation to implement the above-mentioned resolutions [...] The Heads of State or Government stressed the necessity for taking urgent measures for achieving progress towards establishing the New International Economic Order.

The poor and almost completely fruitless results of the efforts made to establish the New International Economic Order – a program that is ever more urgent in view of the greater, deeper and more drastic deterioration that the world economic situation has undergone in the last three years –

contrast sharply with the vigorous and sustained efforts of the Non-Aligned and all underdeveloped countries during that period.

In fact, immediately after the closing of the Sixth Summit Conference, and bearing witness to the stands of the Non-Aligned Countries as regards the pressing need for adopting measures to establish the New International Economic Order, Cuba, as representative of the Movement, proposed in the United Nations formulas in response to the desperate economic and social situation of the Third World. Cuba first of all proposed the establishment of an additional inflow of resources of no less than $300 billion in 1977 real values, to be distributed from the outset in annual amounts of no less than $25 billion and used in the underdeveloped countries. This aid was to adopt the form of grants and long-term soft credits at minimal interest rates.

On that occasion, Cuba made a 10-point summary of the additional steps indispensable in reversing the crisis, and that, owing to their current validity, are worth reaffirming:

Unequal exchange is impoverishing our peoples; and it should cease!

Inflation, which is being exported to us, is impoverishing our peoples; and it should cease!

Protectionism is impoverishing our peoples; and it should cease!

The disequilibrium that exists concerning the exploitation of sea resources is abusive; and it should be abolished!

The financial resources received by the developing countries are insufficient; and should be increased!

Arms expenditures are irrational. They should cease, and the funds thus released should be used to finance development.

The international monetary system that prevails today is bankrupt; and should be replaced!

The debts of the least developed countries and those in a disadvantageous position are impossible to bear and have no solution. They should be cancelled!

Indebtedness oppresses the rest of the developing countries economically; and it should be relieved!

The wide economic gap between the developed countries and the countries that seek development is growing rather than diminishing; and it should be closed!

Furthermore, the Sixth Non-Aligned Summit Conference had suggested that the Committee of the Whole of the UN General Assembly begin preparations for a Special Session of that body in order to launch a Global Negotiation in the areas of commodities, energy, trade, development, and monetary and financial problems. Indeed, in the fall of 1979, the General Assembly unanimously agreed that "global and sustained negotiations" should be prompted during the Eleventh Special Session in 1980, wherein the New General Strategy for Development should also be adopted. It is common knowledge that the Special Session was held in the summer of 1980 and ended in total failure. Some capitalist powers – and notoriously the United States – practically sabotaged the draft, which remained stranded by procedural matters.

The period that bridges over these two Summit Conferences must be analyzed without defeatism, but its balance of accrued economic frustrations must be approached objectively and constructively. Throughout these years the attempts to launch the Global Negotiations not only failed – though the underdeveloped countries have not given them up yet – but, furthermore, important proposals, principles and even achievements of the underdeveloped world were seriously jeopardized due to the aggravating circumstance of a world economic crisis of unprecedented depth and scope in the entire post-war era.

Thus, the Integrated Commodities Program ran aground and agreements on market stabilization were seriously affected by the policies of some capitalist powers, as was the case of the International Sugar Agreement, whose full implementation was prevented by the selfish attitude of the European Economic Community. Moreover, some given principles and even demands won by the underdeveloped countries after long years of struggle were simply overlooked in the Multilateral Trade Negotiations. These negotiations registered a negative balance in fundamental issues, among them, the Generalized System of Preferences, whose benefits were eroded by several billions of dollars.

On the other hand, during these years, the protectionist tide in the market economy countries, instead of slackening, gained momentum thus affecting a number of underdeveloped countries. Instead of growing as requested, Official Development Assistance declined, particularly in real terms. Institutions such as the International Monetary Fund – more than ever in the hands of the United States and a group of capitalist powers – continued to pursue policies contrary to the demands of the underdeveloped countries.

It must be pointed out that the history of frustration of the underdeveloped countries in their efforts to establish a more equitable system of international economic relations antedates the 10-year period that has practically elapsed since the adoption of the program for the New International Economic Order. Actually, it covers a much broader period which starts in the early post-war years, when national liberation movements gained the momentum which resulted in the collapse of colonial empires, UN membership for dozens of new States, and the beginning of the struggle against neo-colonialism, spearheaded by the Movement of Non-Aligned Countries. Throughout those years, the work performed by individual experts, research and study centers and by various UN agencies shed light on the problems of underdevelopment and especially on those which, stemming from inadequate and unfair international economic structures, hampered the attainment of genuine independence, development and progress by the countries of Asia, Africa and Latin America. During that time, several initiatives were put forth – i.e., the First and Second UN Development Decades – which to a certain extent encouraged international cooperation to tackle the problems of underdevelopment, and organizations – such as the Regional Economic Committees and UNCTAD – that carried out research and served as fora for debating and promoting favorable agreements for the underdeveloped countries.

The Non-Aligned Countries and the Group of 77 never hesitated in supporting these initiatives and organizations, not even when the proposals of a dialogue between developed and underdeveloped countries – opposed by some – implied holding negotiations outside the UN framework as was the case of the Paris Conference (1976), and of the Cancun Meeting (1981). The latter was mainly inspired in the Brandt Commission proposals. Though experts and personalities of the underdeveloped world participated in this Commission, its report clearly showed the views of the most enlightened circles in the developed capitalist countries and contained observations and suggestions in favor of the demands raised by the underdeveloped countries, albeit as part of a philosophy reflecting the long-term interests of the capitalist system.

In spite of the fact that Cuba was the Chairman of the Non-Aligned Movement, the United States vetoed Cuba's participation at the Cancun Meeting. In a gesture acknowledged as exemplary, and as evidence of the underdeveloped countries' positive attitude vis-à-vis all fora that could provide possible solutions to their serious problems, Cuba relinquished its right to attend that meeting. But the Cancun Meeting, as is known to all, also ended in total failure mainly on account of the stand taken by the United States.

Indeed, the climax of a process lasting several decades was the adoption, in May 1974, of an initiative by the Non-Aligned Countries, which was later taken up by the Group of 77, supported by the socialist countries and accepted – though reluctantly – by the developed capitalist countries: the program for the establishment of the New International Economic Order. This program – enriched subsequently with agreements adopted by UNIDO, UNCTAD and other conferences – had the historic merit of being the first to be launched at the United Nations through the original action of the underdeveloped countries and with their unanimous support. The program contained sound political stands (anti-colonialism, anti-racism, defense of the right to self-determination and sovereignty over natural resources) and equally fair economic demands (in favor of commodities, official development assistance, an international monetary system reform, etc.).

The sustained action for the implementation of the principles of the New International Economic Order gave strength, coherence and unity to the underdeveloped countries in their untiring pursuit of a world based, not on exploitation, but on international cooperation, a less unfair and more equitable world, a world that would favor, instead of hindering, any effort to break the vicious circle of backwardness and dependence for more than 100 countries where three-quarters of the world population is concentrated together with almost all of the hunger, poverty and even the hopelessness that today overwhelm mankind.

It is thus permissible to anticipate that the difficulties and frustrations met by the Non-Aligned Countries and all underdeveloped countries in their struggle for the materialization of that program, far from discouraging, will spur on the quest for avenues leading to final success.

2

The economic crisis and its impact on the underdeveloped countries

The present cyclical crisis and its complications

The present crisis is part of the typical cyclical course of the developed capitalist economies. Now, however, it has acquired new complications and aggravating dimensions. This is not the place for a theoretical analysis of the issue, yet it is obvious that certain basic observations must be made in this regard if the Non-Aligned Countries are to draw up a realistic and effective strategy in line with the circumstances.

These crises – the most severe phase in the cyclical evolution typical of capitalist development – date back to at least the second quarter of the 19th century. In the course of time, they have tended to produce sharper, deeper and more generalized interruptions of the economic upsurge with world-wide effects. The most notorious crisis was the catastrophic world-wide depression of 1929-1933.

During the period following World War II, and even in the midst of relatively prolonged and generalized expansion, the cyclical evolution was present – although with significant changes in its so-called classical behavior. Thus, the upsurge tended to be longer, while the crises lost their previous international synchronism and sometimes appeared as relatively brief and mild recessive processes.

This pattern changed toward the end of 1973, when, in the midst of an unprecedented upsurge, economic activity was suddenly weakened, turning into a significantly deep crisis throughout the developed capitalist world in 1974 and early 1975.

Despite its severity, this crisis ended in the second half of 1975 with a speedy recovery, which led to an upsurge during the first half of 1976. In the following two years (1977 and 1978) there was a relatively modest, unstable growth rate (between 3.5 and nearly 5 per cent). But this situation barely continued until the first half of 1979. In the second half of 1979, the symptoms heralding the present crisis began to appear. The decline has continued since 1980, thus reaching the depressed levels of today, unprecedented since World War II. It should also be mentioned that the capitalist pattern since 1974-75 – closely resembling that of the '30s in some respects – is considered by some economic circles to have been the beginning of a crisis that continued despite the relative 1976-78 revival and then plunged to its present level.

This description, although short, suggests the characteristics of an unprecedented cyclical course. There is, first of all, the fluctuating brevity of the recovery and boom phases that used to last from eight to ten years but that now could barely be sustained for three or four years. Two other features also give the situation new characteristics.

One is *the coexistence of an apparent recovery and upsurge process (1976-79) coupled with high unemployment rates.* The average unemployment rate in OECD countries reached 5 per cent during the 1974-75 crisis, but never dropped below that level in the following years; and, indeed, increased in 1979 (over 5.5 per cent), 1980 (over 6 per cent) and 1981-82 (over 8 per cent).

The other is *the coexistence of a crisis phase coupled with high inflation rates.* In recent years, inflation (as measured by the consumer price index) has never dropped below 8 per cent per year for OECD countries and has in fact gone over 12 per cent.

The slight drop in inflation levels in recent months is, for example – according to general opinion – inseparably linked to the increased unemployment of over 30 million people in the OECD area.

Another very important aspect is the now internationally acknowledged failure of State policies for the regulation of the cyclical processes in developed market economies. The Keynesian formulas applied during the three decades following World War II proved to be inadequate in coping with the complex events of the '70s. The monetarist formulas – so much in fashion recently and applied with various modifications by most of the capitalist powers – has led to the most spectacular economic disaster of modern times.

It is not just a question of these policies – the alchemy of the "monetary-fiscal mix" – having served merely to maintain and even aggravate the crisis, in addition to taking a tragic social toll. The problem is that these policies have disastrous economic effects on the underdeveloped countries. What is worse, certain governments are trying – either directly or through a number of international agencies – to impose these regressive concepts on the underdeveloped countries, thereby sharpening the impact of the crisis and subjecting them to truly intolerable political, economic and social domestic tensions.

Thus, in the underdeveloped countries, the effects of the crisis have been transmitted in a very dramatic way, worsening the already precarious situation characterized by poor development of their productive forces and the deformation of their socio-economic structures.

For the Third World peoples, the present crisis has meant the almost complete ruin of their economies; the dashing of their hopes for improvement, because of the worsening conditions in trade; and bankruptcy staved off by mortgaging both the future and even the present, expressed in unbearable, unpayable indebtedness – in short, a prospect of hunger, poverty and disease for a painfully growing proportion of impoverished mankind.

In recent years, it has been possible to note, first of all, Third World subordination to the general trends in the developed capitalist world, which passes on the effects of the crisis to the weakest countries.

The crisis is expressed in all its severity in the indicators related to the Third World's foreign economic relations. They clearly show how the negative effects of the cycle are passed on to the underdeveloped countries.

This is particularly evident in the *inflation rates,* which grew 15 per cent more in the non-oil-exporting underdeveloped countries than in the market-economy developed countries in the 1974-75 period. Inflation imported by means of the international monetary and trade system has become an erosive factor in the deteriorated Third World economies which, except in the case of the oil-exporting countries, do not have any defense mechanisms to counter even partially these negative trends.

Similar conclusions may be drawn from the deterioration in the *terms of trade,* which dropped by 15 per cent in the non-oil-exporting countries in the 1974-75 period.

The deterioration of the Third World's foreign economic relations is summed up in the growing deficits in the current accounts of their balances of payments which totaled $83.3 billion in 1974-75. Such negative balances could not be met under these conditions except through more loans – which began the spiral of indebtedness from which the underdeveloped world suffers today.

Thus, the *external debt* grew at an average annual rate of 25.1 per cent between 1973 and 1975, while debt servicing grew at an annual rate of 61.1 per cent in the same period. Starting with the 1974-75 crisis, the external debt began operating as a short-term factor for cushioning the consequences of crises, at the cost of mortgaging the underdeveloped countries' future and generating a growing – and today unbearable – process of economic strangling in those countries.

Later, in 1976, the economies of developed capitalist countries showed high growth rates which, nevertheless, did not surpass levels prior to the crisis. In fact, the available data show that the GDP grew at an average rate of 6.3 per cent in 1973 but only 5.2 per cent in 1976.[1]

Most Third World countries were faced with the same situation, since their growth rates in 1976 were higher than those in 1973 only in the case of the oil-exporting countries.[2]

A process of initially fast recovery began in 1976 but it immediately weakened and became sluggish until about 1979 without culminating in a stable economic upsurge; thus, the system clearly stagnated.

The economies of the underdeveloped countries also suffered from visible stagnation between 1976 and 1979, while their indicators of international economic activity clearly deteriorated. Indeed, during those years, their inflationary differential with the developed capitalist countries increased, reaching 19 per cent in the non-oil-exporting countries in 1976. Similarly, another deterioration in the terms of trade was noted starting in 1978, and, after a short decrease, the trend of increasingly negative balances in the current accounts reappeared. The most significant deterioration, however, was seen in the level of the external debt, which grew at an average annual rate of 22.4 per cent, while its servicing was 31.7 per cent between 1976 and 1979.

Thus, economic recovery did not reach the Third World since increasingly negative trends gathered momentum in its economy during the years following the 1974-75 crisis.

The world economy between 1979 and 1982

From 1979 to 1982, the capitalist economy not only failed to overcome the serious difficulties it had faced since 1974 but also evolved negatively.

Monetarist-style economic policies that have focused attention on fighting inflation – which the ruling circles in the capitalist governments have increasingly come to consider the main cause of all the ills afflicting the capitalist system – have come to the fore in those governments.

Thus, *restrictive policies* that were applied, especially from 1980 onward, have mainly involved reductions in fiscal expenditures. This has meant budgetary cuts for social programs and the reduction of public service jobs – with negative social and political consequences. The monetary manipulations have been even more injurious, however, among them the *increase in interest rates*, since 1979. Thus, the policies applied in recent years have worsened economic recession in all capitalist countries and have not stably reversed the phenomenon of inflation; as a result, the worker's standard of living has deteriorated.

The effects of these measures have been particularly acute in the field of finance, especially in the underdeveloped countries.

Moreover, the disarray and instability of the capitalist economy in this period has also affected the socialist countries, which have also been subjected to growing political hostility by the US Government.

In this context of gloomy prospects, the unfolding of the world economy in 1981 and 1982 brought out the negative trends of preceding years. For the third consecutive year, the Gross Domestic Product of all developed capitalist countries performed poorly in 1982. This reflected the critical situation of the capitalist economy, which has unquestionably been exacerbated in recent years.

The GDP of the OECD member countries in 1981 as compared to 1980 showed a growth rate of only 1.2 per cent, similar to that obtained in 1980, but it declined to -0.5 per cent in 1982 as compared to 1981.

The seven major OECD countries, which account for approximately 84 per cent of the total GDP, did not perform better. After a meager 1.3 per cent growth in 1981, this indicator dropped to 0.5 per cent in 1982. In 1982, only France and Japan achieved growth rates of more than 1 per cent. The remaining countries either practically stagnated (Italy and the United Kingdom) or registered decreases.

The year 1981 was particularly adverse for European capitalist countries, especially for the members of the European Economic Community. The former's GDP decreased by -0.3 per cent, while that of the latter decreased by -0.6 per cent. In both cases, the GDP grew by only 0.25 per cent in 1982.

GROSS DOMESTIC PRODUCT OF DEVELOPED CAPITALIST COUNTRIES (GDP)

	Annual changes (percentage)		
	1980-79	1981-80	1982-81
The 7 major OECD countries			
Canada	−0.1	2.9	−5.0
United States	−0.1	1.9	−1.75
Japan	4.4	3.0	2.5
Federal Republic of Germany	1.9	−0.2	−1.25
Italy	3.9	−0.2	0.75
France	1.2	0.3	1.5
United Kingdom	−1.4	−2.2	0.5
TOTAL	1.1	1.3	−0.5
Remaining OECD countries	1.9	0.7	0.5
TOTAL OECD	1.2	1.2	−0.5
OECD-EUROPE	1.6	−0.3	0.25
OECD-EEC	1.4	−0.6	0.25

SOURCE: Based on OECD. *Main Economic Indicators,* April 1982, p. 180; *Economic Outlook,* no. 32, December 1982, pp. 15-16.

The growth rate of *industrial production* for the group of OECD countries during 1981 was slightly higher than that registered in 1980. However, the decline in industrial production in the OECD area – dropping to -3.5 per cent in 1982 – confirms the existence of a crisis in those countries' industry.

This situation, observed in 1982, is the continuation of a process of stagnation in industrial growth that was becoming a trend in the capitalist countries ever since the 1974-75 crisis. From 1976 to 1979, these countries experienced a slight industrial recovery, but, at the end of 1979, and mainly in 1980, the capitalist economic crisis once again had negative effects on industry in OECD member countries.

OECD INDUSTRIAL PRODUCTION
CHANGES FROM THE PRECEDING YEAR
(Percentage)

	1980	1981	1982
United States	−3.6	2.6	−8.25
Japan	7.0	3.1	1.5
Federal Republic of Germany	0.2	−1.5	−2.5
France	−0.4	−0.9	−1.5
United Kingdom	−9.4	−6.3	0
Italy	5.6	−2.3	−0.25
Canada	−1.8	1.0	−9.25
The major OECD countries	−1.2	0.8	−4.25
TOTAL OECD	−0.8	0.7	−3.5

SOURCE: Based on OECD. *Economic Outlook,* no. 30, December 1981, pp. 12, 61, 67, 72, 78, 84, 89 and 94; *Economic Outlook,* no. 32, December 1982, pp. 15, 67, 74, 79, 85, 91, 96 and 101.

The slight recovery in the growth of industrial production during 1981 mainly occurred in the first half of the year due largely to the United States' growth in industrial production in the first quarter of the year. This occurred at a time when most of the major European capitalist nations' industry was stagnating. However, industrial production in the United States dropped sharply in the second half of 1981, and especially in the last quarter of the year, while continuing to stagnate in the major developed capitalist countries.

Unemployment, which along with industrial production, is one of the indicators which better shows the severity of the cycle's crisis phase, has reached unprecedented levels in recent years. Since the 1974-75 crisis, when 15 million people in the developed capitalist countries were out of work, unemployment has risen without interruption. There were 21.4 million unemployed in 1980 and more than 25 million in 1981; the figure is now estimated to be over 30 million.

It is not just a quantitative problem, although its magnitude makes for a very serious situation. Present unemployment affects almost every branch of the capitalist economy, from public services to branches which

UNEMPLOYMENT RATE
(Per cent of the labor force)

	1980	1981	1982
United States	7.2	7.6	9.5
Japan	2.0	2.2	2.25
Federal Republic of Germany	3.4	4.8	7.0
France	6.3	7.3	8.5
United Kingdom	7.0	10.6	12.25
Italy	7.6	8.5	9.25
Canada	7.5	7.6	11.0
Total of the 7 major OECD countries	5.7	6.5	8.0
Other OECD countries	8.3	8.9	10.5
TOTAL OECD	6.2	7.1	8.5

SOURCE: Based on OECD. *Economic Outlook,* no. 30, December 1981, p. 19; *Economic Outlook,* no. 32, December 1982, p. 35.

historically have been little affected by this problem or have been recently established. In addition, in line with the above, it may be said that there is no part of the capitalist economy that has not been affected. Chronic

CONSUMER PRICE INDEX
(Changes from the preceding year in per cent)
Annual rates

	Average 1961-70	1971-77	1978	1979	1980	1981	12 months ending in Sept. 1982
United States	2.8	6.6	7.7	11.3	13.5	10.4	5.0
Japan	5.8	10.7	3.8	3.6	8.0	4.9	3.2
Federal Republic of Germany	2.7	5.6	2.7	4.1	5.5	5.9	4.9
France	4.0	9.0	9.1	10.8	13.6	13.4	10.1
United Kingdom	4.1	13.9	8.3	13.4	18.0	11.9	7.3
Italy	3.9	13.1	12.1	14.8	21.2	19.5	17.1
Canada	2.7	7.5	9.0	9.1	10.1	12.5	10.4
Total for these 7 countries	3.2	8.1	7.0	9.3	12.2	10.0	6.5
OECD-Europe	3.8	10.0	9.3	10.6	14.2	12.3	9.8
OECD-EEC	3.6	9.6	7.1	9.1	12.3	11.5	9.2
TOTAL OECD	3.3	8.5	8.0	9.8	12.9	10.6	7.3

SOURCE: Based on OECD. *Economic Outlook,* no. 30, December 1981, p.47; no. 32, December 1982, pp. 46 and 163.

unemployment has hit not only workers but even the more privileged social groups.

The pattern of prices in 1981 indicates a slight improvement in the levels of inflation in most of the OECD countries.

A relatively marked trend toward a reduction in price increases may be noted, due to several junctural factors which, in the view of many experts, may not operate in the near future.

Price developments in 1982 showed that, even though a restrictive monetary policy was implemented within the framework of an economic recession, the price rise was not eliminated but only restrained. This is due to the fact that inflation in capitalist countries stems not only from strictly monetary processes but also more complex phenomena derived from deep socio-economic contradictions.

SHORT-TERM INTEREST RATES[a]

	1979	1980	1981	1982[b]
United States	12.10	13.60	12.97	8.03
Japan	8.13	9.90	6.75	6.97
France	12.59	11.56	15.26	13.45
Federal Republic of Germany	9.58	10.27	10.82	7.58
Great Britain	15.84	13.02	14.78	8.83

[a] Interest rates on three-month Treasury notes.
[b] Until October 1982.

SOURCE: Based on OECD. *Main Economic Indicators*, April 1982, p. 24.

LONG-TERM INTEREST RATES[a]

	1979	1980	1981	1982[b]
United States	9.64	11.49	13.72	10.91
Japan	8.64	9.41	7.93	8.45
France	12.14	14.71	17.00	16.44
Federal Republic of Germany	7.90	8.90	9.70	8.30
Great Britain	11.75	12.14	13.89	9.73

[a] Interest rates on long-term (five years or more) government bonds.
[b] Until October 1982.

SOURCE: Based on OECD. *Main Economic Indicators*, April 1982, p. 25; and December 1982, p. 25.

The indiscriminate rise in *interest rates* promoted by the United States Government is, without a doubt, one of the most arbitrary economic measures in recent years. This measure implies serious consequences not only for the US economy itself – it has indeed contributed to deepening the crisis – but has also brought about a serious deterioration of the international financial market, increased Third World external debt servicing, and contributed to stagnation in international trade. Although other factors could be added that also contributed to the existence of high interest rates. They include governments' great need for loans in a context of restrictive monetary policy as a consequence of large budget deficits, the process of eliminating regulations in credit markets, the use of new financial mechanisms in a group of countries as a result of readjustment in the financial credit system (mainly in the United States) and the need of some capitalist countries (Japan and Western Europe) to protect their currencies and prevent decapitalization of their financial markets.

The effects of these factors, together with specific domestic situations and speculative phenomena, resulted in increased interest rates in most OECD countries – which, in turn, had a negative influence on economic developments in those nations.

During these years, the United States' main trade partners criticized the US Government many times, charging it with being largely responsible for the adverse situation in the capitalist economies. Such criticism had also been frequent during the last decade as a result of worsening intercapitalist contradictions, but they were repeated in stronger terms in 1981-1982 since the new Republican Administration forced the rest of the United States' partners to act in the interest of Washington and against those of Japan and Western Europe.

The use of this anti-inflationary policy, together with other factors, favored fast changes in and a tendency for interest rates to rise to very high levels. Moreover, the policy of high interest rates in the United States favored the strengthening of the US dollar, which had suffered a notable deterioration in previous years. Other factors, such as a favorable initial reaction by the international financial community to the new US Government's economic policy, also contributed to the dollar's over-appreciation.

Even though interest rates tended to fall in late 1982, they remained higher than their historic average.

The uncertainty of the financial markets – as a result of an anticipated rise in inflation rates – coupled with the pressures caused by high levels of state indebtedness on the credit markets, brought out a tendency to rising long-term real interest rates.

Changes in the rate of exchange were related to a complex group of factors, including differences in the inflation rates of various countries, interrelationships among interest rates, and the different situations of the current accounts of the balances of payments in the various countries.

During 1981, the OECD countries' *foreign trade* recovered slightly from the depressed levels of 1980, a trend that did not remain in 1982.

One of the factors restraining greater recovery in OECD international trade was the economic crisis in these countries. This was caused by a fall in demand and in the level of exports in intra-OECD trade which began in the second half of 1980. The sustained trade deficit experienced by the major market-economy developed countries as a group has also been significant.

VOLUME OF EXPORTS AND IMPORTS
OF THE OECD COUNTRIES
(Percentage)

	1979	1980	1981	1982
Exports	6.7	5.0	2.3	−1.5
Imports	8.4	−1.5	−1.9	0

SOURCE: Based on OECD. *Economic Outlook,* no. 32, December 1982. Tables 36 and 37, p. 117.

TRADE BALANCE
(Billions of dollars)

	1979	1980	1981	1982
United States	−27.3	−25.3	−27.9	−37.5
Canada	4.0	7.8	6.6	14.0
Japan	1.8	2.1	20.0	18.75
France	−1.4	−13.0	−10.1	−15.5
Federal Republic of Germany	17.5	10.5	17.9	26.0
Italy	−1.0	−16.3	−10.6	−8.0
Great Britain	−7.4	2.8	6.1	0.75
The 7 major OECD countries	−13.9	−31.6	1.9	−1.5
Other OECD countries	−25.5	−42.7	−30.7	−25.25
TOTAL OECD	−39.4	−74.3	−28.8	−26.75
TOTAL EEC	−6.3	−31.1	−5.3	−0.5

SOURCE: Based on OECD. *Economic Outlook,* no. 30, December 1981, table 30, p. 57 and tables 47 and 49, p. 114; *Economic Outlook,* no. 32, December 1982, table 48, p. 121.

As may be noted, the particular situation of the various sub-groupings of OECD countries differs greatly.

This phenomenon can be traced to the unequal economic development of the OECD member countries. It is reflected in their uneven levels in product competitiveness and their different production and foreign trade structures. These differences are also due to their varying degrees of reliance on foreign supplies of raw materials and inequalities in regional concentration of their foreign trade.

Significant changes also took place in the developed capitalist countries' *balances of payments* in 1981 and 1982. The OECD estimated that the deficit in the current accounts of its member countries amounted to $39 billion in 1982 – $30 billion less than the 1980 deficit, that reached the figure of $69 billion.

The most recent effects of the economic crisis in the underdeveloped countries

For the underdeveloped countries as a whole, 1981 and 1982 were years of general economic catastrophe – which added to the permanent economic ruin which characterizes them as a group. Dragged along by the crisis generated in the developed capitalist economies, they – as always – paid the highest price for a situation they had not created, since they were used to soften the crisis' worst effects.

A simultaneous drop in their export prices and the brutally adverse performance of the financial sector in these years resulted in actual strangulation for our countries, starting with plummeting export prices and very high interest rates which sent debt servicing soaring, made new loans extremely expensive or impossible to obtain and reduced investments in production. The deterioration in the terms of trade, the reduction in the volume of exports, the rise in interest rates, and trade and financial barriers – hampering access to foreign loans and imposing harsh loan conditions – were the salient features of the underdeveloped world's economic reality.

Indeed, 1974 and 1975 were bitter years for our countries, but as of 1980, the situation has become even more oppresive in 1981 and 1982, though figures for the latter are still incomplete. In 1974 and 1975 the conditions in which the crisis was faced – especially in the terms of trade – were not so negative as they are now, whereby the financial sector has been most affected. Though a flow of commercial loans and some declining concessionary financing which barely sustained imports was still maintained in those years, the only way to face the prevailing international situation now is by reducing imports and reaching minimum or even negative growth.

The performance of economic growth indicators in 1981 shows the magnitude of the disaster.

Growth of the Gross Domestic Product dropped from close to 3 per cent in 1980 to just 0.6 per cent in 1981. This poor growth is in sharp contrast with the 5.6 per cent annual average reached in the '70s, even more so when compared with the 7 per cent minimum target set by the International Development Strategy for the Third United Nations Development Decade. *Per caput GDP in the underdeveloped countries as a whole fell by more than 1 per cent in 1981.* This had not occurred since the late '50s. On the other hand, this has been the fourth consecutive year in which growth of the GDP has declined.

UNDERDEVELOPED COUNTRIES: REAL RATES OF GROWTH
IN THE GROSS DOMESTIC PRODUCT, 1971-81
(Percentage)

	1971-80	1976-79	1979	1980	1981
Underdeveloped countries	5.6	4.9	4.4	2.9	0.6
Energy exporters	5.5	4.8	4.7	1.4	−0.5
(excluding Iran and Iraq)	6.3	(6.5)	(6.8)	(5.5)	(3.4)
Capital surplus oil-exporting countries[a]	4.8	2.2	1.9	−7.4	−10.1
(excluding Iran and Iraq)	7.2	(6.9)	(8.0)	(1.7)	(−2.7)
Capital deficit oil-exporting countries[b]	6.0	6.4	6.4	6.7	5.4
Energy importers[c]	5.6	5.0	4.2	4.1	1.4

[a] According to the classification made by the Department of Economic and Social Affairs of the United Nations, the capital surplus oil-exporting countries are Brunei, Iran, Iraq, Kuwait, Libya, Qatar, Saudi Arabia and the United Arab Emirates.

[b] The capital deficit energy exporters are Algeria, Angola, Bahrein, Bolivia, Cameroon, the Congo, Ecuador, Egypt, Gabon, Indonesia, Malaysia, Mexico, Nigeria, Oman, Peru, Syria, Trinidad and Tobago, Tunisia and Venezuela.

[c] The rest of the underdeveloped countries are energy importers.

NOTE: Figures in parentheses are estimates.

SOURCE: Based on UN. *World Economic Survey 1981-1982,* New York, 1982, p. 22.

The fall in the GDP was markedly severe in the oil-importing countries. In one year alone, it dropped by about two thirds to 1.4 per cent – one of the lowest rates in the past 25 years. In this large group of countries, where 1.8 billion people live, the deterioration of 4 to 5 per cent in their terms of trade and the crushing debt servicing – mainly caused by the very high interest rates unleashed by the present US administration – led to and absolute drop in per caput income for the whole group. For some countries, this was the second consecutive year in which such a drop had been experienced.

The United Nations[3] pointed out that 27 of the 49 countries on which information was available registered this absolute drop. The year 1981 was not very pleasant for the oil-exporting countries either, for their GDP *dropped* by 0.5 per cent. Cutbacks in their oil production contributed to this, and the Iran-Iraq war was also an aggravating factor. However, excluding Iran and Iraq, the growth of the oil-exporting countries only reached 3.4 per cent, 2 per cent less than in 1980. The capital deficit oil-exporting countries experienced growth rates of 5.4 per cent, falling short of the 6 to 7 per cent in preceding years.

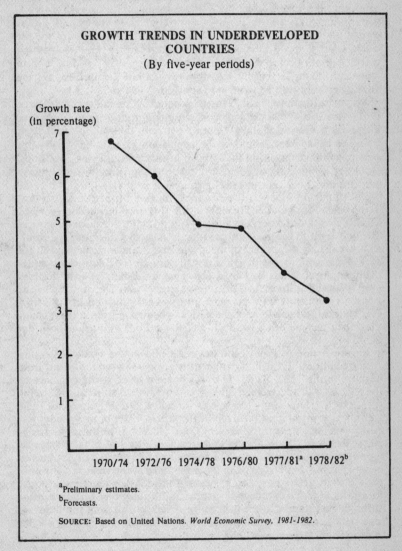

**GROWTH TRENDS IN UNDERDEVELOPED
COUNTRIES**
(By five-year periods)

[a]Preliminary estimates.

[b]Forecasts.

SOURCE: Based on United Nations. *World Economic Survey, 1981-1982.*

In Latin America, 1981 brought a sharp drop in growth. Its GDP had risen by 6.5 per cent in 1979 as compared to 1978 and by 5.8 in 1980 vis-à-vis 1979. In 1981, growth fell to 1.2 per cent, the lowest rate ever recorded since 1945 (according to ECLA, the first year for which reliable figures on the developments of the regional GDP were available), thus being lower than the average demographic growth.[4] This negative trend worsened in 1982, when, according to preliminary ECLA estimates, the GDP dropped by nearly 1 per cent. Consequently, the per caput GDP dropped by slightly over 1 per cent in 1981, something which had not occurred in Latin America since 1959. Of the 19 Latin American countries considered, the growth rate dropped in 17, the GDP decreased in 6 and the per caput GDP fell in 9.

According to the United Nations Economic Commission for Africa, 1981 was a year of disaster and economic ruin for the African continent.[5] The average growth of slightly over 3 per cent attained by the African countries barely keeps ahead of the population growth and shows, at a glance, no improvement in the African masses critical living conditions. Moreover, preliminary estimates made by the same Commission show a decrease of 1.4 per cent in 1982 as compared to 1981.

The situation of the African economy, however, is particularly critical in the field of agriculture. Throughout the '70s, food production averaged a feeble growth of 1.4 per cent a year – around half the population growth. The only term to describe this situation is collective calamity, in a continent where only 44 per cent of the arable land is under plough and 80 per cent of the working population is directly or indirectly dependent on agriculture. Against this backdrop, per caput availability of food declines every year and is lower now than it was in the '60s. The most backward African countries faced even more hunger and starvation in 1981 than ever before. Over one third of the African population lives in these countries, their income being less than half the average in other African nations.

A growth rate of 4 per cent was registered in the non-oil-exporting Asian countries. Though far from satisfactory, this rate was the least negative in the Third World. This was due, however, to the influence of the regional figures of some of the so-called newly "industrialized" countries, NIC's (Hong Kong, Malaysia, Singapore, South Korea and Thailand), which maintained relatively high rates in 1981. In these countries, notwithstanding their controversial growth model – as platforms for transnational exports – based on the exploitation of cheap labor, factors can be noted which raise doubts as to the possibility of maintaining such rates in coming years. These factors are: the persistence of the crisis in the developed capitalist countries, which consume these Asian countries' exports; its effects in terms of reduced demand; and increased protectionist pressure. This together with the emergence of new competitors and unfavorable trends in the external finance sector challenge the stability of the Asian NIC's in the near future.

Seen as a whole, the Third World's prospects for economic growth are gloomy due to the fact that its dependence on the West is dragging the Third World to a persistent crisis. At the end of 1981, 70 per cent of the underdeveloped countries had double-digit inflation rates, which tended to grow in some of the most economically important nations.

Adverse conditions prevailing in the international economy in 1981 were directly reflected in the underdeveloped countries' *trade relations*.

The volume of Third World exports as a whole registered a drop of 4.5 per cent in 1981, thus continuing the negative trend started in 1980, when it dropped by 5.8 per cent. Naturally, these overall figures are also greatly influenced by reductions in the volume of oil exports which dropped by 17 per cent (in surplus capital countries) and by 5 per cent (in capital deficit oil-exporting countries). The non-oil-exporting underdeveloped countries (the vast majority) experienced a 4 per cent increase in their volume of exports – opposed to nearly 8 per cent registered until 1980.

Trade, however, is not so adversely affected by this as by the extremely negative performance of the terms of trade and its impact on the volume of imports of the non-oil-exporting underdeveloped countries, on which growth possibilities and even their peoples' standards of living depend considerably.

In 1981, these countries drastically reduced the growth of their imports, which only reached 2 per cent compared to the already low, unsatisfactory 5 per cent in preceding years. This obviously represents a violent contraction due to non-existent or too costly commercial and other financing.

Primary commodity price fluctuations have been simply disastrous. In 1981, non-oil primary commodity prices taken as a whole dropped by 15.6 per cent. The sub-grouping of food prices was the worse hit with an overall drop of 21.3 per cent.

Taking into consideration that prices for manufacturing exports by the developed capitalist countries dropped by 5 per cent, basically due to the appreciation of the dollar caused by US Government policies, it may be concluded that in the year under examination primary commodity exporters registered a drop of some 11 per cent in their prices as compared to manufactured goods. Between 1978 and 1981 the non-oil-exporting underdeveloped countries suffered a deterioration in their terms of trade of about 20 per cent.

The drop in prices in 1981 and 1982 – veritable collapses in some cases – meant losses of at least $8 billion for the Third World.

In this context, *the drop in oil prices* deserves special attention.

Although annual average oil prices were 10 per cent higher in 1981 than in 1980, important changes in the oil market took place in 1981 that notably modified the 1974-1980 marketing features of this fuel.

In 1981, the simultaneous impact of the crisis and the consecuent reduction in economic activity, together with energy-saving and conservation measures, radically changed the situation prevailing since 1974. Average consumption, measured in millions of barrels a day, fell to below 60 million (59.8), in constrast to 1979 (64.7) and even 1980 (62.6). In two years, world consumption dropped by nearly 8 per cent.

OPEC responded to this decline by reducing production to avoid even sharper price falls. In November 1981, world production fell to 55.5 million barrels, 4.6 per cent less than for the same month the preceding year. This reduction, in turn, reduced OPEC's share in world production from 48 per cent in 1979 to 38 per cent in 1981. Oil exporters such as Algeria, Libya and Nigeria reduced their total production by nearly 30 per cent.

The fall in demand made prices drop for the first time since 1974 and although there were fluctuations in 1981, in early 1982 the price per barrel was $34.18, $1.31 less (3.6 per cent) than in the preceding year.

However, the behavior of spot prices during 1981 seems to be even more expressive of the oil market's actual situation than the official sale prices. In the second quarter of the year, spot prices fell below official prices, also reflecting changes in the reserve policy of major consumers. High interest rates, which render the maintenance of big reserves more costly, led them to cutbacks in stocks, and contributed to further depress demand.

Other pressures are being exerted to push down OPEC prices still further, such as the decision of English and Norwegian national firms to sell oil at three to four dollars under the OPEC prices in the context of a contracting sellers market. This makes the maintenance of differentials improbable, as might occur in years when the market is strong. Early in 1980, price differentials ranged from $1.5 for Indonesian oil to $8.5 for Libyan oil, higher than the Saudi price.

In 1981, various United Nations sources announced that, by 1985, Argentina, Brazil and Chile in Latin America, and Cameroon, the Ivory Coast and the Sudan in Africa will become self-reliant in terms of oil.

Moreover, notwithstanding the continuous disputes in the present trade crisis, with the United States, the European Economic Community and Japan constantly accusing one another, the underdeveloped countries face the attempts to "protect" Western markets against exports from the Third World. This is another way in which developed capitalist countries try to mitigate domestic imbalances brought about by their crisis – by raising *trade barriers* which pressure and harm the underdeveloped countries.

In this connection the so-called non-tariff barriers have grown in importance, reducing the real value of the liberalizing agreements reached in the Tokyo Round. Of the wide range of non-tariff barriers, the so-called voluntary restraints on exports – actually, prices cuts lest even greater restraints were imposed – continued operating in 1981. A recent study showed that in 1974 about two fifths of all trade by developed capitalist countries was subject to non-tariff barriers, while in 1980 the proportion had grown to three fifths.[6]

In the *financial sphere*, the developments registered in 1981 proved that the stifling conditions that prevailed – and continue to prevail – together with the aforementioned deterioration in primary commodity prices account for the catastrophic situation previously examined.

The crisis generated in the developed capitalist economies and the irrational economic policy implemented by the US Government which exacerbates the negative effects of the crisis can be clearly seen in the field of finances in underdeveloped countries. The irrational and aggressive economic policy of so-called "adjustment", which claims to fight inflation and bring monetary variables to the fore, has had two important effects: the sharp rise in interest rates and the appreciation of the US dollar during most of 1981 and on into 1982.

The simultaneous action of high interest rates and the dollar appreciation increased Third World external-debt servicing to an impressive $131 billion at the end of 1982.

The critical financial situation was immediately reflected in the deficit of the current accounts balance of payments. The worst hit were the non-oil-underdeveloped countries, which had a deficit of $77.5 billion. Also the oil-exporting countries, previously referred to as capital deficit countries, accumulated an imbalance on current accounts amounting to $15.5 billion.

BALANCE OF PAYMENTS ON CURRENT ACCOUNTS OF THE UNDERDEVELOPED COUNTRIES
(Billions of dollars)

	1978	1979	1980	1981
Underdeveloped countries	−34.0	10.6	35.9	−11.5
Capital surplus oil-exporting countries	19.0	65.9	103.7	81.5
Capital deficit oil-exporting countries	−22.8	−7.1	0.9	−15.5
Non-oil countries	−30.2	−48.2	−68.7	−77.5

Source: Based on UN. *World Economic Survey 1981-1982*, New York, 1982, p. 63.

The year 1981 was another growing deterioration in the current accounts of non-oil underdeveloped countries. In Latin America, the deficit grew from a little over $28 billion in 1980 to more than $33.7 billion in 1981. In this area, although net capital inflows rose from around $26.5 billion in 1979-80 to nearly $31.8 billion in 1981, they failed to totally finance the deficit in current accounts, resulting in an overall balance of payments deficit of nearly $2 billion.

The overwhelming burden of the high interest rates can also be understood in the case of non-oil underdeveloped countries by comparing the percentage of their total payments to foreign capital between 1976 and 1981. It is truly impressive to observe that the payment of interests as a percentage and in comparison with the payment of profit to foreign capital has almost doubled in this short period, with greater intensity in 1980 and 1981. This shows that *in recent years financial mechanisms have been the key imperialist factors in the resource drain. They have had a stronger impact than direct investment of foreign capital, highlighting the phenomenon of growing "bankification" of the international economy* mentioned by some writers.

NON-OIL UNDERDEVELOPED COUNTRIES. PAYMENTS OF INTERESTS
AND FOR CAPITAL INFLOWS AS
PERCENTAGES OF TOTAL PAYMENTS TO FOREIGN CAPITAL
(Percentages)

	1976	1977	1978	1979	1980	1981
Payments for direct investment inflows	3.4	4.1	4.2	3.5	3.0	3.0
Payments of interests	11.1	10.8	13.1	16.4	19.9	27.5
TOTAL	14.5	14.9	17.3	18.9	22.9	30.5

SOURCE: Based on UN. *World Economic Survey, 1981-1982,* New York, 1982, p. 66. (Information collected from 49 countries).

According to the United Nations, the so-called "non-debt-creating" financial flows (official aid and direct investment) financed approximately 40 per cent of the current account deficit of the non-oil countries in 1976, while in 1981 this figure fell to less than 25 per cent.

The capital surplus oil exporting countries have had in the high interest rates a financial ally, due to the large amount of external financial assets they obtained from 1975 to 1981.

The severity of the crisis and the negative burden – particularly of a financial nature – it implies has made a large number of countries implement "adjustment" policies which are not based on their own decisions or sovereign choice of alternatives as part of a development strategy. These "adjustment" policies have forced emergency responses to the atmosphere of crisis and, above all, to the US and British policies of shifting the main weight of the so-called adjustment on to the Third World. The Third World is confronted with a *fait accompli* and many countries are encouraged to adopt restrictive measures in investments, imports and obviously growth itself, in an attempt to reduce external deficits. Not even the policies aimed at attracting private transnational capital – allegedly to reduce these deficits – have been able to succeed, since *capital prefers to remain as financial capital drawing high interest rates, rather than as investment in production*. The results are highly eloquent as shown by a great number of indicators, many of which have already been mentioned. Another indicator is the state of the reserves in non-oil countries.

At the end of 1979, these countries' reserves were enough to cover nearly four months of imports – a situation by no means favorable – but by the end of 1981 only 2.5 months could be covered. This average, however, masks the dramatic situation of a large number of countries well below that amount. In fact, approximately half the non-oil countries (some fifty) had reserves for less than two months, and some thirty could not even cover a single month. Taken as a whole, the non-oil countries' reserve in late 1981 was approximately $8 billion below late 1980, an impressive drain.

These countries financed their depressed economic activity in 1981 – among other ways – by taking on onerous debts with the transnational commercial banks ($30 billion) and loans from the International Monetary Fund subject to humiliating conditionality clauses ($4.6 billion).

The Third World external debt, considered by many authors to be uncollectable and unpayable in strictly technical terms because of its staggering size, awesome growth rate and worsening conditions, is probably one of the clearest expressions of the irrationality and unviability of an obsolete international economic order. The very fact that this order has found it absolutely necessary to include in its operations the accumulation of a debt which implies the permanent bankruptcy of the vast majority vis-à-vis a tiny minority clearly indicates its absurd and harmful nature.

The Latin American external debt is a good example of this. In 1981 it grew by about 15 per cent, reaching nearly $240 billion (disimbursed gross external debt). At the end of 1980, it amounted to $208 billion. In absolute terms, the gross external debt doubled in 1978-1981.

Main trends in 1982

During 1982, the international economy showed the following crucial aspects:[7]

- the effects of the monetary-oriented economic policy implemented in the major developed capitalist countries;
- growing international trade tensions; and
- the growing deterioration of the underdeveloped countries' economic situation basically stemming from the worsening of their trade and the international financial situation.

The economic situation of the developed capitalist countries has continued to be a decisive factor in the evolution of the world economy in 1982.

The heralded recovery of the developed capitalist countries did not materialize in 1982. In this regard, more recent estimates show that the average of the Gross National Product in the seven major market-economy developed countries declined by 0.5 per cent, while for 1983 OECD anticipates a minimal 1.8 per cent growth.[8]

This was evidenced particularly in the case of the United States, which has continued to endure the longest and deepest crisis since World War II. In 1982, the US Gross National Product dropped by 1.75 per cent. In the main capitalist world power, industrial production – a decisive indicator in US economic evolution – has continuosly declined since August, 1981; high interest rates have persisted; consumer prices have kept climbing although at lower rates; and unemployment reached 10.8 per cent in December, 1982.

The gloomy outlook of interest rates on account of budget deficits amounting to $111 billion in the 1981-82 fiscal year should also be added to this. US official sources assess the deficit for the 1982-83 fiscal year at over $190 billion. In such conditions it is difficult to assume a short-term, stable, significant decline in interest rates, a factor which, on the other hand, is deemed decisive for a substantial revival of the capitalist economy as a whole, including the underdeveloped countries.

International trade prospects are similarly disturbing, especially in terms of the rise in protectionism resulting from the trade war Japan, the United States and the EEC have been engaged in. The violations of most-favored-nation treatment and the increase in non-tariff barriers are the most salient developments in this situation, all of which has led to the failure of the GATT Ministerial Meeting in November, 1982.

MID-YEAR PROJECTIONS FOR THE MAIN WORLD TRADE VARIABLES IN 1982

(Average annual rate of change in percentage)

	Volume of exports	Volume of imports
World economy	1.5	1.5
Developed market economies	2.5	1
Underdeveloped countries	−2.5	2
Capital surplus countries	−20	5
Other energy-exporting countries	2	–
Net energy-importing countries	5	2

SOURCE: Based on UN. *World Economic Survey, 1981-1982*, New York, 1982, p. 56.

In the field of trade, the underdeveloped countries' prospects are closely inter-related with the possible recovery of the developed capitalist countries whose projections are far from encouraging.

MID-YEAR PROJECTIONS FOR PRICE CHANGES IN INTERNATIONAL TRADE IN 1982
(Average change in percentages compared to the preceding year)

Non-oil primary commodities	−4
Food	−10
Tropical beverages	2
Oils and oil seeds	−11
Agricultural raw materials	−7
Minerals and metals	2
Crude oil	−5

SOURCE: Based on UN. *World Economic Survey, 1981-1982,* New York, 1982, p. 59.

Similar projections were made for prices of the main exports from Third World countries in 1982, as can be seen in the table above.

However, more recent estimates indicate that world trade decreased in 1982 and that, in that same year, there was a 15 per cent fall in prices of all non-oil primary commodities: 18 per cent in food, 13 per cent in agricultural raw materials, and 12 per cent in minerals and metals.[9]

However, the worsening of the underdeveloped countries' economic situation in 1982 stands out more clearly in the field of finances.

MID-YEAR PROJECTIONS OF THE CURRENT ACCOUNT BALANCE IN UNDERDEVELOPED COUNTRIES IN 1982
(Billions of dollars)

Underdeveloped countries	−62.5
Capital surplus countries	32.5
Other net energy-exporting countries	−20
Net energy-importing countries	−75

SOURCE: Based on UN. *World Economic Survey, 1981-1982,* New York, 1982, p. 63.

In 1982, external borrowing grew vis-à-vis increasingly severe credit restraints and the absence of solutions by the IMF and the World Bank. Thus, in the course of 1982, external debt reschedulings were requested, particularly by Latin American countries. In such conditions, it is perfectly understandable that the Third World's external debt amounted to around $626 billion in 1982.[10]

To conclude, in a paragraph from a recent United Nations report it was said that 1982 could be regarded as a year in which the growth of developing countries would again be unusually sluggish with little or no increases in investment. This could jeopardize the prospects of growth throughout the first half of the decade. The report claimed that, if there was no significant improvement in the international economic situation, the clear possibility of a regression in many of the weakest developing countries could not be excluded.[11]

3

Commodities and other trade problems

Developments of world trade in the 1970's

Although between 1980 and 1982 world trade experienced a sudden deceleration due to the severe capitalist economic crisis in the 1970's and even before, trade increased at rates higher than those of world production. Numerous authors highly commended this impetus by linking it to the evolution of the international division of labor and the increasing interrelationship between national economies and markets. Although the sharp drop of the past three years indicated the intensity of the international economic crisis, such impetus in trade has been used to claim an alleged economic prosperity in the post-war period, that would exemplify the improvable, but basically correct functioning of the present international economic order.

VARIATION OF EXPORTS AND WORLD PRODUCTION 1963-1981 (Annual average percentage of volume variation)			
	1963-73	*1973-81*	*1981*
World production of goods	6	3	1
World exports	8.5	3.5	0

SOURCE: Based on GATT extracts. *El comercio internacional, 1981-1982*, Geneva, 1982, pp. 2-3.

Obviously, the evolution of world trade is a highly significant matter for the Third World. This stems from the significance of trade expansion for the underdeveloped countries, their quantitative and qualitative share, the articulation of the growth in trade with the development process as a whole, the ways and means through which international trade may act as a dynamic driving force for structural change and a factor for overcoming underdevelopment, backwardness and poverty.

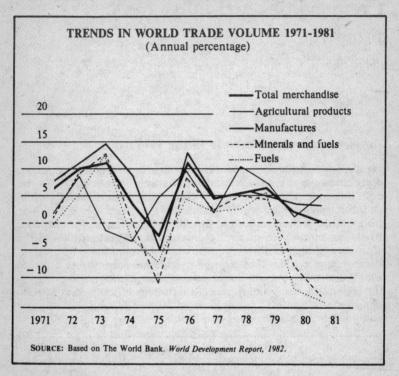

TRENDS IN WORLD TRADE VOLUME 1971-1981
(Annual percentage)

SOURCE: Based on The World Bank. *World Development Report, 1982.*

The expansion of trade recorded since the end of World War II has reflected a wide range of economic and other processes and developments, including the comparatively long period of growth without sudden drops in the developed capitalist countries; the impact of scientific-technological revolution; the establishment of the so-called consumer society; the relative trade liberalization established (now undergoing a serious crisis); the significant upsurge of transnational corporations, and – less significant than expected – the introduction of Third-World-generated trends in world trade.

This trade expansion, however, as well as the basic features of present international trade also emphasize, firstly, the precarious situation of the Third World, the inability of trade to push forward a development which it actually hinders, while reflecting the deep inequities of the present system of international economic relations. This trade situation is unable to promote development in the underdeveloped countries and also represents one of the exploitation devices to further widen the gap between the affluent West and the underdeveloped periphery.

It is necessary to recall some of the basic features of international trade, since they are forceful starting points for both understanding reality and trying to transform it.

The first basic feature is the *share of the underdeveloped countries in world trade*. This highly significant indicator clearly shows how the gap between developed capitalist countries and the Third World has grown; thus, in 1980, the former had further increased their predominance in world exports, surpassing the percentage reached in 1950 and keeping an upward trend only temporarily affected by oil price increases while holding a decisive qualitative superiority.

In turn, the Third World's share in world exports in 1980 was lower than that of 1950 – a regression that not even the high 1974-1980 oil prices have been able to stop. From 1950 to 1973 it plunged – from 30.8 per cent to 19.2 per cent –, increasing accordingly with the 1974 oil price increases.

The non-oil underdeveloped countries, where 75 per cent of the Third World population lives, have experienced a true collapse in their trading position due to this sharp drop. As can be observed in the following table, these countries accounted for 23.6 per cent of world exports in 1950. In 1980, the figure declined to 11.2 per cent.

The above-mentioned trade collapse shows strong effects in the productive sphere and the available technology. Thus, in 1950-1977, the per caput Gross Domestic Product in 1970 US dollars increased by $2 576 in the United States, by $1 771 in the European Economic Community countries and only by $126 in the Third World countries taken as a whole, another critical expression of the abyss separating the two.

The gradual displacement of the Third World in trade is coupled with trends observed in *the geographic orientation of world trade*. The developed capitalist countries prefer to channel more than 70 per cent of their overall trade among themselves, while with the underdeveloped countries they exchange a little over 20 per cent, over one third of which is with OPEC member countries. The underdeveloped countries also trade more than 70 per cent with the West, while trading about 25 per cent among themselves – following a slow upward trend showing a slight 5 per cent growth in a decade. Approximately 4 per cent of Third World trade goes to the markets of the socialist countries.

On the other hand, *the world trade structure by types of goods* adapts to the well-known trend of the increasing predominance of manufactured goods, the sustained decrease of agricultural products and the rise in the value of fuels.

It is obvious that, apart from the occasional rise in oil prices which generates increases in their export value and the relative diminishing of the

SHARE OF MAJOR GROUPS OF COUNTRIES IN WORLD EXPORTS
(Percentage)

	1950	1955	1960	1965	1970	1973	1974	1975	1976	1977	1978	1979	1980
Developed capitalist countries	61.1	64.5	66.8	68.8	71.3	70.8	64.6	66.0	64.7	64.6	67.0	65.2	63.1
Underdeveloped countries (total)	30.8	25.5	21.7	19.6	18.0	19.1	27.0	24.2	25.9	25.8	23.3	25.6	28.1
Oil-exporting underdeveloped countries	7.2	8.1	7.5	7.1	6.7	8.1	16.2	14.1	15.0	14.6	12.3	14.5	16.9
Non-oil underdeveloped countries	23.6	17.4	14.2	12.5	11.3	11.0	10.8	10.1	10.9	11.2	11.0	11.1	11.2
Socialist countries	8.1	10.0	11.7	11.6	10.6	10.1	8.6	9.7	9.4	9.6	9.2	9.2	8.9

SOURCE: Based on UNCTAD data. *Handbook of International Trade and Development Statistics*, 1981, p. 25.

share of manufactured goods, the latter represent the most dynamic and strategic sector of world trade, while the worst lot, befalls agricultural products representing the most vulnerable type of product with the most declining trends. From 1963 to 1980 alone, the share of agricultural products in world exports was reduced practically by half.

WORLD TRADE STRUCTURE BY TYPES OF GOODS

(Percentage)

	1963	1973	1976	1978	1979	1980
Agricultural products	29	21	17	16	16	15
Non-fuel minerals	6	6	4	4	4	5
Fuels	10	11	20	17	20	24
Manufactured goods	52	61	57	60	58	55

SOURCE: Based on GATT. *El comercio internacional, 1980-1981,* Geneva, 1981, p. 4.

Therefore, the share in world trade of underdeveloped countries, particularly the oil-importing ones, has gradually decreased, and most of them remain tied to exports of primary commodities, which still account for more than 60 per cent of Third World export revenues and are the weakest export sector.

In 1980 – regarded as a relatively good year for Third World trade as compared with the disaster of 1981 and 1982 – the industrialized countries imported $135.9 billion CIF from the non-oil underdeveloped countries.[1] Of this figure, 55 per cent were primary commodities and 43 per cent was recorded as imports of manufactured goods, which seems to be a somewhat balanced structure. However, the real significance of these manufacture imports is evidenced when their composition and origin are known.

The export structure of the non-oil underdeveloped countries in 1980 shows that in that year those countries exported manufactures which only accounted for 9 per cent of the total world export of manufactured goods. However, the weakness of these exports of manufactured goods is clearly seen in their internal composition. It is in garments where this group of countries has the largest share in the world total (37 per cent), followed by textiles (20 per cent) and various finished consumer goods (17 per cent), including footwear, sporting and travel goods, toys, and so on.

In turn, the percentage of strategic chemicals, products of the machine and electrical industries, and iron and steel, does not surpass 5 per cent, clearly showing that most of the exported manufactured goods are textiles and garments. These products are the typical representatives of an industrial production in which the use of abundant and cheap labor to operate simple technologies yields high profit rates for the transnational corporations which control the so-called fibre-textile-garments complex.

The aforesaid is confirmed by the fact that 70 per cent of the manufactured goods imported by the industrialized countries in 1980 came from the group of four or five South-East Asian countries, where in recent years a ready-made garments and consumer-goods industry has strongly established itself, based largely on the action of transnational subsidiaries, whose main incentive is cheap labor.

All this is summarized in the 1980 trade balances between developed capitalist and non-oil underdeveloped countries. That year, industrialized countries experienced a deficit of $48.2 billion in primary commodities, but this deficit was amply outweighed with a $60.4 billion surplus in manufactured goods.

TRADE BALANCE BETWEEN MARKET-ECONOMY DEVELOPED COUNTRIES AND OIL-IMPORTING UNDERDEVELOPED COUNTRIES

(Billions of dollars)

	1973	1980
Manufactured goods	23.7	60.4
Primary commodities	−20.7	−48.2
Balance (all goods)	3.0	12.2

SOURCE: Based on GATT. *El comercio internacional en 1980-1981,* Geneva 1981, p. 24.

If the trade of manufactured goods is examined by type, it can be readily noted that the strategic productions of the machine, electrical, and iron and steel industries, and chemicals recorded a considerable surplus of $77.7 billion, which greatly surpasses deficits in primary commodities, textiles and garments, thus delivering to the developed countries – in a year of comparatively high prices for primary commodities – a trade surplus amounting to $12.2 billion from their trade with the group of countries which, due to their lack of energy sources and the degree of underdevelopment in most of them, make up the poorest grouping in world economy.

Between 1973 and 1980 alone, the products from the machine and electrical industries increased the surplus they contribute to the industrialized countries from $19.7 billion to $54.6 billion, acting as the fundamental basis for these countries' trade surplus.

TRADE BALANCE BETWEEN MARKET–ECONOMY DEVELOPED
AND OIL–IMPORTING UNDERDEVELOPED COUNTRIES. TRADE
IN MANUFACTURED GOODS

(Billions of dollars)

	1973	1980
Products of the machine and electrical industries	19.7	54.6
Iron and steel	2.8	6.6
Chemicals	4.9	16.5
Sub-total	27.4	77.7
Various finished consumer goods	−0.9	−5.7
Garments	−3.0	−12.4
Various semi-manufactured goods	−0.2	1.0
Textiles	0.4	−0.2
Total manufactured goods	23.7	60.4

SOURCE: Based on GATT. *El comercio internacional en 1980-1981*, Geneva, 1981, p. 24.

What has been said so far, is but a review of well-known facts proven by statistic figures and empirical evidence. The figures show the gradual displacement of the Third World's share in world trade, its dependence upon the most vulnerable and low-priced goods, and a trade growth in manufactured goods, which could presumably reflect a new form of dependence, while transferring to light manufacturing the technological backwardness, trade imbalance and economic subordination traditionally characteristic of commodities.

Commodities and international trade

But these are not all the negative aspects of world trade in the Third World.

As stated above, over 60 per cent of the underdeveloped countries' export revenues comes from the marketing of commodities. They have the worst lot in international trade. In the past two years they have experienced a true economic disaster with serious consequences for the Third World.

The fact that there are very few (no more than 10) Third World countries with significant exports of manufactured goods, and that oil exporters are also a very small group, gives a clear economic picture of some 100 underdeveloped countries dependent mostly on commodity exports (food, agricultural raw materials, mineral raw materials). In Latin America – the most industrialized region of the Third World – commodity exports constituted almost 50 per cent of total exports. Oil-exporting countries excluded, the share of commodities accounts for about 80 per cent of total regional exports.

The question of commodities continues to be significant for the Third World. Actually, dependence on commodities is one of the features which more globally and deeply links and identifies substantial common interests within the Third World.

Numerous surveys have evidenced the disadvantaged position of commodities. It is needless to repeat well-known facts, such as the increasing substitution of synthetic products for natural commodities, which poses a constant threat to our economies. Their negative price trends can be observed in both the short and long term, although the trends in real prices over long periods are especially revealing and definitely challenge certain optimistic short-term perceptions generally held by economists of the Western developed world.

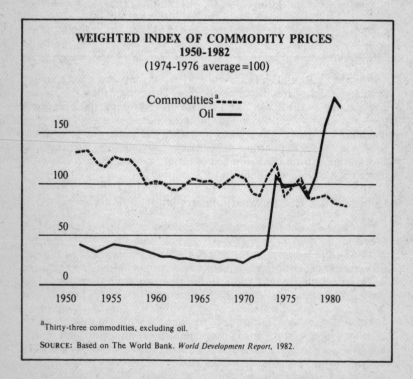

WEIGHTED INDEX OF COMMODITY PRICES
1950-1982
(1974-1976 average =100)

Commodities[a]
Oil

[a]Thirty-three commodities, excluding oil.

SOURCE: Based on The World Bank. *World Development Report,* 1982.

On considering the movement of real prices in the 1960-1981 period, a significant picture of what has happened with the export revenues of the majority of Third World countries is observed, not to mention the catastrophic price situation that has so seriously affected our countries in 1981.

A recent FAO survey analyzed the real price trends of 15 agricultural commodities accounting for exports valued at over $80 billion annually.[2] Following are some paragraphs from this survey. The data alone speak for themself.

Sugar: In early September 1981, current prices had dropped again below 9 cents per pound and real prices had reverted to the levels of twenty years before.

After September 1982, the situation of sugar prices worsened, current prices dropping below 6 cents a pound, which in terms of real purchasing power is less than 2 cents at 1960 prices.

Coffee: By mid-1981, prices had dropped in real terms to the low average level of the early '60s.

It should be noted that, due to the poor performance of prices, exporters were forced to increase the volumes of traded coffee from 2.6 million tons in 1960-1962 to 3.6 million in 1978-1980 in order to maintain their export revenues.

Cocoa beans: In real terms, the drop proved excessive and continued pushing the cocoa prices by mid-1981 back to the levels existing in the mid-1960's, and below those of the 1940's.

Obviously, since the global trade volume has not increased compared with the early 1960's, the real value of all export revenues from cocoa beans has decreased. Ghana in particular has been adversely affected, since its current export volume is half the level reached in the early 1960's.

Tea: In fact, the real auction prices of tea, on an annual basis, are likely to be one third of the 1960 level. Therefore, although the volume of world trade in tea has increased by 60 per cent in the past twenty years, the real export revenue value has considerably decreased.

Bananas: Although a sharp upward trend in current prices was characteristic in the 1970's, in real terms the banana prices have declined by over 20 per cent in the past twenty years.

Banana exporters have also had to increase their exports by two thirds during the past twenty years in order to precariously maintain their export revenues.

Rice: On the contrary, in real terms, the trend in the past twenty years has been downwards: real rice prices in recent years have been lower that in any other period during the past two decades.

To maintain their export revenues it has been necessary to increase marketed volumes from 6-7 million tons in the early '60s to some 12 million in 1981.

Jute: As a result of the unfavorable market situation in the recent 1980-1981 harvest, world market prices for average-quality jute were set about

$290 per ton at current terms, one third of that existing 20 years ago in real terms.

Sisal: The resulting incentives to intensify sisal cutting, together with a reduction in polypropilene resin prices, weakened the prices of the fibre and of the sisal packthread for agricultural use, which started in early 1980 and lasted to this date, reducing real price and placing it close to the early '70s depressed levels and at 40 per cent below those for 1960.

Natural rubber: In 1981, prices were a little higher than in the early 1970's as a result of the serious recession which negatively affected demand in 1980, and 60 per cent below the 1960 level.

Rubber exporters have managed to sustain their export revenues through considerable efforts, increasing the trade volume by 60 per cent as compared to 1960.

According to the FAO study, beef, soy beans, palm oil, cotton and other commodities suffered similar price drops. These examples show the sustained long-term trend toward decreased real prices, coupled with occasionally extreme peaks and troughs, all of which shape the intense process that stifles the trade relations between our countries and the developed capitalist countries.

As can be noted, many of the exporters of these commodities have been able to keep real export revenues at the 1960 levels only by delivering increasing amounts – as much as 60 per cent or more over the amounts required in 1960.

In general, FAO holds the view that between 1970 and 1978 alone, real incomes from exports of all commodities decreased by 7 per cent for the low-income African countries and 23 per cent for Asia.

Furthermore, long-term trends in real prices have revealed the weak position of minerals as commodities. Thus, in the world trade of aluminum, bauxite, copper and iron ore, prices deflated by the manufactured exports price index in 1979 were lower than the level reached in 1955.[3]

The downward trend in real prices is accompanied by occasional extreme peaks and troughs which are well known in our countries and which prevent even an elementary planning of export revenues. This produces spasmodic performance in our economies which originate fleeting moments of less poverty followed by an abrupt fall into bankruptcy and indebtedness. Traditionally, we have been in this vicious circle, occupying a more depressed position with every new cycle.

Under such circumstances, it is perfectly understandable that, between 1980 and 1981, twenty countries were forced to request the IMF's so-called compensatory financing, and that the available funds under the European Economic Community STABEX plan were insufficient to cope with the African, Pacific and Caribbean countries' deficits.

Our status as primary producers and exporters places us at the lowest step on the world economic ladder and deprives us of revenues badly needed for the life and development of the broad Third World masses.

The UNCTAD Secretariat has estimated that, had the underdeveloped countries reached the semi-processing stage for ten of their export commodities in 1975, the revenues from unprocessed products, amounting to $19.7 billion, would have risen by $27.2 billion.[4]

No matter how dramatically adverse long-term trends have been, immediate prospects are catastrophic.

The crisis originated in developed capitalist economies has also had a destructive impact on the underdeveloped countries' foreign trade. In 1981 and 1982, although figures for the latter are still incomplete, the fluctuations in prices were simply disastrous for Third World exports.

As was already mentioned, considering commodities as a whole (except oil), the decrease in prices in 1981 was 15.6 per cent, whereas for the food sub-group it reached 21.3 per cent. Between 1978 and 1981, the non-oil underdeveloped countries witnessed a deterioration of about 20 per cent in their terms of trade.

CHANGES IN PRICES OF COMMODITIES
(Percentage)

	1981	1982
Non-oil primary commodities	−15.6	−15.0
Foodstuffs	−21.3	−18.0
Tropical beverages	−18.9 ⎫	
Oils and oleaginous seeds	−13.0 ⎭	−13.0
Minerals and metals	−12.3	−12.0

SOURCE: Based on UN. *World Economic Survey, 1981-1982,* New York, 1982, p. 59, and UNCTAD estimates.

Some drops in commodity prices were truly sharp. Sugar prices, which were 42 cents a pound in October, 1980, dropped 70 per cent by December, 1981, and almost 85 per cent by November, 1982, hitting a low of 6 cents a pound. *These price drops produced losses in 1981 which the UN Economic and Social Affairs Secretariat conservatively estimates at some $8 billion.*

As stated, the deterioration in the terms of trade was extremely marked for the Third World in recent years. This deterioration, a phenomenon which our countries have suffered as a permanent, long-term trend irrespective of occasional fluctuations, has been the subject of many surveys that have proved its negative performance. The abundant statistical data used by UNCTAD, ECLA, FAO and other international agencies illustrate this reality.

But even more revealing is the concrete expression of unequal exchange in our countries and the increasingly disadvantageous position of commodities. The FAO Director-General has referred to the problem as follows:

> The constant deterioration of the terms of trade can be verified through the following phenomena: at the end of the past decade the profits from exporting one ton of bananas could purchase only half the steel it could buy ten years before. The case of wheat is even worse. In 1976, 16 tons of wheat could be bought for a ton of cocoa beans. Current prices only allow for the purchase of 9 tons of wheat for a ton of cocoa beans.[5]

To illustrate this phenomenon of growing and unjust unequal exchange between developed and underdeveloped countries, there are other examples in addition to those presented by the FAO Director-General, including the incidence of oil prices:

- In 1960, 6.3 tons of oil could be purchased with the sale of a ton of sugar. In 1982 only 0.7 tons of oil could be bought for a ton of sugar.

- In 1960, 37.3 tons of fertilizers could be bought for a ton of coffee. In 1982 only 15.8 tons could be bought for a ton of coffee.

- In 1960, with the sale of a ton of bananas 13 tons of oil could be bought. In 1982 only 1.6 tons could be bought.

- In 1959, with the income from the sale of 24 tons of sugar, one 60HP tractor could be purchased. By late 1982, 115 tons of sugar were needed to buy that same tractor.

- In 1959, with the income from the sale of 6 tons of jute fibre, a 7-8 ton truck could be purchased. By late 1982, 26 tons of jute fibre were needed to buy that same truck.

- In 1959, with the income from the sale of one ton of copper wire, 39 X-ray tubes for medical purposes could be purchased. By late 1982, only 3 X-ray tubes could be bought with that same ton.

Estimates based on the following sources: *US Exports,* September-December, 1981, US Department of Commerce; *Comercio Exterior de Cuba 1959,* Junta Central de Planificación, 1961; and data from the Instituto de Coyuntura of the Ministry of Foreign Trade of Cuba.

The last two years have meant an economic and, surely, trade disaster in all Third World regions. In Africa, exports were lower in 1981 than in the previous year. The region accumulated a trade deficit of some $12 billion, or a loss of about 5 per cent of its Gross Domestic Product.

A particularly marked expression of the adverse terms of trade is the aforementioned deceleration of export growth in non-oil underdeveloped countries which, in 1981, reached only 4 per cent as compared to near 8 per cent up to 1980. But even more dramatic in significance for potential growth and living standards in most of the Third World is the drastic reduction of imports in 1981. The growth rate of imports dropped to only 2 per cent as compared to levels above 5 per cent in previous years.

This violent contraction has been an involuntary, urgent and painful measure resulting from the unavailable or extremely costly development financing, and even trade financing. This reveals the intensity and severity of the present economic situation in the Third World, where the situation in commodities implies disaster for 1.8 billion people in more than 100 countries.

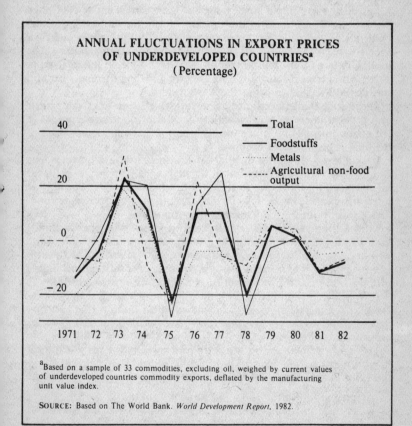

**ANNUAL FLUCTUATIONS IN EXPORT PRICES
OF UNDERDEVELOPED COUNTRIES[a]**
(Percentage)

———— Total

———— Foodstuffs

·········· Metals

– – – – Agricultural non-food
output

40

20

0

– 20

1971 72 73 74 75 76 77 78 79 80 81 82

[a]Based on a sample of 33 commodities, excluding oil, weighed by current values of underdeveloped countries commodity exports, deflated by the manufacturing unit value index.

SOURCE: Based on The World Bank. *World Development Report*, 1982.

Commodities and transnational corporations

An UNCTAD survey published in 1976 estimated that the share of the final price received by producer countries from the marketing of commodities is extremely low.[6] Shares are under 10 per cent for iron and bauxite; 20-40 per cent for tea, coffee, cocoa beans, citrus fruits, bananas and jute, and about 50 per cent for sugar.

If to the above it were added that export prices include transportation and other local costs, then the producer's share is really negligible.

Another recent UNCTAD survey has thoroughly demonstrated how small the cotton producers' share is in the fibre and textile production-marketing complex. The direct producer receives about 6.4 per cent of the final retail price of a ready-made denim garment. That is, he receives 52 cents for a piece sold at $8.04 retail (1974).[7]

In recent years, various studies, some of them carried out by the United Nations, have penetrated to a certain extent into the intricate manipulations of the transnationals, disclosing their harmful operations and their sophisticated techniques of exploitation. Though the transnationals will be dealt with in greater detail further on, it is impossible, in this analysis of Third World trade problems, to avoid referring to the particularly harmful role played by these corporations in this field.

These huge transnational conglomerates which seek to establish their own peculiar international economic order, are by no means innocent of the erratic fluctuations in commodity prices and the minimum share of the final price producing countries receive.

It should be recognized firstly that transnationals exert tremendous control over commodity marketing. Though widely known, this fundamental fact does not always receive the attention it deserves. Actually, all international trade in primary commodities exported by developing countries continues under the transnationals' control.[8]

The decision-making power of these corporations over price setting is such *that any Third World demand for the reassessment of its trade with a view to coping with unequal exchange must include – in order to be coherent and get to the root of the problem – the eradication of transnational control over marketing and the transfer of trade mechanisms to these nations.*

It is really important that, apart from hides and skins, transnational control over the marketing of 18 commodities which make up the vast majority of Third World exports ranges between 50-60 per cent, and 85-95 per cent for 11 of these products.

This overwhelming control is exerted by a few corporations which trade in more than one commodity. The above-mentioned UNCTAD survey on the scope of the power of the transnationals states:

> At present, 15 large trading corporations control 85-90 per cent of world trade in cotton. They exert similar control over the markets of many other primary commodities, such as the leaf-tobacco market,

where 85-90 per cent of international trade is directly controlled by six transnationals; the banana market, 70-75 per cent controlled by three corporations; and cocoa beans, where five corporations control more than 75 per cent of world trade, just to mention four of the major commodities.[9]

UNDERDEVELOPED COUNTRIES' EXPORTS BY TRANSNATIONAL CORPORATIONS 1976

	Total exports (millions of dollars)	Percentage marketed by transnationals
Foodstuffs		
Cocoa beans	1 737	85
Bananas	793	70-75
Tobacco	1 079	85-90
Tea	827	85
Coffee	7 831	85-90
Sugar	4 881	60
Rice	1 102	70
Wheat	449	85-90
Agricultural raw materials		
Hides and skins	29	2
Natural rubber	2 202	70-75
Cotton	2 692	85-90
Jute	172	85-90
Forestry products	4 169	90
Minerals and metals		
Crude oil	29 14	7
Copper	3 03	85-9
Iron ore	1 25	90-9
Bauxite	518	90-95
Tin	60	75
Phosphates	850	50-60

NOTE: The oil, copper, iron ore, tin, hides and skins data correspond to 1973.

SOURCE : Based on UNCTAD. *Dimensiones del poder de las empresas transnacionales,* p. 61.

More recently, in the international economy there have emerged the so-called general trading companies, huge marketing corporations handling thousands of products (estimated at 20-25 thousand products each), ranging from coffee to metals and even diverse manufactured goods.

For instance, in the case of the cotton market, the following paragraph based on the aforementioned UNCTAD report is eloquent in itself:

> Contrary to the widespread myth of price formation in a free market, a small group of speculators and big corporations trading in various commodities exert a powerful and marked influence on short-term movements of world cotton prices. Long-term movements are also determined by other factors, including prices and business activities of the major chemical and petrochemical corporations. Therefore, socialist and developing countries, producing more than 80 per cent of world cotton only play a marginal role in short- and long-term movements of world cotton prices and are confined to accepting price fluctuations and enduring its potentially harmful effects, particularly for the countries dependent on cotton exports as the major source of hard currency and funds for development.[10]

Actually, these huge corporations set a price, take over production and sell it at the established price in any quantity the market may absorb. These are the so-called "managed prices", fixed by the seller to maximize monopoly profits and thereby compensate, through large-scale operations, for eventual drops in profits from one product by increasing profits on others, and also by shrewdly taking advantage of the interrelationship of different products.

These monopolies also profit from the inadequacy of the traditional product-by-product analyses, which conceal the relationship among numerous products linked into production-marketing complexes, as is the case of the raw cotton/cotton trade/yarn/textiles/garments/textile machinery chain, which in turn is linked by mutual effects to the oil/natural gas/petrochemical products/chemical fibres chain.

Considering the fact that transnationals take in 80-90 per cent of the retail price in the marketing of most commodities, an understanding of the deterioration in the terms of trade acquires new characteristics, as revealed by an UNCTAD survey on bananas.[11]

In this context, the well-known terms of trade indicators, based on usual trade statistics, can hardly express the real economic benefits for underdeveloped countries, since a price increase under the prevailing conditions without eliminating the intervention of transnationals would only contribute a marginal share to the national producers, and would instead widen the gap between such producers and the increasing share appropriated by transnationals.

In July 1981, the transnational corporations of the developed capitalist countries controlled 80 per cent of the world's merchant fleet, including the so-called unregistered fleet; 12 per cent was in the hands of the underdeveloped countries, and the remainder controlled by other countries. This means that through the payment of monopolistic freight charges set by the international conferences on ocean transport, abundant resources in hard currency are extracted from our countries, thus increasing the balance of payments deficit.

Manufacture exports from Third World countries

Underdeveloped countries have rejected the classic notion – originated in developed capitalist countries, updated with various additions and transformed into an economic policy – that seeks to divide the world into an industrialized area with advanced technology and a primary-commodity-producing area. This old and persistent notion is based on a climatic determinism or on the availability of already acquired resources, and of late it has been presented with sophisticated econometric subtleties. But all its variants have been rejected by our countries, which refuse to admit as a sole and supposedly favorable status what history has undoubtedly proven to be the materialization and deepening of backwardness and poverty.

In the last two decades the underdeveloped countries' share in world exports of manufactured goods has considerably increased, coinciding with the correct decision to advance in the industrialization of the Third World as the only strategically valid way to overcome underdevelopment and gain access to modern technology.

Nevertheless, the relationship between part of this industrialization process and the transnational corporations arouses serious concern when evidenced that *a new form of dependence is being imposed upon our countries, thus turning them into exporters of simple manufactured goods, trapped in the network of transnational production-marketing systems, while continuing to import capital and capital goods which determine the course of development.*

Thus arises an industrialization structure, which some authors have called "subsidiary", since it is based on production and trading subsidiaries of transnational corporations, imposing patterns alien to real national requirements and benefiting from cheap labor for their highly profitable and uncontrolled activities.

The textiles and garments industry is not the only, but quantitatively the most important agent in this process. The way in which the various stages of its industrial process are distributed offers a clear picture of the export boom in textile products.

The chain begins with the preparation of yarn – the first processing stage – which is high-labor and low-capital intensive. Growth in textile manufacturing has largely concentrated on this stage in recent years. The Third World share in world yarn production increased from 19 per cent in 1950 to almost 40 per cent in 1979.[12]

The following stage – weaving – which is more capital-intensive and requires high automation and concentration, is still controlled by developed capitalist countries, and based there. The third stage – the garments industry –, where mechanization and automation are less viable, is still based in underdeveloped low-wage countries and often executed by small manufacturing units.

Finally, the last stage – the manufacture and sale of textile machinery – requires advanced technology and a complex design, on which the future of the entire sector largely depends. The share of the underdeveloped countries in this stage clearly reveals the power relationship in the textile sector. They hold less than 5 per cent of the textile machinery export market with little possibilities of increasing it.

In regard to this process briefly detailed here, UNCTAD has stated:

> The oligopoly of conglomerates has brought about two features on industrialization in the developing countries. First, the transfer of subsidia.ies and industrial capital, mainly to six or seven developing countries, has strengthened divisions within the so-called Third World, so that the phrase "industrialization of the Third World" means above all, in reality, the expansion of manufacturing in that small group of countries. Second, the oligopolistic corporations appropriate a considerable part of the benefits from such industrialization, even if they share them with a growing, but still subordinated section of industrial entrepreneurs of the developing countries. As a result, the distribution of benefits among these industrializing countries is also limited and unequal.[13]

But, leaving aside the textile sector and approaching the problem more globally, the situation is equally clear.

The following table offers an overall picture of the phenomenon of transnational "subsidiarization" and the extent of the control exerted by these corporations in Latin America. According to these figures, 33.1 per cent of all US imports from Latin America come from the local subsidiaries of US transnationals. In the case of manufactured goods, the share goes up to 51 per cent.

On the other hand, total exports to US-based parent companies from US transnational subsidiaries in that region increased from 69 to 85 per cent between 1971 and 1975. These exports were taken as manufactured exports growth and as convincing proof of ongoing industrial development in a number of Latin American countries, although, in fact, what they show is that a high percentage of foreign trade in manufactured goods and, obviously, of production takes place outside the control and decisions of the national economic authority.

Thus the so-called *"captive trade" system* arises turning international trade into a caricature of itself – many authors consider that no less than 40 per cent of world trade has these characteristics – since trade flows are established within the subsidiary network of the transnational corporation. Exports that are not really exports are recorded as such, and prices are set,

UNITED STATES IMPORTS FROM LATIN AMERICAN COUNTRIES, TOTAL AND ORIGINATED IN US SUBSIDIARIES, CLASSIFIED ACCORDING TO THE DEGREE OF ELABORATION, 1977
(Million dollars and percentages)

	Total imports	Percentage from subsidiaries	Primary commodities	Percentage from subsidiaries	Semi-manufactures	Percentage from subsidiaries	Manufactures	Percentage from subsidiaries
Argentina	386.0	6.8	114.6	2.1	100.5	7.0	167.5	9.2
Brazil	2 230.7	18.5	1 082.9	4.9	368.2	15.5	755.6	38.4
Mexico	4 647.3	48.3	2 080.0	30.5	547.6	28.5	1 803.6	70.8
Bolivia	160.3	4.4	115.4	4.2	42.4	3.4	1.3	9.1
Chile	229.4	5.0	65.6	10.3	139.0	3.0	15.4	2.9
Colombia	824.6	13.4	646.1	12.5	28.5	3.7	141.2	17.3
Ecuador	604.0	14.0	515.3	15.8	73.6	0.5	11.2	10.2
Peru	488.9	7.4	264.9	3.0	154.8	3.2	47.3	8.1
Venezuela	4 065.5	25.6	1 859.9	17.7	374.6	13.8	1 814.0	36.0
Costa Rica	293.9	24.7	255.2	21.6	3.8	0.4	32.6	50.4
El Salvador	426.2	17.2	328.8	0.4	1.6	6.7	91.2	74.9
Guatemala	377.5	6.4	361.7	5.7	4.3	5.1	5.7	7.1
Honduras	255.3	40.2	233.9	40.5	5.6	7.5	13.9	46.7
Nicaragua	180.2	17.7	156.1	18.9	4.2	12.9	18.3	8.1
Paraguay	23.4	5.3	12.8	6.1	5.3	0.1	4.9	5.4
Uruguay	88.2	3.9	4.2	1.9	11.2	0.4	72.3	4.2
Haiti	169.9	27.5	46.7	33.2	17.7	9.7	101.1	28.4
Panama	158.9	39.6	113.8	27.2	6.0	24.3	34.2	85.5
Dominican Republic	625.7	13.0	482.8	5.6	59.0	18.0	71.5	48.0
Guyana	55.9	6.1	45.8	6.5	7.2	0.0	2.1	2.6
Jamaica	346.3	86.7	216.2	95.2	108.4	76.6	19.8	53.2
Suriname	120.5	33.9	58.9	38.8	59.7	30.0	0.6	0.7
Trinidad and Tobago	1 655.9	77.3	753.4	81.5	207.4	54.3	689.4	79.8
TOTAL 23 countries	18 414.4	33.1	9 815.0	23.7	2 330.6	22.0	5 914.7	51.0
TOTAL FROM SUBSIDIARIES	6 100.4		322.1		512.3		3 014.5	

SOURCE: Based on ECLA. *Las relaciones económicas externas de América Latina en los años ochenta*, p. 39.

whose goal is not the equitable remuneration of the labor spent by national producers, but rather the transfer of profits from one subsidiary to another with the purpose of maximizing profits within the conglomerate as a whole.

These transfer prices notably differ from the so-called normal prices and their effects are as important as the financial transfers characteristic of the transnational corporations. As profits are important after taxes, transnational corporations can reduce tax payments to a minimum by manipulating prices in order to relocate the profits obtained in countries with heavy taxation toward those with lower tax rates.

Another procedure is to inflate the costs of goods imported from the subsidiaries in order to evade government controls aimed at preventing the retail profit margins from surpassing a certain percentage of imported goods prices or of production costs. Transfer prices are also manipulated in order to withdraw profits and treasury funds from weak-currency countries and evade restrictions on hard currency withdrawals.

The outcome is a distorted international trade; transfer prices that function as parts of the mechanism of commercial exploitation and unequal exchange; a diminished national capability to manage the economy and direct development; a newly fashioned dependence of unalterable essence; misleading international statistics suggesting a positive course where real trends point to an intensification of underdevelopment and growing plunder.

It is impossible to describe the international trade of the underdeveloped countries – be it in commodities or in manufactured goods – without finding in the transnationals and in the economic policies of the countries where the parent companies are based, the main obstacle to the development of the Third World. To ignore the action of these conglomerates would be to follow the philosophy of an ostrich: burying one's head in the sand. Without a coordinated strategy and concerned actions vis-à-vis transnational corporations, little progress could be achieved in steering away from the present catastrophic course in terms of trade expansion and the use of trade as a development factor.

Old and new protectionism

Since its inception the capitalist system has, for all practical purposes, been linked to protectionist theories and policies. Fifteenth-, sixteenth and seventeenth-century mercantilism is perhaps the earliest antecedent of the present protectionist wave that is currently affecting our countries with particular intensity.

For the underdeveloped countries, protectionism can be an instrument to defend incipient industrial production and the employment it generates against the competition of the developed countries; but it becomes historically unfair when countries with powerful economies implement selfish measures that retard the development of the immense majority of peoples whose backwardness is the result of centuries of colonial and neo-colonial exploitation on which the opulence of a small group of nations was built.

The reality our countries have experienced has been cruelly simple. The major capitalist powers have implemented protectionist measures which have adversely affected us whenever they have deemed it convenient, while repeatedly claiming to be devoted supporters of trade liberalization and deeply concerned over the likelihood of escalating protectionism interfering with the alleged free functioning of international markets.

These protectionist policies block access to markets or make the products exported by underdeveloped countries less competitive.

Before focusing our attention on the effects of protectionism on the Third World it should be noted that in the field of trade, protectionism in its various forms – as a policy tool in interimperialist rivalry – is but a capitalist reaction to the crisis and a manifestation of the struggle between transnationalized sectors of the ruling classes interested in a more internationalized and open economy and domestic monopolistic sectors with a domestic market base in the developed countries. In this intricate and complex rivalry what is really at stake is who will produce what in the future with all its implications or, in other words, market control in the '80s and beyond.

Control over markets and Third World sources of supply plays a significant role in this rivalry. In this context, protectionism is used to discourage undesirable production, and liberalization is invoked in order to penetrate the markets of countries or groups of countries.

It is no secret that protectionism has evolved. It has become more sophisticated and more effective where trade barriers are concerned. There has been a shift from tariff-to the so-called non-tariff barriers which characterize neo-protectionism today.

Nowadays, the defenders of neo-protectionism charge some Third World countries which have increased their manufactures exports with disrupting the market, while ignoring the advantages of transnational corporations in this process. In the manufacturing sector, however, there was an insignificant increase of 1.2 to 2 per cent in OECD countries' imports from the Third World as a percentage of their domestic consumption, over 15 years (1960-1975). This goes to show that these imports continue to be negligible as compared to the potential consumption of those countries and that the supposed invasion of Western markets by Third World manufactured goods is far from real.

If they level these charges against the few countries which have increased their manufactures exports, what will happen in the future when inevitably more countries export more manufactured goods?

It is also timely to recall that in the 1960's and early 1970's a number of Western authors held that, because of their inflexibility, fixed exchange rates were the root cause of protectionist measures. At present, however, there are floating exchange rates and yet the so-called structural adjustment in developed countries continues to rely on protectionism as a major component to correct the balance of payments and subsidize non-competitive industries.

The *old tariffs* have yielded to non-tariff barriers, but they have not disappeared. They still operate and constitute a factor of pressure, as shown in the Tokyo Round of Multilateral Trade Negotiations within the framework of GATT. During these negotiations a new reduction in the average weighted rate of the nominal tariff in the United States, the European Economic Community and Japan was agreed upon. However, this seeming progress in trade liberalization contains very negative elements that were unavoidable given those countries' adamant opposition during the protracted and complex process of negotiations.

Indeed, there are still many digressions regarding the average rate, which imply high levels of effective protection for certain products that are very important in our economies. The so-called tariff escalation was established as a principle, imposing heavier duties on products that involve more processing, all of which goes to prove that pressures aimed at keeping the Third World in its traditional role of primary exporter continue to be ever-present. Finally, the tariff reduction agreed upon in Tokyo did away with the preference margins resulting from the Generalized Systems of Preferences (GSP) of the United States, the EEC and Japan without even establishing compensations for other products not included in such systems. For years, the underdeveloped countries persistently called for the implementation of the GSP on the understanding that it contained significant concessions.

The Tokyo Round revealed the very dubious nature of such concessions and virtually annulled them, thus causing a net potential loss of $1 billion, considering the GSP of the United States, the EEC and Japan.[14]

The possibility of overcoming the serious deficiencies in tariff systems resulting from the Tokyo Round is remote, since a new round of negotiations is not envisaged in coming years and because in every negotiation within the framework of GATT the same basic principles prevail, i.e., the principles of most favoured nation, non-discrimination and reciprocity. It is widely known that the underdeveloped countries get the thin end of the wedge.

The so-called special treatment for underdeveloped countries adopted in Tokyo and to be implemented in agreements emanating from there – subsidies and compensatory rights, anti-dumping measures, import licenses, fair pricing, technical obstacles to trade and purchases by the public sector – does not modify the essence of such agreements. This is because the special treatment which boils down to exempting a certain country from a certain duty or recognizing certain particular situations is not all-encompassing. Negotiations are required in each case to put its provisions into effect. Furthermore, none of the agreements incorporated the principle of direct and stable access to developed countries' markets; instead, each of them did incorporate the so-called gradation principle, which leaves to the other party the application of special treatment according to its assessment of the country's level of development on the basis of a case-by-case decision. All this is very far from the preferential, stable and direct treatment to which our countries aspire as a legitimate demand in order to make headway in the field of trade.

In general, the Tokyo Round fell very short of the needs and expectations of our countries. The institutionalization of principles such as gradation, the impossibility of reaching agreements on matters such as safeguard clauses (which leave to the developed countries' discretion the possibility of applying discriminatory measures whenever they deem it convenient), the inadequacy and conditionality of the so-called special treatment, all of these are factors producing strong Third World insatisfaction with the last round of multilateral trade negotiations and with the present international economic order. It is a fact that the aforementioned negotiations convened by GATT were above all aimed at settling trade problems among the US, the EEC and Japan. The needs and aspirations of the Third World were a marginal issue; thus, it is not surprising that the results do not reflect the interests of our countries.

ECLA has expressed the following view, which is applicable not only to Latin American, but also to all underdeveloped countries:

> These countries were unable to have their situation and aspirations adequately considered, and their demands in the negotiations on products or in the new standards for international trade were not satisfied. Therefore, their future participation will be hampered by the difficulties in taking part in the system's decision-making process within a framework that has institutionalized – or seeks to institutionalize in the near future – concepts which do not meet the trade needs of the developing countries.[15]

The 38th Session of the GATT Contracting Parties held in Geneva, in November, 1982, did not achieve any significant results for the underdeveloped countries either. Once again their demands were ignored and the debates centered mainly on trade contradictions between the United States and the European Economic Community.

On the other hand, *non-tariff barriers* are, at present, the most effective instrument for discrimination and market obstruction. Subtlety, variety and covertness are the prime features of this type of barrier. They include an infinite number of protectionist practices – UNCTAD has identified some 700 – which range from government subsidies, quantitative restrictions, health standards and technical standards to deliberately complex administrative procedures. Another alternative is the so-called official or private "agreements on organized free trade", which are but restrictions accepted under threat of worse reprisals.

This wide range of protectionist measures, including the obstinate and rigid agricultural protectionism against the Third World practiced by the EEC, causes as yet unquantified losses due to the elusive nature of non-tariff measures.

Nevertheless, according to ECLA,[16] a review of twenty groups of non-tariff measures shows that they affected sales amounting to $8 billion in 1979, in other words, more than 50 per cent of all Latin American exports to the US, the EEC and Japan, excluding oil. Some sources estimate that approximately three fifths of the developed capitalist trade is currently subject to non-tariff barriers.

Fully in effect is the discriminatory and punitive US Foreign Trade Act – an elaborate sampling of barriers and exclusions on political and ideological grounds, which even include OPEC membership. This act includes the inevitable provisions on trade retaliation against underdeveloped countries which, exercising their sovereign right over their natural resources and economic activities, nationalize US property without "prompt and effective compensation" and even against those which, in order to protect their exports, participate in producers associations that, in the US Governments' view, are damaging to US interests. On several ocassions, the US authorities have tried to impose trade bans on their transnational subsidiaries in underdeveloped countries, as in the case of Argentina and other countries in their trade relations with Cuba.

Recent trends toward the appreciation of the US dollar, fostered by the current US Administration's policies, aggravate the contradictions among the major developed capitalist countries and, *inter alia*, contribute to increase the US balance of trade deficit – over $42 billion in 1982, a new record in the history of that country. These developments intensify protectionist trends in the US economy, which increasingly affect the Third World and forecast an important source of protectionist pressures as long as these policies are in effect.

The European Economic Community's sugar policy consists in strongly subsidizing inefficient domestic production and exporting increasing tonnages to the world market. It has played a significant role in the low effectiveness of the International Sugar Agreement – to which it has refused to adhere – and in the sharpest commodity price drop in the last three years. Also, in 1980 the EEC raised from 59 to 136 the number of so-called "sensitive" products exported by underdeveloped countries that, in order to have access to the EEC market, are subject to restrictive quotas.

Eight years after the launching of the program for the New International Economic Order, after the two so-called Development Decades and after numerous authors within and without the United Nations have shown in detail the unfavorable trade situation of our countries resulting from a persistent unequal exchange which exhausts some scarce resources, the position of the Third World in international trade is probably worse than ever before.

The measures proposed as possible solutions or as paliatives – of debatable efficiency – remain more or less at a standstill or very far from their original projections.

The few agreements on products reached so far are also at a standstill or in open crisis. The prospects of new agreements are uncertain. And the goals of the Integrated Commodity Program and its main component, the Common Fund, are still very far from being achieved.

Indexing has been persistently rejected by market-economy developed countries, which have even refused to discuss it.

Producers associations have been accused, boycotted and portrayed as satanic factors that disrupt markets and unleash crises. They have been victims of threats and discrimination.

Compensatory financing for drops in export revenues is still restricted to the context of ominous IMF dictates and its interventionist policy of conditions, while the STABEX system's attractive mechanisms have a restricted scope due to the limited resources it channels and the neo-colonial burden it bears.

At the deepest point of its worst crisis, it is historically imperative for the Third World – now more than ever before – to break the vicious circle of its trade inferiority and turn international trade into a true element for independent national development.

4
Monetary and financial questions

The international monetary system and the underdeveloped countries

The international monetary-financial crisis mainly affects the underdeveloped countries and constitutes one of the most visible manifestations of the bankruptcy of the present system of economic relations that capitalism has imposed on the world.

Throughout the last ten years, the economies of the Third World countries have been particularly hard hit by the disintegration of the system of fixed exchange rates, the appearance of enormous deficits in the balance of payments in their current accounts, galloping inflation and shortages of financial resources that can be used under acceptable conditions – with this phenomenon exacerbated by an excessive increase in interest rates and the resulting unprecedented rise in their external debts.

The origins of this chaotic situation go back to the crisis of the monetary-financial system imposed by the United States following World War II.

That system – agreed to under pressure at the well-known Bretton Woods Conference, in 1944 – gave the US dollar a privileged position as the main international reserve asset, comparable, in practice, to gold itself. In this way, the undisputable hegemony of that country in the monetary-financial sphere was established, through the well-oiled mechanisms of domination of the International Monetary Fund (IMF) and the International Bank for Reconstruction and Development (IBRD), better known as the World Bank.

The monetary-financial system thus created effectively guaranteed the United States' virtually unchallenged dominance over the international economy. Its massive exports of capital, reconstruction programs in Europe and military expenditures were generously financed by means of the simple expedient of monetary expansion. Logically, this presupposed a hegemonic economy and especially gold reserves to appropriately back the dollars in circulation.

These conditions no longer held, however, when the international economic panorama changed as of the late 1950's.

The US economy began to feel the effects of increasing competition from Western Europe and Japan starting at that time.

The extreme extent to which the self-financing capacity this system gave the United States was used, together with the maintenance of the anachronistic, unjust structure of the IMF, began to undermine its very existence from the early 1960's on. It was then, following the period of the "dollar shortage" in the developed capitalist countries, that the United States began to finance its privileged place in the international economy by issuing more dollars which had less and less gold cover or backing in other convertible currencies or real demand derived from the growth of goods and service exports. The great investment drive of US transnational corporations in those years, the growth of "aid" programs with political strings attached and the inordinate increase in the parasitic nature of its economy, which generated a growing amount of imports of all kinds and increasing military expenditures, were largely based on the policy known by all commercial banks as "creating money with a stroke of the pen," without any backing other than the credibility and coercive political force of the country.

The following data give an idea of that policy:

INTERNATIONAL POSITION OF THE DOLLAR
(Billions of dollars)

	Gold reserves	Liabilities in foreign hands
1960	17.8[a]	40.9[c]
1970	11.1[a]	97.7[c]
1980	11.2[b]	202.9[d]

SOURCE : Based on:
[a]*Economic Report of the President, 1969*, USGPO, p. 330.
[b]*Federal Reserve Bulletin*, November 1982, p. 455.
[c]*International Economic Report of the President 1975*, USGPO, p. 143.
[d]OECD. *Main Economic Indicators*, December 1982, p. 86.

The progressive accumulation of large amounts of dollars abroad decisively contributed to the creation of the speculative market of Eurodollars and undermined the base of the central reserve currency system, whose liquidity level became uncontrollable. Thus, this policy was one of the primary sources of the acceleration of the inflationary process initiated in the late 1960's, which has reached unprecedented levels in the international economy.

SHARE IN WORLD EXPORTS
(Percentage)

	1960[a]	1980[b]
United States	16.0	10.9
Japan	3.2	6.4
Federal Republic of Germany	8.8	9.5

SOURCE : Based on:
[a]*International Economic Report of the President 1975*, p. 131.
[b]*Economic Report of the President 1982*, p. 352.

In spite of these circumstances, the dollar remained artificially overvalued until 1971. When fixed parity and gold convertibility of the dollar were abandoned, with the result that the gold price was no longer pegged to the dollar, and the successive dollar devaluations in 1971 and 1973, the monetary system created at Bretton Woods came to an end. A new and as yet inconclusive stage of disorder and even monetary warfare in the international economy was ushered in. This was characterized by floating exchange rates, growing inflation, and the disorderly and asymmetrical creation of liquidity in the international financial market.

The successive amendments to the system adopted in 1969 and 1976 – in an unsuccessful process of reform, which in fact institutionalized the present monetary-financial disorder – failed to achieve the hoped-for stability of the post-war period. US economic hegemony, which had been the basis of the system, is now being challenged by Western Europe and Japan, thanks to their real and growing economic power.

The creation of Special Drawing Rights (SDR) in 1970, an instrument that was supposed to become the main reserve asset and replace the dollar, was a symptom of the incongruities manifested in the system. These changes did not meet the real need to transform the present international monetary system, however, and these expectations never materialized, though Special Drawing Rights did show the changes in the balance of forces between the United States and the rest of the developed capitalist world in recent years.

Nevertheless, the crisis of the international monetary system has hit the underdeveloped countries harder.

First of all, *fluctuations in exchange rates* have led to constant uncertainty; in the case of those currencies that have depreciated, this has resulted in the reduction of the real value of export earnings and of the level of foreign exchange reserves and has made it practically impossible to have any economic programming in the underdeveloped countries that use so-called hard currencies as their main reserve assets.

This has been especially hard on countries, such as the ones in Latin America, whose currencies and international reserves are tied to the dollar.

TRENDS IN US DOLLAR EXCHANGE RATES IN TERMS OF THE MAIN CURRENCIES OF THE CAPITALIST WORLD
(1975 = 100)

	1975	1976	1977	1978	1979	1980	1981	1982
Effective exchange rates	100	105.2	104.7	95.7	93.7	93.9	105.7	114.1

Source : Based on IMF. *International Financial Statistics,* May 1978 and May 1982.

In this case, it should be emphasized that the overvaluation of the dollar during 1981 and 1982 responded to the rise in the interest rates in the United States that took place as part of its restrictive monetary policy. This measure had negative effects on the external debts of the Latin American countries – as in the rest of the Third World – for it increased the cost of foreign financing, especially debt servicing.

Secondly, high *inflation rates* have also had very negative effects on the economy of the Third World in recent years.

WORLD INFLATION BY GROUPS OF COUNTRIES
Measured through annual changes in the consumer price index

(Percentage)

	1973	1974	1975	1976	1977	1978	1979	1980	1981
Seven major developed capitalist countries	7.5	13.3	11.0	8.0	8.1	7.0	9.3	12.2	10.0
Underdeveloped countries									
Oil-exporters	11.3	17.0	18.8	16.8	15.5	10.6	10.5	12.6	13.1
Oil-importers	22.1	28.7	27.0	27.6	27.0	23.6	29.0	36.9	37.2

Source : Based on IMF. *Informe anual* 1982; OECD. *Economic Outlook,* July 1982.

Inflation – whose root causes include the monopoly practice of price fixing and the sudden increase in unproductive government expenditures, especially military expenditures, in the developed capitalist countries during the last few years – has unquestionably become one of the clearest expressions of the irrationality of the system of economic relations prevailing in the market economy countries.

The inflation generated by the internationalization of economic activities in the 1970's shattered the Keynesian mechanisms of economic control that had been applied for many years. As a result, the formerly strengthening effect of inflationary spending by the governments in the capitalist countries to stimulate economic growth was lost.

At the same time, the inflation generated in the most advanced countries of that system has been passed on with a vengeance to the underdeveloped world, ensuring high profit margins for the transnational corporations through price mechanisms that increasingly impoverish and asphyxiate the underdeveloped countries.

Finally, the problem of *international liquidity* has also had a negative influence on the economies of Third World countries, as has the inadequate and distorting role played by the IMF.

As may be seen in the table below, not only is the amount of resources assigned by the IMF for compensating for the deficits in the current accounts of the underdeveloped countries clearly insufficient, the proportion of this support is decreasing.

BALANCE OF CURRENT TRANSACTIONS
AND RESOURCES ASSIGNED BY
THE INTERNATIONAL MONETARY FUND TO THE NON-OIL
UNDERDEVELOPED COUNTRIES
(Billions of dollars)

	1976	1977	1978	1979	1980	1981	1982[a]	1976-82
Balance of current transactions (1)	−32.0	−28.3	−39.2	−58.9	−86.2	−99.0	−97.0	−440.6
Total resources assigned by the IMF (2)	2.4	2.2	1.0	2.5	3.5	5.5	5.8	22.9
Percentage compensation 2:1	7.5	7.8	2.6	4.2	4.0	5.6	5.9	5.2

[a] Estimated.

SOURCE : Based on data in the IMF 1982 Report.

This organization's policy has not responded correctly to the crying needs of the underdeveloped world, since it has completely ignored the structural nature of the underdeveloped countries' balance of payments problems; limited all except short-term, compensatory financing; and attached strings that entail a high social, economic and political price and go against our peoples' interests and sovereignty. Moreover, the IMF has been shown to be – even recently – a veritable gendarme of the most reactionary interests of international financial capital.

Early last February 1983, when the IMF revised its members' quotas, the Group of 24 – made up of government representatives of Asia, Africa and Latin America – repeated its call for a 100 per cent increase in these quotas and the issuing of Special Drawing Rights (SDR). The demand for increased quotas, particularly in favor of the underdeveloped countries, was legitimately based on the worsening of the world economic crisis and its impact on these countries. Important circles of world public opinion supported the Group of 24 in this demand.

However, the IMF, as usual, ignored those proposals. Quotas were increased by less than 50 per cent, i. e., from 61 billion in SDR to 90 billion, and this increase was distributed in such a way that it benefited a group of powers – France, the Federal Republic of Germany and Japan, among others – at the expense of the underdeveloped countries. The issue of new Special Drawing Rights, as had been demanded, was not agreed on. And although the funds of the so-called General Agreement on Loans were increased, this agreement continued subject to the control of the eleven industrial powers plus, recently, Saudi Arabia – which, as the suppliers of the funds, decide who are to receive the loans.

This limited quota increase approved by the IMF contrasts with what the underdeveloped countries need to face the currently pressing state of their balance of payments (not to mention the large-scale flow of resources that would be necessary to emerge from the crisis and advance development). *In point of fact, only a small share of this quota increase will go to the underdeveloped countries and that small share, in turn, is but a fraction of the losses in foreign exchange that these countries have suffered since the last quota increase in late 1980.* Indeed, in 1981-1982 estimates put the losses in foreign exchange at $85 billion ($40 billion in decreased export revenues; $37 billion in increased debt servicing; and $5-10 billion in new loans).

The small share that the underdeveloped countries will receive of the recently approved IMF quota increase is no more than an insignificant paliative, albeit extremely costly in political, economic and social terms. Access to the loan possibilities offered by that quota increase requires going through the humiliation of that institution's increasingly stringent and interventionist conditionality clauses. Thus the Fund's traditional inflexibility is revealed today more explicitly than ever in the tremendous gap between the scant resources it contributes and the immense needs of the underdeveloped countries; between the meager, barely, short-term solutions and the serious depth and historic magnitude of the problems; between what it offers and what it demands in exchange. It is a formula that does not get to the bottom of the economic tragedy of the Third World. The need to replace the imperialist "petty cash box", that is, the IMF, with a new, equitable and universal international monetary and financial system would seem to be imperative.

The last few years have witnessed an unprecedented expansion in the activities of *transnational banks* in the underdeveloped world. The causes of this expansion are related in one way or another with the development of the transnational corporations; the internationalization of production; and, above all, the economic crisis and its effects, in both the developed capitalist and underdeveloped countries.

It was the private banks, acting above all through such relatively new mechanisms as the Euromarket, that have exerted pressures, in accord with the IMF, to force the debtor countries to apply economic policy measures that harm the most vital interests of Third World peoples. Thus, the underdeveloped countries have been trapped in the market network of highly speculative and restrictive capital. This, together with the deficits in their trade and payments transactions, has led to a critical situation with regard to paying the cumulative negative balances.

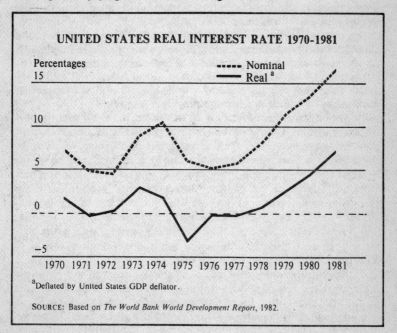

UNITED STATES REAL INTEREST RATE 1970-1981

Percentages

----- Nominal
—— Real [a]

[a]Deflated by United States GDP deflator.

SOURCE: Based on *The World Bank World Development Report*, 1982.

THREE-MONTH INTERBANK RATE OF INTEREST OFFERED (LIBOR) ANNUAL AVERAGE OF RELATED EUROMONEY

(Annual percentage)

	1979	1980	1981	1982
US dollar	11.9	14.1	16.9	13.2
French franc	11.2	12.5	17.9	19.6
Pound sterling	14.0	16.7	13.9	12.3
FRG deutsche mark	6.1	9.1	11.7	8.6
Japanese yen	6.1	11.5	7.7	7.0

SOURCE : 1979 – Based on effective rates at the end of the month, compiled in 1979 Euromoney (monthly numbers).
1980-1982 – Based on the average daily rates.

In addition, attempts were made to control inflation with restrictive monetary policies that have not only exacerbated the economic crisis and reduced markets but also implied the implementation of measures that have caused interest rates to rise to the highest levels recorded since the post-war period – and, therefore, created a tense situation given the cost of obtaining short-term loans.

The solutions proposed for these difficulties by the ruling circles in the United States have been domestic economic austerity and the unlimited, no-strings-attached opening of their economies to the supposedly beneficial action of international private capital – a combination of *further reducing the already very low standard of living and allowing the transnational corporations to operate at low cost and without restrictions.*

Efforts are being made even now, in its decline, to use the international monetary system to back up the hard-line policy that is a basic element in ensuring the survival of the present system of economic relations. In this regard, the International Monetary Fund has strengthened the strings attached to its credits and is firmly imposing its well-known role as supervisor and auditor of the underdeveloped countries' economies, telling them they should accept its neo-colonialist prescriptions of devaluation, austerity and the opening of their economies to merchandise and investments from the developed capitalist countries – in addition to paying high interest rates determined by the capital market and submitting to strictly regulated short-term payment programs.

It is sad to recall the many cases of progressive governments on which these measures were imposed, wrapped up in technocratic considerations. Meanwhile, every time the developed capitalist countries have found themselves in difficulties, the IMF has served as a guarantor and agent for mobilizing capital. A clear example of the conduct of this agency was its recent loan of more than a billion dollars to South Africa, with utter contempt for the other African countries and the international community.

Development requires enormous efforts and great cost. Only by eliminating the neo-colonial nature of the international monetary system – and especially that of such instruments as the IMF – will it be possible to undertake the transformations that are absolutely necessary. No international agency in which a small group of five countries provides the capital, controls 40 per cent of the votes and thus imposes its will on more than 110 underdeveloped countries can serve the interests of the latter.

Foreign financing for development and the external debt

The deformation of the economic structures that foreign domination has imposed throughout history on the Third World has meant our peoples have been faced with the impossibility of generating, on their own, the financial resources that are indispensable for overcoming backwardness.

Now, when an overwhelming financial burden is seriously threatening the economies of the underdeveloped countries and when spiraling indebtedness appears to be leading to disaster on an unforeseeable scale, the Third World's problems of foreign financing necessarily come to the fore.

For some years now, it has been evident to the international community that the only way to overcome underdevelopment is by obtaining foreign financial resources under fair conditions. That has not, however, been the main motivation for the flow of financial resources to the underdeveloped countries in recent years. The sharp worsening of the Third World's international economic relations while an appreciable volume of surplus capital was available in the developed capitalist world created the conditions for turning flows of financing into a generator of even greater indebtedness, dependence and domination for the poorest countries.

An objective analysis shows that this foreign financing – which has often been termed "for development" simply because it is directed to the Third World – has not contributed at all to overcoming the aftermath of colonialism and neo-colonialism.

In fact, the uncontrollable growth of the underdeveloped countries' external debts is not a reflection of logical consequences of a development process which necessarily involves foreign financing imbalances. It is rooted in the growing deterioration of economic relations between the most advanced capitalist countries and the peoples of the Third World.

This becomes manifest, in the first place, in trade relations, especially in those of the group of non-oil-exporting countries, whose terms of trade deteriorated by around 13 per cent between 1973 and 1981, giving rise to a deficit of more than $355 billion in their trade balance in that period.

The developed capitalist countries' control over world trade, the reduced diversity of the Third World's exports and its great dependence on imports have kept these countries from increasing their export income and forced them to accept unfavorable terms of trade that have more than doubled their trade deficits in just three years.

The seriousness of the growing trade imbalances has been accentuated in recent times through deficits in servicing operations. The balance of this for the period, also presents a deficit (of $76 billion).

All the above showed an overall deficit in the current accounts of their balance of payments which, according to the IMF, amounted to more than $476 billion between 1973 and 1982.

It should also be pointed out that the drain in the form of servicing operations continues to contribute greatly to the unrestricted, uncontrolled activites of the transnationals, through remittances of profits from the underdeveloped countries where they are located to their parent companies in other parts of the world. Studies of the balances of payments of the underdeveloped countries show that, during the 1970-78 period, the direct investments that entered those countries totaled $42.2 billion, whereas repatriated profits rose to $100.218 million. In other words, $2.37 left those countries in profits for every dollar invested, thus strengthening the balances of payments of the developed capitalist countries.[1]

Foreign investments have therefore been an important factor of deterioration in the underdeveloped world's balance of payments and an element contributing to its external debt.

Just as the financial resources transferred to the Third World have served only to compensate in the short term for the disequilibriums in its balance of payments and have not had any real weight in the process of development, a growing process of indebtedness has been generated in those countries.

EXTERNAL DEBT PAID BY THE UNDERDEVELOPED COUNTRIES
AT THE END OF THE YEAR
(Billions of dollars)

	1975	1976	1977	1978	1979	1980	1981[a]	1982[a]
Total debt	179.1	216.9	264.6	336.6	397.3	456.2	524.0	626.0
Annual average change (percentage)	24	21	22	27	18	15	15	19.5

[a] Estimates.

Source : Based on OECD. *Development Co - Operation Review, 1981,* Paris, 1981, p. 218; OECD. *Resumen de la deuda anual de los paises en desarrollo de 1982,* AP, December 16, 1982.

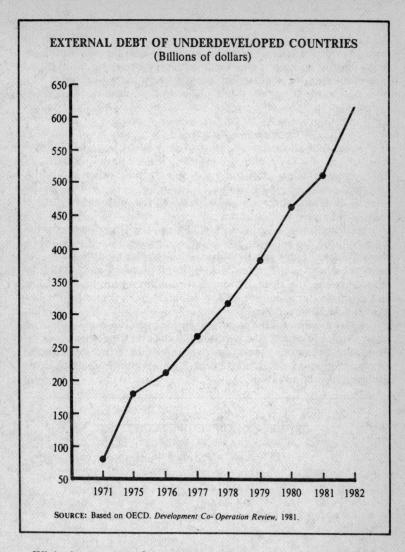

EXTERNAL DEBT OF UNDERDEVELOPED COUNTRIES
(Billions of dollars)

SOURCE: Based on OECD. *Development Co-Operation Review,* 1981.

While the economy of the underdeveloped world grew as a whole at a rate of 3.2 per cent between 1978 and 1982, its exports fell by an average annual rate of 1.7 per cent and its debt rose by 16.8 per cent in the same period.[2]

This fabulous amount of financial resources has mainly been used to cover the deficits in the underdeveloped countries' current accounts, caused by the unjust nature of their economic relations with the developed capitalist countries. In the last two years, this process has become untenable for the underdeveloped countries, due to the drop in the demand for their products, stemming from the acute crisis in the developed market economies and also to the negative results of the financial policies in the international capital market. This has meant, as we shall see, shorter duration and grace periods, higher interest rates and fewer opportunities for obtaining new credits.

Obviously, this indebtedness that spiraled particularly in the 1970's has now outstripped all forecasts to reach a dizzy speed that makes it ever more difficult for Third World countries to meet their obligations.

The burden of this indebtedness is such that it is crushing not only all possibilities for economic growth but also the possibilities for guaranteeing the low levels of consumption that are characteristic of most of the underdeveloped countries which are very dependent on imports.

Several studies show that every child born in the Third World now has a debt of $260, but since the debt grows much faster than the population there is a considerable growth in the annual debt per inhabitant – that is, every inhabitant in the underdeveloped world will owe around $500 by 1985. Of course, this figure is even higher in some regions than in others. In Latin America, where around $300 billion is owed, the debt per inhabitant is already around $1000.[3]

The very dynamics of the process of indebtedness, however, while making it possible to cushion the effects of the crisis on the economies of the Third World countries to some extent, has itself become a source of enrichment for transnational finance capital. This is clearly expressed in the evolution of debt servicing.

TOTAL ANNUAL DEBT SERVICE OF THE UNDERDEVELOPED COUNTRIES
(Billions of dollars)

	1975	1976	1977	1978	1979	1980	1981[a]	1982[a]
Debt service total	26.2	32.2	41.0	56.9	73.6	91.2	111.7	131.3
Interest	9.5	11.8	14.3	19.8	26.0	34.9	46.5	–
Amortization	16.7	20.4	26.7	37.1	47.6	56.3	65.2	–
Annual average growth rate of debt service total (%)	19	23	27	39	29	24	22	17.5

[a] Estimates.

SOURCE : Based on OECD. *Development Co-Operation Review, 1981,* Paris, 1981, p. 218; OECD. *Resumen de la deuda anual de los países en desarrollo de 1982,* AP, December 16, 1982.

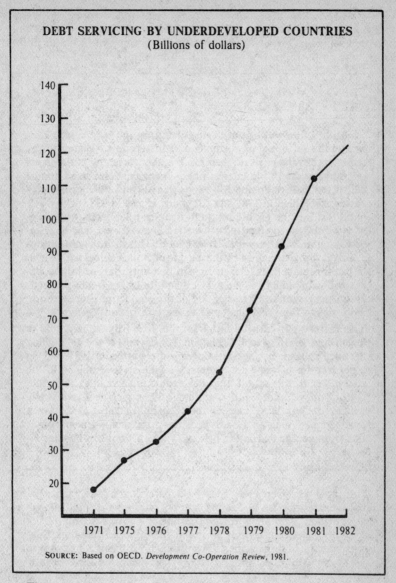

DEBT SERVICING BY UNDERDEVELOPED COUNTRIES
(Billions of dollars)

SOURCE: Based on OECD. *Development Co-Operation Review*, 1981.

These data show that, between 1978 and 1982, debt service grew at an annual average rate of 23.3 per cent – at a greater rate than the increase of the debt itself. In other words, *it is increasingly necessary to ask for loans in order to be able to pay what is already owed.* Thus, according to World Bank estimates, the real net transfer of financial resources to the Third World was equal to only 22 per cent of the total amount of loans in 1980.[4]

THE PARADOXICAL MECHANISM OF FEEDBACK FROM THE EXTERNAL DEBT

For the oil-importing developing countries, the large disequilibriums in the balance of payments in current accounts – aggravated by the impact of the crisis on their exports, the worsening of the terms of trade and the rise in interest rates – were expressed in an annual deficit that rose to around $80 billion in 1979 and 1980, greatly surpassed $90 billion in 1981 and continued to rise in 1982. The result of all this was the rapid increase in their external debts, which, depending on the method of calculation that is used, are now approaching or have surpassed $600 billion. This debt, whose magnitude was first determined by the need to obtain resources with which to pay for the deficits in their current accounts, has, with time, become a factor adding to the deficit – and, in fact, a feedback mechanism that takes an increasing toll of the product of peoples' work, more than a third of which goes to the transnational banks.

This may be proved with data from the World Bank, according to which debt servicing took $99 billion (85 per cent) of the $117 billion obtained as loans by the underdeveloped countries in 1981, leaving a net transfer of resources of only $18 billion ($600 million in the case of Latin America). Things have come to such an extreme that the underdeveloped countries are incurring in new debts practically for the sole purpose of meeting the obligations created by their own indebtedness. Such an absurd, perverted, irrational phenomenon as this is unprecedented in the history of international economic relations.

This spiral was given a new boost between 1979 and 1981, thanks to the indiscriminate increase in floating interest rates on the international financial market. According to OECD estimates, these rose from 12 to an average of 18 per cent a year. For the underdeveloped countries, this increase represented disbursements calculated at $2 billion more for every 1 per cent increase in the interest rate, which meant an increase in payments of an additional $13 billion by our exhausted economies in 1981 alone.[5]

Interest, which constituted 30.3 per cent of debt servicing in 1971, had risen to 41.6 per cent of the total ten years later.

This also shows that the export of loan capital has become the most lucrative form of capital investment in the Third World. Interest payments constituted 90 per cent of foreign capital earnings in the non-oil-exporting underdeveloped countries in 1981.[6]

As a result of all this, the share of the total value of the underdeveloped world's exports that went to debt servicing rose from 14 to 21.2 per cent between 1973 and 1982, and to almost 37 per cent in the Third World oil-importing countries.[7]

Capital flows from private banks in the last few years were important in worsening the Third World's conditions of foreign financing.

PARTICIPATION BY THE DIFFERENT CAPITAL FLOWS IN UNDERDEVELOPED COUNTRIES FOREIGN FINANCING
(Percentage of the total)

	1970	1980	1982
Official credits	32	25	23
Private credits	39	45	51
Direct investments	8	15	14

SOURCE : Based on *The World Bank World Development Report 1982*, p. 35.

The growing proportion of the flows of financing to the Third World that is provided by private banks is largely due to the effects of the capitalist economic crisis, which has caused a drop in the profit rate in the developed capitalist countries and, consequently, an increase in the export of private capital to the Third World in search of greater profits.

CREDIT CONDITIONS IMPOSED ON THE UNDERDEVELOPED COUNTRIES
(Percentage)

	1972	1981
Total interest rate	4.6	10.2
Floating interest rate	7.9	18.0
Concessionary loan factor	28	11[a]

[a] 1980 data.

SOURCE : Based on OECD. *Development Co-Operation Review, 1981*, Paris, 1981, p. 70; World Bank, *Informe Anual, 1980*, Washington, 1980, p. 155; The World Bank. *Annual Report, 1982*, Washington, 1982, p. 143.

The fact that the major flow of resources was granted on non-concessionary conditions – which amounted to $321.1 billion between 1973 and 1981 – has led to a worsening in the general conditions under which the credits were granted to the underdeveloped countries in the last decade.

To this worsening of credit conditions from private sources is added a relative reduction in the level of official flows of financing in the form of development aid.

In fact, the target established in the United Nations International Development Strategy, which calls for setting aside 0.7 per cent of the Gross National Product of the developed countries as official development assistance, has repeatedly not been met for several years. According to World Bank data, between 1975 and 1981 the official assistance for development by developed capitalist countries averaged 0.35 per cent of the annual GNP, that is, half of the planned amount.

The worsening of international financial conditions for the underdeveloped countries, particulary in the last two years, have forced them to carry out an increasingly generalized process of rescheduling their external debts, through which they try to overcome, at least temporarily, their most immediate financial obstacles.

Thus, according to several estimates, debts to the amount of $10.8 billion were refinanced in 1981 and $40 billion in 1982, with the rescheduling involving 21 Third World countries.

TRENDS IN THE UNDERDEVELOPED WORLD'S DEBT AND PAYMENTS, 1982-90

If present international finance and trade trends are maintained, the future in store for the Third World could not be more disquieting.

Estimates made on the basis of the present situation clearly show that, in just seven years, it will be impossible for the underdeveloped countries' economies to pay the enormous cost of financial servicing and survive.

It seems intolerable that these payments could come to absorb nearly 40 per cent of this group of countries' total export earnings by 1990. Nevertheless, this situation is dwarfed by the one that may affect the oil-importing underdeveloped countries – that is, the majority – that may be forced to use nearly 80 per cent of their export income to cover interest and amortization. In absolute terms, this would reduce by half their already short supply of foreign exchange for acquiring imports of goods and services – the $142 billion available for this purpose in 1982 would be cut to only $71 billion by 1990. For countries whose economic structures are very dependent on imports, this would lead to virtual paralysis.

EXTERNAL DEBT TRENDS AND SOME EFFECTS FOR THE UNDERDEVELOPED COUNTRIES BETWEEN 1983-1990

(Billions of dollars at current prices)

	External debt		Debt service payments[a]		Exports[b]		Relation between servicing and exports (%)		Financing required to balance current deficits[a]		
											Cumulative deficit 1983-90
	1982	1990	1982	1990	1982	1990	1982	1990	1982	1990	1983-90
All the underdeveloped countries	597.6	1473.5	119.0	361.0	561.4	922.6	21.2	39.1	109.2	559.7	2719.7
Oil importers	417.7	1050.7	81.9	264.0	223.8	334.5	36.6	78.9	82.4	397.6	1968.2
Oil exporters	179.9	422.8	37.1	97.0	337.6	588.1	10.9	16.5	26.8	162.1	751.5

METHODOLOGICAL NOTE: Trend estimates were based on data from the sources given in each case.

Quadratic functions of the $y = a + bx + cx^2$ type were used for the debt, service payments and deficits in current accounts; based on the real information of the 1976-82 period, they fulfilled the basic hypotheses of the model, expressed in the following determination coefficients:

Total debt: all: 0.9989; oil importers: 0.9998; oil exporters: 0.9958.
Servicing payments: all: 0.9790; oil importers: 0.9962; oil exporters: 0.9816.
Current accounts balances: all: 0.8900; oil importers: 0.8483; oil exporters: 0.5128.
Median rates of values betwen maximums and minimums taken from the World Bank's *Informe sobre el Desarrollo Mundial, 1982*, p. 33, were used as the basic for estimating exports of goods.

SOURCE : Based on:

[a] World Bank. *Informe sobre el Desarrollo Mundial, 1982*, pp. 13 and 15.
[b] UNCTAD. *Handbook of International Trade and Development Statistics*, 1981.

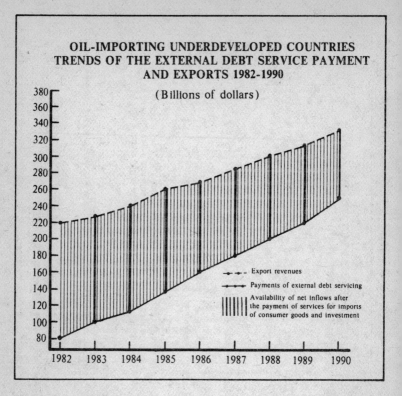

OIL-IMPORTING UNDERDEVELOPED COUNTRIES TRENDS OF THE EXTERNAL DEBT SERVICE PAYMENT AND EXPORTS 1982-1990

(Billions of dollars)

- Export revenues
- Payments of external debt servicing
- Availability of net inflows after the payment of services for imports of consumer goods and investment

Monetary-financial problems now constitute a revealing symptom of the contradictions gripping the system of neo-colonial domination. The present monetary-financial crisis endangers the very existence of the now bankrupt international financial system, victim to powerful interests, internal antagonisms and speculative mechanisms. This situation demands radical changes.

5
Agriculture and food

Over 20 years have elapsed since the World Indicative Plan for Agricultural Development (WIP) was presented within the framework of FAO in 1962. It reflected the difficult food and agricultural development situation at the time and established the guidelines for a program that was, by 1985, to make hunger and undernourishment mere bitter memories of an unpleasant past for the peoples of the Third World and turn the agricultural sector into a dynamic development factor instead of a traditionally stagnant and weak sector.

Over eight years have, likewise, elapsed since the World Food Conference in Rome (1974), urgently convened in view of the massive famines and alarming decrease of food reserves recorded during those years. On that occasion, the Conference solemnly declared that hunger and undernourishment should be stamped out on the planet in ten years and called on all nations to cooperate in an enormous effort for international food security.

The total failure of these endeavors to achieve the basic and essential objective of supplying all human beings with enough food to develop their potentialities for enjoying a full life is today more evident than ever. Over 500 million hungry people – a terrifying and skyrocketing figure – are turning into a tragic irony the good intentions of the aforementioned World Indicative Plan of reaching a calorie-intake level equal to the projected demand in the Third World by 1975, and that this intake surpass by 10 per cent the required levels by 1985. By now it is perfectly obvious that the eradication of hunger by 1984 – as stated by the World Food Conference – is simply one more well-meant although unsuccessful attempt of the kind that characterize the path of our countries' negotiating position in the world economy.

The so-called food crisis is not a recent phenomenon, although the current deep economic crisis contributes to its worsening. Strictly speaking, the food crisis, understood as widespread hunger and malnutrition among broad masses of the population – so paradoxically in contrast with food overconsumption by some minorities – has always been an unavoidable component of colonialism, neo-colonialism and underdevelopment. The food crisis must be considered by the majority of the underdeveloped world as a secular, permanent condition of their precarious life. For them, the hypothetical recovery of the developed capitalist economies has almost no meaning, since not even the greatest economic booms of the system have been able to prevent the presence of hunger and undernourishment in the Third World. For the hundreds of millions of hungry people living in that world, the food crisis is not a mere conceptual reference, but rather a tragic daily experience, a disgraceful reality for all mankind.

At a time when man is travelling to outer space and works true wonders in science and technology, per caput food production decreased in 52 underdeveloped countries from 1971 to 1980. While in many developed countries greater attention is being paid to the growing incidence of diseases related to overeating and hundreds of millions of dollars are spent on feeding pets, in India alone, according to FAO, there are 201 million seriously undernourished human beings; 33 million in Indonesia; 27 million in Bangladesh; 14 million in Nigeria; 12 million in Brazil, Ethiopia and Pakistan; 10 million in the Philippines; 6 million in Afghanistan; 5 million in Burma, Colombia and Thailand. Over 40 per cent of the population of Chad, Haiti, Mali and Mauritania go hungry.

The painful truth is that, despite the goals to eradicate it, hunger persists and tends to grow. In the '70s, food production increased by an annual 3 per cent in the Third World, thus falling short by 25 per cent of the rate established by the UN International Development Strategy, and, should the present trends continue, the number of hungry people would rise to no less than 750 million by the 21st century.

And all this is happening in the midst of an unbridled arms race, senseless both because of its essence, dangerousness and dimensions, and because of the contrast between the huge resources spent in developing means for man's extermination and our peoples' vital and daily needs. Indeed, US spending budgeted for the development of the MX missile in 1983 alone – $2.5 billion – could have financed the total amount of African wheat imports in 1979 or total Asian rice imports that same year, or the cost of developing 10 million hectares of pastureland in the Third World, or the cost of flood control in 2 million hectares of land.

Agricultural and food production in the Third World

The underdeveloped countries' agricultural production reached an average yearly growth rate of approximately 3 per cent in 1969-71 and 1981. This average, nevertheless, showed important regional variations. Thus, Africa only reached a 2 per cent average annual growth rate, while Latin America's was 3.6 per cent.

AGRICULTURAL PRODUCTION INDEX
(1969-1971 = 100)

	1979	1980	1981
Underdeveloped countries	127	131	137
Africa	114	118	122
Far East	129	132	140
Latin America	133	135	143
Near East	130	133	136

SOURCE : Based on FAO. *El estado mundial de la agricultura y la alimentación, 1981*. p. 5.

From 1975 to 1980, however, per caput world food production grew at the very low rate of 0.3 per cent yearly. During the past 20 years, over 70 countries of the underdeveloped world have witnessed a net decline in per caput food production and, in some of them, an absolute reduction in the output volume. Concerning cereal production, the per caput decreased in at least 66 underdeveloped countries, 31 of which were African.

According to figures of the US Department of Agriculture, the per caput growth of agricultural output in developed nations was 8 per cent in 1980 with respect to average levels in 1969-1971, while no growth was recorded in the Third World.

Actually, in the past 20 years, food output in underdeveloped nations has lagged behind food demand, a tendency that, according to FAO's studies, will continue at least until the end of the century unless present conditions concerning the food production, marketing and distribution change substantially.[1]

PER CAPUT FOOD OUPUT INDEX
(1969-1971 = 100)

	1972	1974	1976	1978	1980
Developed capitalist countries	101	105	107	111	111
Underveloped countries	97	99	102	105	103
Africa	97	96	94	90	89
Latin America	98	101	105	107	108
Near East	103	103	110	106	104
Far East	95	97	102	108	105

SOURCE : Based on UN. *Statistical Yearbook 1979-80*. p. 15.

The situation resulting from the present trends acquires truly disastrous dimensions for the whole of Africa, where the continent's average indicates that per caput food availability today is lower than that of 1960 and where food output growth is approximately half of the population's growth.

In the face of such situations, FAO has estimated that in 1977 the developed countries' food supplies as a whole met 133 per cent of their needs on average.

The underdeveloped countries' enormous backwardness where food production is concerned, especially in Africa, can be noted in the table above.

CEREAL PRODUCTION IN UNDERVELOPED COUNTRIES
(Thousands of metric tons)

	1978	1979	1980	Average annual change 1971-80 (%)
Total production	452 869	433 482	464 205	2.5
Africa	46 804	44 392	46 210	0.6
Latin America	85 173	83 910	87 369	2.1
Near East	53 984	55 475	56 269	2.6
Far East	266 908	249 705	274 357	3.1
Wheat	91 922	97 472	95 570	3.3
Rice	204 609	186 567	213 971	3.1
Maize	78 320	75 569	81 099	1.6

SOURCE : Based on FAO. *El estado mundial de la agricultura y la alimentación. 1981.* pp. 129-131.

In this examination, special emphasis should be made on cereal production.

It should be stressed that, according to a FAO survey in 1978 about 530 million metric tons of cereals – 36 per cent of world consumption – were used for animal feed and, if rice is excluded – almost exclusively for human consumption – this ratio rises to 43 per cent. In addition, of all cereals cattle consume, in 1978 maize accounted for 42 per cent. Thus, in spite of it being the main staple for many underdeveloped nations, 61 per cent of the world maize consumption that year was devoted to cattle feed.[2]

VOLUMES OF CEREAL USED FOR FEEDING
1975-1977
(Millions of tons)

	Human		Animal	
Developed countries	164.1	28%	413.0	72%
Underdeveloped countries				
Africa	42.4	93	2.9	7
Latin America	42.8	59	29.6	41
Near East	39.1	77	11.9	23
Rest of Asia	413.8	92	35.3	8
Others	0.3	96	–	4
WORLD TOTAL	702.5	59	492.7	41

SOURCE : Based on FAO data. *Ceres* magazine, no. 77. 1980. p. 6.

UNDERVELOPED COUNTRIES' LIVESTOCK PRODUCTS
(Thousands of metric tons)

	1978	1979	1980	Average annual change 1971-80 (%)
Meat	25 815	26 553	27 586	3.7
Milk	95 957	98 503	99 645	3.0
Eggs	4 414	4 685	5 040	6.0

SOURCE : Based on FAO. *El estado mundial de la agricultura y la alimentación, 1981,* pp. 129-132.

Livestock-related products showed a slight growth in the '70s.

Other agricultural productions of greater importance for the Third World have practically stagnated in the last decade – in the case of coffee and cocoa – and have even dropped, as in the case of dry legumes. Nevertheless, if the 1978-1980 three-year period is examined, decreasing tendencies are also noted in tubers, sugar and tobacco, all of which indicates the worsening of key commodity supplies for a large number of underdeveloped countries.

An obvious expression of that negative situation is that, according to FAO data, by the mid-1970's, the underdeveloped countries, which, have more than 65 per cent of the world population, only produced 38 per cent of the food, while output per agricultural worker, at 1975 prices, was $550 per year, while in developed countries it was $5 220.

OUTPUT OF OTHER AGRICULTURAL COMMODITIES IN UNDERDEVELOPED COUNTRIES
(Thousands of metric tons)

	1978	1979	1980	Average annual change 1971-80 (%)
Tubers	188 059	187 327	187 110	1.8
Dry legumes	25 002	24 411	21 935	−0.9
Citrus fruit	22 862	23 589	26 116	5.5
Vegetable oils	90 339	91 072	97 922	3.7
Sugar	46 256	45 426	42 304	2.0
Green coffee	4 673	4 933	4 687	0.2
Cocoa beans	1 451	1 619	1 616	0.3
Cotton fiber	5 612	6 768	6 198	1.1
Tobacco	2 402	2 290	2 274	2.8

SOURCE : Based on FAO. *El estado mundial de la agricultura y la alimentación, 1981.* pp. 129-132.

FERTILIZER OUTPUT AND CONSUMPTION

	Total production (thousands of metric tons)	Per caput production (kg)	Total consumption (thousands of metric tons)	Per caput consumption (kg)
Market-economy developed countries	60 608	77.7	49 623	63.6
Underdeveloped countries:	12 437	5.7	20 462	9.5
Africa	735	2.0	1 183	3,2
Latin America	3 184	8.8	6 751	18.8
Near East	2 372	11.2	2 970	14.0
Far East	6 107	5.0	9 537	7.8
Others	39	7.7	21	4.4
Centrally-planned economies	45 721	32.7	41 586	29.7

SOURCE : Based on FAO. *Ceres* magazine, July-August 1981.

In 1979-80, the world produced a total of 118.7 million metric tons of chemical *fertilizers* (NPK), of which 111.7 million were consumed. This figure meant a 3.4 per cent increase with respect to the previous year. Europe produced 30 per cent, North America 27 per cent, and the USSR 18 per cent, i.e., as a whole, 75 per cent of the world total. This same group of countries consumed 66 per cent of the total. While per caput fertilizer consumption was 63.6 kg in the developed capitalist countries, in the underdeveloped countries it was 9.5 and, specifically, in Africa, 3.2.

Arable surface area per agricultural worker – an indicator of the technological development in relation to the extension of land a man can work – increased in 1961-1965 and 1978 from less than 6 to 9 hectares in developed countries, while in the Third World, except for a slight increase in Latin America, it dropped to levels averaging 1.3 hectares.

Likewise, the present degree of *mechanization* of agriculture in the Third World is a clear expression of its extreme technological weakness. In 1977, 88.4 per cent of all tractors in the world were in developed countries; 61.5 per cent of them in North America and Western Europe, regions which only have 22.4 per cent of the world's cultivated land. The Third World only had 11.6 per cent of all tractors and Africa, in particular, with its dramatic food problems, only had 1.0 per cent of all tractors. On the other hand, only 5.2 per cent of the world's harvesters are in underdeveloped countries.

According to FAO data, in 1980 the total amount of arable land under irrigation in underdeveloped countries was 105 million hectares, or some 14 per cent of all arable land in those countries. Only 60 per cent of the former was fully equipped.

In the year 2000 the projected 40 per cent increase of irrigated lands in those countries will bring the figures to 148 million hectares, or 16 per cent of all arable lands in those countries. Hence, the annual growth rate would be 1.7 per cent less than that obtained in recent years. Equipped areas are also projected to reach 73 per cent. Considering an average cost of $2 380 per hectare, the required total investment will surpass $100 billion.

Those irrigated areas, if efficiently exploited, could yield 50 per cent of the entire agricultural output of the underdeveloped world. Nevertheless, this will not be so. By the end of the century, 84 per cent of the Third World's arable land will still lack irrigation and will yield 59 per cent of its entire agricultural output. The United Nations has estimated that water requirements for irrigation, which amounted to 70 per cent of all the water used by man in the late '70s, will double by the year 2000.

But water is in shortage in many Third World regions. Huge resources are required to protect the sources and build up new reserves by constructing big and small dams for agricultural, industrial and human consumption – avoiding the loss of large volumes which flow into the seas –, changing courses of rivers, enriching phreatic zones wherever pos-

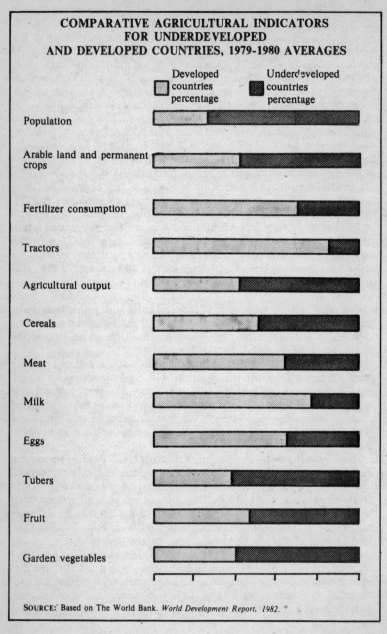

COMPARATIVE AGRICULTURAL INDICATORS
FOR UNDERDEVELOPED
AND DEVELOPED COUNTRIES, 1979-1980 AVERAGES

Developed countries percentage

Underdeveloped countries percentage

Population

Arable land and permanent crops

Fertilizer consumption

Tractors

Agricultural output

Cereals

Meat

Milk

Eggs

Tubers

Fruit

Garden vegetables

SOURCE: Based on The World Bank. *World Development Report, 1982.*

sible and making use of the results achieved in the production of artificial rain, and of all means made available to man by science and technology to increase fresh water resources.

The years that have elapsed and the experience gained have dissipated the hopes for the solution of agricultural and food problems arising from some of the spectacular results of the so-called Green Revolution.

Modernization of agriculture in certain Third World areas, based on the use of scientific advances without altering the internal and external socio-economic structures that constitute the basis for agricultural backward-ness, was a clear expression of scientific-technological progress and socio-economic failure and evidenced that agricultural and hunger problems are not only of a technological-productive nature, but that they are mainly derived from social structures and relations of domination.

Indeed, the introduction of fertilizers and pesticides combined with new varieties of high-yield agricultural crops – wheat, rice, maize, sorghum, millet, potatoes, legumes, with qualities such as greater resistance to disease, greater capacity to absorb soil and sunlight nutrients, greater tol-erance to cold weather and droughts, shorter growth periods, etc. – are important achievements that cannot be disregarded. But the largest food output has been clearly insufficient to meet the problem of mass hunger, while other very important social effects such as the creation of jobs in agriculture, the reduction of the rural exodus to the cities and preventing the increase of inequalities in land tenure and exploitation, have been ag-gravated by the advent of the Green Revolution.

New scientific-technological methods demand capital for their applica-tion and are only accessible to rich farmers and agro-food transnationals. Although new varieties might not demand mechanization, they do create economic incentives for its introduction, replacing labor by machines, and increasing unemployment. The machines and the new varieties demand larger land areas, leading to the purchase of lands from producers who cannot bear modernization costs. This results in a greater concentration of land tenure, greater income inequality, higher unemployment and, finally, malnutrition, since the poor and the unemployed lack the income needed to purchase the new food being produced.

In this analysis, it is also impossible to disregard the action of agro-food transnationals in the present Third World agricultural and food situation. Their role has been the subject of studies that have showed the great re-sponsibility they have in this field. They have been appropriately termed veritable dealers in the underdeveloped countries' wants since their eco-nomic power and big profits have been built on the hunger and weak ag-ricultural sectors of the Third World. Thus, they are reluctant to change the structures that have served as their basis and their source of profits.

The transnationals' negative action in agriculture and food is evidenced in various ways, such as the appropriation of the best lands in some coun-tries, the imposition of crop and food patterns alien to domestic needs, the monopolistic control over internal and external marketing mechanisms, including the basic agricultural inputs like fertilizers, machinery, equipment, herbicides and others.

These agro-food transnationals have worked intensively during the past decade, promoting a producer-exporter complex for the markets of developed capitalist countries or for urban consumption of high-income small minorities in underdeveloped countries.

They have forcefully established themselves in numerous Third World countries, manufacturing food for large marketing networks making up the transnational conglomerate. Through their financial, technological and trading power, they have thus imposed production and consumption patterns alien to the food consumption interests of the broad masses.

This has resulted in the mass replacement of the traditional crops that helped feed the people, often grown by small farmers, in order to establish export crops which do not meet consumption needs nor adapt to the recipient countries' historical-cultural patterns. This forceful destruction of traditional crops to promote agro-exporting productions within transnationally controlled systems is widely evident in many Third World countries that have become net importers of foodstuffs that they traditionally exported and that are an important part of national eating habits. Countries that were traditionally maize and beans exporters and consumers today import tens of millions of dollars' worth of those products as a result of the mass destruction of their crops to plant other highly profitable produce for the transnationals.

Fisheries production

Fisheries production, another main food for human consumption, that provides 15 per cent of world protein intake, showed a very slow, and even negative movement in underdeveloped countries at the end of the last decade.

FISHERIES PRODUCTION 1978-1980
(Millions of tons)

	1978	1979	1980	Change (per cent) 1979-80	1971-80
World total	70.4	71.2	71.8	0.9	1.5
Developed countries	37.2	37.2	38.0	2.2	1.2
Underdeveloped countries	33.2	34.0	33.8	−0.6	1.9

SOURCE : Based on FAO. *El estado mundial de la agricultura y la alimentación, 1981,* p. 35.

According to FAO, as can be seen above, in 1981 world production of fish, crustaceans and shellfish amounted to 71.8 million tons, a growth of less than 1 per cent as compared with the preceding year.

In terms of per caput catches, the figures also illustrate the differences between developed and underdeveloped countries. According to FAO data, in 1980, world per caput fish catch was 32.6 kilograms in the developed countries, whereas in the underdeveloped countries it was only 10.5 kilograms.

Of fisheries production in 1981, some 29 per cent of the catch was used for animal feed, according to the same source.

In assessing the development of world fishing activity, underdeveloped countries' progress in defending their rights to the sea, must be considered.

The Convention on the Law of the Sea, recently endorsed by 119 States sets forth the main claims regarding territorial seas, economic zones, fishing rights, seabed resources and others made by Third World countries since 1958.

It is important to recall here that for the first time an international legal system for the use and exploitation of the sea was established. It should be noted that this offers the opportunity of standing up collectively against the transnationals' insatiable voracity over three quarters of the globe's surface – waters and seabed – where, aside from rich fishery sources, immense mineral reserves are found in the nodules of exploitable areas, estimated at 23 billion dry tons containing diverse basic metals, chiefly 290 million tons of nickel, 240 million tons of copper, 60 million tons of cobalt, 6 billion tons of manganese, etc.

It is common knowledge that the United States obstinately and selfishly opposed the Convention and refused to endorse it, thereby giving further proof of the contradiction between the interests of the monopolies and the vital interests of the peoples of the Third World.

On the other hand, world aquaculture production in 1980 increased to a little over 8.7 million tons, 37 per cent of which was fish, 25 per cent sea algae and the rest crustaceans and shellfish. By 1981, 15 per cent of world fish production was obtained from inland waters.

It should be mentioned that, in contrast with the developed countries' share of the world's fisheries production from the sea, the underdeveloped countries catch over 80 per cent of the total from inland waters. This is due to the shortage of resources for deep-sea fishing that is intensively practiced by developed countries with high-technology fishing fleets.

It should also be noted that natural weather conditions and the large volumes of inland waters in underdeveloped countries favor the potential development of this type of fisheries production. The overall growth rate was 6.9 per cent from 1976 to 1980.

Food trade

Faced with a considerable deficit in their food production with respect to population growth, the underdeveloped countries have been globally forced to increase their food imports.

In 1975, the underdeveloped countries generated 42 per cent of the worlds' total agricultural exports and absorbed 25 per cent of imports. In 1980, these figures had changed considerably: only 38 per cent of total exports were generated by our countries, while imports rose to 30 per cent. From 1963 to 1975, the underdeveloped countries' food imports increased by an annual average growth rate of 5.4 per cent in the case of cereals, 4.3 per cent in meat and 4.8 per cent in milk and dairy products.

Cereal production and imports clearly illustrate the plummeting trend in agriculture. FAO estimates that the wheat and secondary cereal imports by the underdeveloped countries in 1981-1982 increased to 87-90 million tons. In the Third World, per caput cereal production decreased at a 1 per cent annual rate from 1976 to 1980. During that same period and along these same lines, cereal imports increased at an annual rate of 14 per cent.

	WORLD CEREAL TRADE (Millions of tons)				
	1934-38	*1948-52*	*1960*	*1970*	*1978*
Developed countries	−11	+4	+20	+38	+70
Underdeveloped countries	+12	−5	−19	−38	−65
Latin America	+9	+1	0	+4	0
Africa	+1	0	−2	−5	−12
Asia	+2	−6	−17	−37	−53

+ net exports
− net imports

SOURCE : Based on FAO and US Department of Agriculture data.

The impact of this dramatic situation in our countries' trade balance is very concrete and eloquent. In 1980 alone, the difference between food exports and imports resulted in a deficit of $13 929 million for the underdeveloped countries. Low-income countries, where food imports hardly mitigate the hunger of millions of people, accounted for 32.2 per cent of that figure.

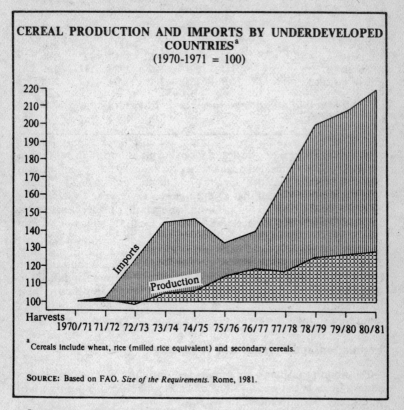

CEREAL PRODUCTION AND IMPORTS BY UNDERDEVELOPED COUNTRIES[a]
(1970-1971 = 100)

[a] Cereals include wheat, rice (milled rice equivalent) and secondary cereals.

SOURCE: Based on FAO. *Size of the Requirements.* Rome, 1981.

It is estimated that the real food prices, in constant values, will have doubled by the year 2000. An eloquent anticipation of this reality is the fact that retail food prices in market-economy underdeveloped countries increased by some 26 per cent in 1980, that is, twice the 1979 increase.

Price performance, decisively manipulated by large marketing transnationals showed a more accelerated trend to increase in cereals, whose production and marketing is strongly controlled by a group of developed capitalist countries. which profited most from it.

As may be noted in the table *infra,* the food imported by the underdeveloped countries during the '70s, at market prices, was 20 per cent more expensive every year and in 1980 amounted to $52.3 billion, one third more than the preceding year.

UNIT VALUE INDEX OF WORLD AGRICULTURAL EXPORTS
PRODUCTS BY MAJOR GROUPS
(1969-1971 = 100)

	1972	1973	1974	1975	1976	1979
Food	116	157	216	232	205	211
Cereals	105	159	245	249	222	298
Fodder	114	291	196	170	188	226
Raw materials	107	155	211	173	189	200

SOURCE : Based on FAO. *El estado mundial de la agricultura y la alimentación*, Rome, 1979.

According to recent estimates, African countries import 26 per cent of the food they consume, although on that continent 80 per cent of the economically active population directly or indirectly depends on agriculture, and it can be anticipated that an even greater decrease in their self-reliance will occur by the year 2000. Given these negative tendencies, it is not surprising that the underdeveloped countries spent $17 billion in 1979 on cereals alone – their major source of calories – which account for a significant percentage of their total export revenues.

The results of these huge expenditures, seen within the context of the critical and growing deterioration of the terms of trade, are not difficult to imagine. They imply a constant increase in external dependence to meet food requirements and the loss of the scarce foreign currency resources that could be used to develop agriculture and the economy in general.

Population and agricultural lands

The world population's accelerated and uncontrolled growth is an important factor in the present situation and in the world's immediate prospects for food and agricultural output.

When compared to 1970, by the year 2000 there will be 4 more people/sq. km. in North America, while in southern Asia there will be 140. Such an increase is, in itself, higher than the present population density of Europe – 85 people/sq. km. This means that, according to the present growth rate, by the year 2000 there will be 390 inhabitants/sq. km. of arable land in southern Asia, i.e., 10 times more than in the United States.[3]

From 1950 to 1975, the proportion of the rural population in Third World countries decreased from 84 per cent to 73 per cent, and it is estimated that it will be around 60 per cent by the year 2000. In absolute terms, however, the rural population increased by 680 million in those 25 years, and it is estimated that in the last quarter of the century it will increase by 850 million.

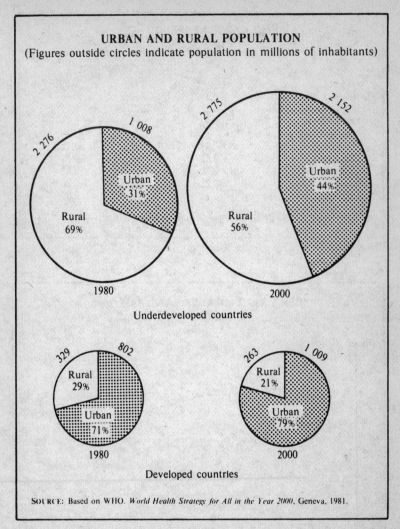

URBAN AND RURAL POPULATION
(Figures outside circles indicate population in millions of inhabitants)

2 276 — *1 008*

Urban
31%

Rural
69%

1980

2 775 — *2 152*

Urban
44%

Rural
56%

2000

Underdeveloped countries

329 — *802*

Rural
29%

Urban
71%

1980

263 — *1 009*

Rural
21%

Urban
79%

2000

Developed countries

SOURCE: Based on WHO, *World Health Strategy for All in the Year 2000*, Geneva, 1981.

The world's total land surface is 13.5 billion hectares; 59 per cent of which (8 billion) is deserts, high-salinity lands, frozen lands and mountains. Some 1.5 billion hectares of land are under cultivation, 11 per cent of the total surface. Maximum arable land availability is 2 425 million hectares.

With the present productivity levels in underdeveloped countries, 0.9 hectares per capita would be needed to reach the developed countries'

PER CAPUT ARABLE LAND
(Hectares)

	1971-1975	1985	2000
		Projections	
Developed countries	0.55	0.50	0.46
Underdeveloped countries	0.35	0.27	0.19
Latin America	0.47	0.38	0.28
Northern Africa and Middle East	0.47	0.33	0.22
Other African countries	0.62	0.49	0.32
Southern Asia	0.26	0.19	0.13
South East Asia	0.35	0.28	0.20
East Asia	0.13	0.11	0.08

SOURCE : Based on *The Global 2000 Report to the President*, USGPO, p. 99.

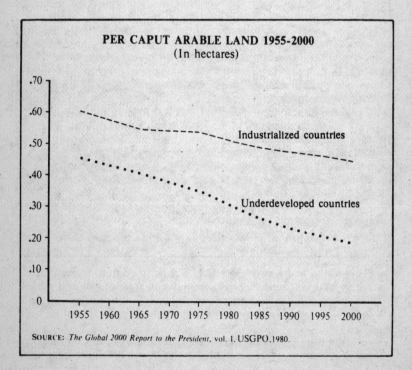

PER CAPUT ARABLE LAND 1955-2000
(In hectares)

SOURCE: *The Global 2000 Report to the President*, vol. 1, USGPO, 1980.

consumption levels. There will be an increasing number of human beings in the underdeveloped countries who will hypothetically depend on one hectare of cultivated land. But, will those countries be economically and technologically capable of increasing land yields in order to ensure sufficient output?

Increased land yield, a vital and decisive element in coping with the growing food crisis in the underdeveloped world, demands attention in regard to many factors: land tenure, forms of land use; advanced technology and, very specially, financial resources – so uncertain, unattainable and burdensome for the broad masses of farmers.

The huge economic effort required for Africa's food self-reliance, for example, is reflected in FAO's projection for the year 2000. Investments in the continent's agricultural sector for that year should be 2.5 times higher than in 1980 – 6 billion dollars – reaching 9.3 billion by 1990 and 15.4 billion by the year 2000.

FAO believes that, with an adequate level of investments, it would be possible to increase agricultural output by a 4 per cent annual average in this decade and 3.7 per cent from 1990 to the year 2000 in the Third World countries. As a result of those increases, agricultural output in the underdeveloped countries would double by the end of the century. However, the attainment of these ambitious goals presupposes putting 100 million additional hectares of land under cultivation in this decade and another 100 million in the following decade, plus the irrigation of an additional 57 million hectares, a significant improvement in current irrigation systems, increased use of fertilizers and pesticides, the development of mechanization and improved seeds. To accomplish this, it will be necessary to invest $57 billion per year until 1990 and $78 billion per year from then until the year 2000. Such important efforts also imply significant changes in price policies and world trade to facilitate agricultural expansion and the marketing of a greater share of the underdeveloped countries' production in the developed world, as well as the necessary international assistance for financing, projecting and implementing large-scale agricultural schemes in the Third World.

Another important factor in the Third World's agricultural problems is the obsolete land tenure structure.

In many Third World regions agriculture is still based on latifundia. Latifundia-dominated agriculture relies on extensive production techniques, promotes underutilization of available lands and ever-greater exploitation of cheap labor, and impedes the appropriate use of machines. The underutilization of resources that latifundia-dominated agriculture entails – in the midst of serious land shortages – can be readily observed in regions such as Latin America. A 1966 FAO survey on 6 countries of this region showed that on average 5 out of every 6 hectares were not under cultivation in large estates.[4] Nothing seems to indicate that this situation has changed substantially since then.

LAND DISTRIBUTION CIRCA 1970

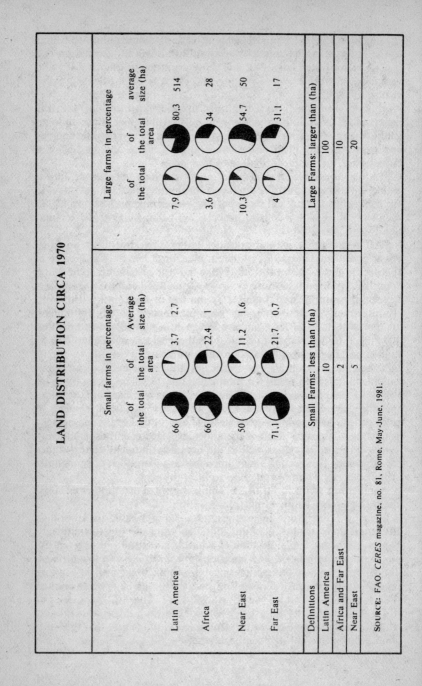

	Small farms in percentage		
	of the total	of the total area	Average size (ha)
Latin America	66	3.7	2.7
Africa	66	22.4	1
Near East	50	11.2	1.6
Far East	71.1	21.7	0.7

	Large farms in percentage		
	of the total	of the total area	average size (ha)
Latin America	7.9	80.3	514
Africa	3.6	34	28
Near East	10.3	54.7	50
Far East	4	31.1	17

Definitions	Small Farms: less than (ha)	Large Farms: larger than (ha)
Latin America	10	100
Africa and Far East	2	10
Near East	5	20

SOURCE: FAO. *CERES* magazine. no. 81, Rome, May-June, 1981.

The existence of minifundia produces similar problems. Minifundia – on many occasions related to subsistence agriculture – put very serious obstacles in the way of applying modern agricultural technology to a large number of crops.

Latifundia and minifundia, within a complex context of colonial heritage and neo-colonial dependence, and at times linked to the continuation of forms of production which antedated market economies, help to explain the terrible state of agriculture in the Third World. Such is the case of shifting agriculture, a practice which characterizes the production of more than 167 million small farmers and landless peasant families, or the eternal pilgrimage of nomad shepherds in arid lands constantly seeking water and feed for their herds. According to FAO data, about 25 per cent of rural households in the Near East, 31 per cent in the Far East, 34 per cent in Latin America and 10 per cent in Africa, were made up by landless farmers by the end of the '70s.

The huge inequalities in land distribution can be clearly observed in situations such as that of the Far East, where small farms (under 2 hectares) accounted for 71.1 per cent of all farms in 1970, covering 21.7 per cent of the total area. The average size of these tiny farms was 0.7 hectares. In Africa, 66 per cent of the farms covered 22.4 per cent of the total area, some farms averaging only 1 hectare. On the other hand, large farms in Latin America (over 100 hectares) accounted only for 7.9 per cent of all farms, but covered 80.3 per cent of the total area – the average size being 514 hectares – which shows the predominance of latifundia.

The agrarian reform implies a more just, equitable and rational land redistribution and much more: it allows for the introduction of higher forms of agricultural management, such as cooperatives and socially owned agro-industrial complexes and the application of modern technologies capable of optimizing the impaired results of traditional agriculture. Therefore, while implying a deeply just social measure, the agrarian reform would mean a substantial contribution to the solution of the Third World's food problems by expanding agricultural production and promoting a more equitable income distribution.

Agriculture and environment

To all the factors affecting the agricultural and food crisis examined so far, it is necesary to add man's actions on the environment, which are increasingly causing unprecedented changes in the stability, organization, balance, interaction and even the survival of the Earth's main ecological systems. The destabilizing processes stemming from the action of man promote and supplement the transforming action of natural factors over the environment.

Thus, mankind should witness with great concern how year after year this degrading action over nature is evidenced through increased desertification, rapid erosion of agricultural soils, growing water pollution and the depletion of water sources, deforestation and other related phenomena. The large ecosystems, on whose organic balance and stability the life of the planet has developed for millennia are today, more than ever before, threatened in terms of their very survival. However, this world-wide phenomenon has specific traits, common origins and maybe even more devastating and already irreversible results in the underdeveloped countries.

One could ask though, what the definition of ecosystems, biological stability, pollution, environmental degradation, etc., would mean for the huge illiterate and hungry masses of the underdeveloped world whose daily struggle is only aimed at mere survival. Could one tell the Sahel nomad shepherd – who in a perennial effort to survive travels with his herds through calcinated lands seeking water and food – that this millenary practice is the most important factor in rapid desertification and that it should cease? Without a previous socio-economic solution that would guarantee a change and new prospects for that inhuman way of life, little can be done to prevent his negative action on nature.

Moreover, little ground could be gained in understanding, much less in counteracting, the serious consequences of the shifting agriculture practiced by millions of landless peasants unless a previous solution is found to unjust land tenure, archaic agricultural forms of production and deplorable living conditions. On the other hand, could tropical countries with vast wooded areas – generally the Earth's poorest – now be asked to stop exploiting their huge forest resources to prevent the serious world ecological and climatic alterations this would entail without previously ensuring their basic development resources and more just and fruitful relations for their peoples?

Market-economy developed countries are directly responsible for a large part of environmental degradation. Air, inland water and ocean pollution, the huge amounts of chemical and nuclear waste deposited in the atmosphere, the soil, the water and the sea are part of the constant environmental aggression against those countries. Transnationals, which are to blame for the exploitation and depletion of mineral, forest and agricultural resources in many underdeveloped countries, have been transfering to these countries highly polluting industrial plants, generally with outdated technology, without ever making supplementary investments to dispose of their toxic waste.

A basic fact always to be borne in mind when examining these processes is that history shows that the course of this destructive phenomenon can be checked and righted. There are well-known examples of transformation – by man's will and intelligence and with the necessary resources – of deserts such as the US Dust Bowl, Kara Kum in the USSR, or the swampy frozen tundras of Northern Siberia. Now then, in the case of our countries, political will, rationality and the very instinct of survival must go hand in hand with international actions to back up domestic efforts.

Erosion

Erosion is one of the determining factors in the process of deterioration, fertility loss and degradation of most of the planet's agricultural soils. It is also the most important concomitant factor in the desertification of vast regions of the underdeveloped world.

Due to the natural features of soils and weather, together with social, economic and cultural factors that lead to backward forms of agricultural and livestock exploitation, erosion in torrid zones constitutes a much more serious phenomenon than in other areas of the world. Subsistance agriculture, with soil overutilization and loss of topsoil; negative agricultural practices, such as burning, typical of shifting agriculture; inadequate crop management; severe droughts, accompanied by constant winds and very often followed by heavy rainfall, are elements that condition and determine the process of erosion.

The loss of agricultural soils is rapidly advancing in tropical countries as a result of erosion. According to FAO publications, it is estimated that rain and wind erosion, in varying degrees, affects up to 75 per cent of the arable land in the American continent. A survey made by the International Union for Conservation of Nature and Natural Resources published by UNESCO states that in India, for example, of a total area of 3.3 million sq. km., soils are gradually eroding in some 1.5 million.[5]

In 800 000 sq. km. alone, estimated annual soil loss amounts to 600 million tons that are washed away to the sea or deposited in dykes and rivers.[6] Suffice it to mention that nature needs 100 to 400 years to produce a one-centimeter-thick topsoil.

A joint FAO/UNEP study estimated that 35 per cent of the African soils north of the Equator and 60 per cent of the arable land in the Near East, among others, suffer considerable damage due to erosion, flooding or salinity.

Desertification

Coupled with the overall growth of over 2 per cent of world population per annum, direct actions of natural and human factors transform a large part of arable lands into desert. In the past centuries, it is estimated that the desertification process has affected over 9 million sq. km., i.e., a surface similar to that of the Sahara. In the sub-Saharan countries alone, there are 685 million hectares of desert lands.

The Earth's desert and semi-desert areas today represent some one fifth of the land surface. Every year, nevertheless, 6 million additional hectares are swallowed by the desert. This means that, at the present rate, from 1983 to the year 2000 over 100 million hectares will have been lost: one million sq. km. will have become deserts.

The large territories located around the Earth's arid zones, with little rainfall and short wet periods, scarce vegetation which is largely fragile and recovers poorly, have year after year contributed new territory to deserts, in the face of man's overexploitative and devastating action. In the Sudan, for instance, the Sahara advanced 200 kilometers southward in 17 years. The Atacam desert in South America and the Thar in Asia are advancing at an increasing pace. The growth of population and of herds, added to the critical weather conditions in those regions, produce – due to overgrazing – the irreversible destruction of the poor existing vegetation. Not only is vegetation depleted, but also the scarce water sources available, practically destroying all forms of life. The nomads' need for firewood and other plant waste for cooking and heating, round out man's destructive work. FAO estimates, for example, that in one desert province of the Sudan alone, 548 million trees or bushes are burnt for these purposes every year.

FAO also believes that there are 2 billion hectares of land under cultivation in Asia, Africa and Latin America showing a "high" or "very high" desertification risk, i.e., that face a more or less direct or serious danger of becoming arid lands unsuitable for cultivation.

1980   2000   2020

If soil deterioration continues at the present rate, in the next 20-40 years one third of the world's arable land (represented by the stalk of wheat) will have been destroyed. By the year 2000 only half the world's untapped productive forest land (represented by the tree) will remain, and the world population (represented by the human figure) will have grown by 50 per cent.

SOURCE: Based on the *UNESCO Courier* magazine, Paris, May 1980.

On the other hand, also according to FAO estimates, agriculture loses 125 thousand hectares of irrigation lands yearly due to salinization, alkalization or the transformation of soils into swamps. At that rate, it has been estimated that by the year 2000 almost 3 million hectares will have been lost for these reasons. Although this phenomenon is common in developed and underdeveloped countries, its impact will obviously be more serious in the latter, considering their lower agricultural technological development, the predominance of extensive land utilization methods, difficulties in adding new surface areas to agricultural production and the fact that the endangered soils are generally the most productive ones.

In addition to the aforementioned factors, there is the annual loss of thousands of sq. km. of arable land to urbanization, industrial facilities, highways, railways, airports, high-voltage power lines, facilities for social sports, military uses, etc.

Therefore, among all the problems facing mankind, the loss of arable areas is one of the most pressing and serious.

Deforestation

Undoubtedly, another of the most pressing problems mankind will have to face in the most immediate future, not only because of its economic consequences but also its implications for the destruction of the Earth's ecological balance, is the accelerated process of deforestation, especially in the underdeveloped world.

One fourth of the Earth's surface was covered by forests by the middle of this century. By 1978, the total forest area had already been reduced to a little over 2.5 billion hectares, that is, 20 per cent of the total surface.

Every year some 20 million hectares of woodland disappear, mostly in underdeveloped countries. This means that every minute over 20 hectares of forests are being felled, burnt or destroyed in our countries. At that rate, the Earth's tropical jungles will be totally destroyed in less than 35 years. By the end of the century, only half of the present surface of untapped productive tropical forests will remain standing.

The main causes of this process of increasing forest devastation are summarized in the following:

- Shifting agriculture and other inappropriate agricultural practices resulting from the growing food requirements of the hungry majorities of the underdeveloped world.
- Economic requirements of tropical countries.
- Forest exploitation as a source of profit.
- Growing timber demands of the developed nations.
- Intensive felling to obtain firewood for heating and cooking, the exclusive energy source for almost 2 billion inhabitants of the Third World.

According to FAO data, the production of wood for industrial construction was 155 million cubic meters in 1975 and it is anticipated that it will increase to 325 million cubic meters by the year 2000. In 1978, nevertheless, 1420 million cubic meters were used in underdeveloped countries for charcoal and firewood, that is, 40 per cent of these countries' energy consumption that year. On the other hand, total reforestation covered only 900 thousand hectares per year.

According to US projections, forest land in the developed countries will decrease only 0.5 per cent by the year 2000, while there will be a 40 per cent decrease in the underdeveloped world. If present trends continue, during the first quarter of the next century – only 40 years from now – all physically accessible forests in the underdeveloped countries will have disappeared.

The disastrous consequences the disappearance of forests presuppose for all of mankind are already being felt in the form of environmental pollution, rainfall alterations, uncontrolled flooding and draught, desertification, erosion, weather deterioration, the loss of river and underground water sources, soil fertility loss and a decline in agricultural production. It can be seen in the rapid and indiscriminate disappearance of hundreds of thousands of plant and animal species from the face of the Earth even before man is able to describe them and much less learn about their potential in medicine and other aspects of our life. Coupled with this, a unique and irreparable genetic wealth that took nature hundreds of thousands and even millions of years to develop, will also disappear. Thus, one of the most useful, necessary and essential systems of life in the Earth is being destroyed at an accelerated pace.

To these effects one must add the long list of phenomena that have already increasingly occurred due to man's neglect of the Earth's ecological balance. To mention but a few, let us recall phenomena such as the growing concentrations of carbon dioxide in the atmosphere and their still undetermined harmful effects, the loss of ozone in the stratosphere, increased radiation, atmospheric and oceanic radioactive pollution, the introduction of huge volumes of toxic materials in the environment, acid rain, the criminal squandering of non-renewable resources, the salinization and alkalization of the best arable lands, and the many more examples of man's ecological irresponsibility.

Gloomy agriculture and food prospects in the Third World

All of the aforementioned reveals the existence of highly negative trends for the underdeveloped countries in the field of agriculture and food. In 1981, FAO extrapolated these tendencies up to the year 2000 and summarized them in the following aspects:

- By the year 2000, some 34 countries, representing half of the population of the 90 countries studied, would have a calorie supply well below minimun requirements.

- Continuing agricultural output trends would have the following main results: increasing hunger and malnutrition, decreasing self-suffi-

118

ciency in food and an enormous increase in cereal import requirements.

- Poor agricultural output and productivity growth will have even more serious effects considering that, between 1980 and the year 2000, there will be an additional 1.6 billion people in the Third World.

- When analyzing the dynamics of demand and production regionally, FAO concludes that the growth in output in Africa (2.6 per cent) would lag far behind the growth in demand (3.4 per cent). In the Near East and in Latin America, output would not meet demand either, while in the group of the poorest countries, there would be a 25 per cent shortfall.

- The agricultural imports of the underdeveloped countries would absorb no less than 95 per cent of their agricultural export earnings, drastically limiting their possibilities for obtaining favorable trade balances.

- The agricultural exports of Africa would not compensate for more than half its agricultural imports by the year 2000.

- The so-called less advanced countries would have agricultural imports two and a half times their agricultural exports.

- The developed countries' net cereal surplus would reach 213 million tons at a time when the Third World would be faced with a deficit of 165 million tons.

- The underdeveloped countries' commodity stocks such as sugar, citrus fruits, vegetable oils and oil seeds would greatly surpass the industrialized countries' import demands due to the protectionism practiced against Third World economies, blocking access to those markets.

- Third World cereal imports would rise extremely fast, moving from the 80 million ton figure in 1978-79 to 135 million in 1990 and 226 million by the year 2000. The financial cost of these imports at 1979 constant prices would be staggering: $37 billion.

- The total number of rural families will increase faster than the arable lands under exploitation in every region, except for Latin America. This implies a decrease in the average size of farms in Africa, the Near East and Asia, and a corresponding increase in the number of landless agricultural laborers. The great landowners would absorb the land of the weakest farmers whose land area would be too small to be economically viable. This would lead to an even more inequitable distribution of the means of production and of income.

To these gloomy prospects contained in the FAO surveys must be added ecological factors such as erosion, desertification, deforestation, depletion and pollution of water sources and other forms of degradation of the Earth's agricultural lands which demand huge efforts from mankind to preserve and recover resources in this, a most vital sphere for survival.

6
Industrialization and economic development

Industrialization is a decisive process for the Third World's economic development, a need nobody dares deny, even though there are diverse opinions when attempts are made to establish its specific characteristics, mechanisms and periods for each country. Unquestionably, the industrialization of the Third World is equivalent, in strategic terms, to laying the main technological and material base for development. The classical model that postulates that agriculture and raw materials are specialized enough for the underdeveloped countries, leaving industrial production in the hands of the developed countries, does nothing but try to perpetuat a model which our countries firmly reject as irrational, unequal and unjust.

Today, it is perfectly clear that industrialization – as a process whose effects are felt in all sectors of the economy, mobilizing a growing portion of national resources for the development of technically advanced economic structures that can produce consumer goods and investments and guaranteeing its own economic and technological reproduction – is a historic imperative for our countries; it is the path that we should take in order to have access to development, modern technology and contemporary civilization itself.

It is well known that the industrialization of the underdeveloped world is presented as a process of even greater complexity and involves even greater difficulties than the processes through which the industrial development of England was effected in the early days of the capitalist system, Germany and the United States later on, and even the Soviet Union starting in 1917. It cannot be ignored that the levels of industrial production in most of the underdeveloped countries are only a fifth to a third as high as the levels reached by czarist Russia just before the 1917 revolution and that it is estimated that the levels of industrial work productivity in Asia and Africa are only a twentieth to a fifteenth as high as in the United States.

Economic history does not record such enormous differences in earlier processes of industrialization. The high-speed dynamics of the present

121

scientific-technical revolution is leaving the underdeveloped countries farther and farther behind.

When attempts are made to describe the Third World, one of the most abbreviated and direct ways of doing so is to say that only 9 per cent of the world's industrial output is generated in it. Moreover, this mere 9 per cent is almost completely made up by industries employing out-dated technologies and most of it is trapped in the production, technology, finance and trade networks of the transnational corporations. Furthermore, this small, weak and dependent industry is concentrated in just a few countries of the Third World.

The industrial growth of the Third World

In terms of industrial growth, it is impossible to agree with those who maintain that there is an impetuous industrial expansion in the Third World.

It is true that there is rapid growth of the industrial output as compared to other sectors of the economy and an accelerated – and distorted – displacement of the rural population to the urban areas, with the virtual abandonment of the rural areas and an ever more accelerated growth of the known urban concentrations in the form of huge, unmanageable cities with an industrial façade and large slums in a few countries.

The positive meaning of this statistically significant industrial growth is debatable, but there are few examples of it, and, rather than illustrate a general trend toward industrial growth in the Third World, it points up the absence even of a slight significant growth in more than 100 underdeveloped countries.

In fact, the underdeveloped countries' share in the world industrial output in 1960 was 6.9 per cent. More than 20 years later, our share had risen to the small figure mentioned above, as a result of that negligible increase.

The Second General Conference of the United Nations Industrial Development Organization (UNIDO), held in Lima in 1975, approved the socalled Lima Program, according to which the underdeveloped countries should reach two main goals by the year 2000: a 25 per cent share in world industrial production and a 30 per cent share in world trade in manufactured goods, as a logical expression of the growth of industrial capacity in the Third World.

Although we will not pause now to comment on these goals, which place the accent more on the quantitative aspect that on the essential meaning of industrial growth, it is already only too well known that the continuation of the present trends would result in our arriving at the year 2000 in even worse conditions in the sphere of industrial development. UNIDO itself predicts that, if the present trends are maintained, the underdeveloped countries – that in 1977 contributed less than 9 per cent of world industrial production – will be contributing only 13.5 per cent of world production in the year 2000 – that is, they will be in an even worse relative position, in view of forecasts of demographic growth.

The underdeveloped countries' share in world industry is truly marginal, though it is a statistically established fact that the growth rate for manufactured goods in the underdeveloped countries in the last 25 years has been higher than that of the developed capitalist countries and only lower than that of the socialist countries.

Nevertheless, this relatively accelerated industrial growth – which, however, is not fast enough – presents some other characteristics which should be kept in mind to appropriately understand it.

One aspect of the greatest importance is that *the underdeveloped countries' share in world industry is much lower in the branches employing the most complex industrial technology.*

At the branch level, growth has taken place in areas lagging behind in technological development, having little scientific content as compared to the advanced branches and constituting industries of the technological rearguard, with high labor intensity and low wages, that are greatly attractive for transnational capital.

Significantly, industrial growth has not taken place in nuclear energy, chemistry, the petrochemical and aerospace industries and advanced electronics – although it has in the assembly of simple electronic parts – but there has been growth in the textile and garment industries, and to a lesser extent in the leather, cellulose and paper industries and in the processed food industry, which does nothing to alleviate the hunger of hundreds of millions of people.

In the same context, *the Third World's industry is also characterized by the very primitive level at which it exploits and processes its natural resources.* The relationship between the exploitation of its natural resources and their industrial processing as manufactured goods reveals the primary nature of this industry. While the underdeveloped countries contribute 25.6 per cent of the mining of metals, they produce only 4.1 per cent of the metal manufactures in the world. With 31.2 per cent of the world's oil and gas, they produce only 7.5 per cent of world output in the important chemical and petrochemical branch.

It isn't a case only of the underdeveloped countries' participating to an insignificant extent in processing their own natural resources; rather, the figures also show *the breaking apart of their economies both within and between sectors – that is, the extreme weakness of the links between their sectors and branches.* There is not enough integration in their intersectorial relations linking the industrial processing of raw materials with final consumer, semi-finished and capital goods.

Mining in the Third World grew at an average annual rate of 1.6 per cent between 1975 and 1980 while the production of metal manufactured goods grew by 6.2 per cent. This was due to the fact that the industry functions on the basis of imported components rather than by processing national resources in an internally integrated economy. This, then, is an industry concentrated in the most primary activities, with weak processing of national resources, and inadequate linkage with other internal sectors and branches – one that mainly functions on the basis of imported components, which increases the pressure on the balances of trade and payments.

THE UNDERDEVELOPED COUNTRIES' SHARE IN WORLD INDUSTRY
(Percentage)

	1963	1970	1975	1980
Mining	17.6	20.0	20.7	19.6
Metal mining	25.4	23.8	24.0	25.6
Metal manufactured products	2.0	3.0	4.0	4.1
Oil and gas	29.4	34.0	33.5	31.2
Chemistry	8.0	7.4	7.7	7.5
Textiles	15.2	16.3	17.6	17.4
Clothing	8.0	9.1	11.9	11.8
Processed foods	12.5	13.4	14.1	15.2
Wood	6.3	7.0	7.2	8.0
Paper	4.9	5.5	7.6	7.9

SOURCE : Based on UN. *La croissance de l'industrie mondiale,* 1969 and 1970 editions; *Yearbook of Industrial Statistics,* 1977; *Monthly Bulletin of Statistics,* 1980 and 1981.

Moreover, this wretched industry also shows some other unfavorable characteristics. *The insignificant level of production of capital goods (means of production) that guarantee economic and technological reproduction, using its own production as a basis for self-sustained development, may be even more serious.*

UNIDO has commented that:

Most of the developing countries have little participation in the production of capital goods. Typically, their industries turn out simple products made to order for small enterprises that process foods, do repairs, turn out textiles, work metal, etc. The complex, high-precision capital goods are imported within the framework of favorable trade and investment policies.[1]

UNIDO further states that:

The branches that are related to mechanical activities are those least represented in the developing countries. In the case of iron and steel, a relatively large number of the developing countries (49 out of 96) have some manufacturing activity, but production in many of these countries was limited to processing domestic or imported scrap iron.[2]

Going beyond the necessarily cautious language of the United Nations, it is very eloquent that the underdeveloped countries produce 8 per cent of the wood manufactured in the world but only 0.1 per cent of the machines for working it . With 28.5 per cent of the world agricultural production, they produce only 6.9 per cent of its agricultural tools and machinery, 40 per cent of which are plows, the most primitive tool. Only 6.6 per cent of the world spinning machines; 8 per cent of its electric motors; 3 per cent of its lathes; 1.7 per cent of its milling machines; 0.9 per cent of its machines for pressing, forging and rolling metals; and 0.06 per cent of its metal-cutting machines are produced in the Third World.

Even in the auto industry, in which intensive propaganda has been made in the past few years concerning its redeployment to underdeveloped countries, their share of world production in 1979 was only 5.8 per cent. In this industry, 90 per cent of which is controlled by transnational corporations, the underdeveloped countries, with very few exceptions, are assigned the phase of assembling imported parts.

The Third World's industrial dependence on imports is not limited to the auto sector but is characteristic of these countries' entire industrial structure.

Examples abound, but we will cite just one more: according to UNIDO data, only 30 per cent of the non-combustible mineral extracted in the Third World was turned into ingots there. Moreover – most significantly – this proportion remained constant between 1950 and 1973.

Naturally, in the industrial reality of the underdeveloped world, the transnational corporations – the subject, because of their importance, of further consideration – bear a high degree of responsibility. It would not be exaggerated to say that their activities are largely responsible for the distorted industrial growth of the past 15 years.

A very revealing aspect of capitalist industry is the high degree of control that the transnational monopolies wield over it.

This control over industrial production – together with their control over capital, technology and marketing – enables the transnationals to impose their model of growth not only in the developed capitalist countries but also in the countries of the Third World, causing serious imbalances in the distribution of world industry.

It only remains, therefore, to point out another well-defined characteristic of the Third World's industrial growth. This is the *strong concentration of the underdeveloped world's industrial production in a few countries, with a tendency to increase that concentration.* In short, five countries were responsible for 61.4 per cent of the industrial output of the underdeveloped world in 1980. In 1975, they were responsible for 56.7 per cent. This means that more than

115 countries shared less than 40 per cent of this production. During the period of the underdeveloped countries' most rapid manufacturing growth (1966-75), 69 per cent of the increase took place in only nine of them.

DEGREE OF CONTROL OF WORLD CAPITALIST INDUSTRY HELD BY THE 866 LARGEST TRANSNATIONAL CORPORATIONS
(Percentage)

	1967	*1977*
Manufactured goods	70.2	76.5
Food, beverages and tobacco	64.2	73.8
Textiles, footwear and clothes	18.5	17.7
Paper and wood products	17.3	34.1
Chemicals	66.0	61.2
Metallurgy and non-metallic products	68.1	80.0
Metal products	74.5	64.6
Commercial and passenger vehicles	n.a.	90.6

SOURCE : Based on UN. *La croissance de l'industrie mondiale*, 1969 and 1970 editions; *Yearbook of Industrial Statistics*, 1977 edition. *Monthly Bulletin of Statistics*. November and February 1980. *Fortune* magazine,1968 and 1978, various issues.

SHARE IN THE UNDERDEVELOPED COUNTRIES' INDUSTRIAL PRODUCTION
(Percentage)

	1963	*1970*	*1975*	*1980*
Brazil	14.0	14.3	16.7	18.8
South Korea	1.4	3.5	7.1	12.1
India	18.8	14.9	12.1	12.0
Mexico	9.1	10.7	10.2	10.7
Argentina	11.1	11.9	10.6	7.8
TOTAL	54.4	55.3	56.7	61.4

SOURCE : Based on UN. *Yearbook of Industrial Statistics*, 1979 and 1980 editions.

The five countries that appear in the table accounted for 79 per cent of the underdeveloped countries' industrial production growth between 1975 and 1980. The trend is toward greater participation by this small group of countries, which are followed, in descending order of importance, by Indonesia, Pakistan, Venezuela, Colombia, Iran, the Philippines, Chile and Egypt, each with less than 5 per cent participation. If to the first five countries, Hong Kong, Taiwan and Singapore are added in regard to manufactures exports, these eight countries will then account for more than 70 per cent of all Third World's exports of manufactured goods.

The obvious conclusion to be drawn from the preceding information is that the vast majority of the underdeveloped countries have virtually no industrialization, or it has barely begun to reach significant proportions.

In spite of some affirmations to the effect that world industry is producing a so-called restructuring that is described as impressive, the really impressive thing is that 69.2 per cent of the world's industrial work force is found in the Third World and that it generates less than 9 per cent of the world industrial production; the really impressive thing is the tenacious persistence of a panorama in which industry in more than 100 countries is no more than a small sample of semi-artisanal activities at definitely obsolete technological levels, producing for a limited domestic market and subsisting precariously thanks to protectionist policies by the public sector and the further reduction of its workers' standard of living.

The accent should be placed not on the supposed dynamism of current industrialization but on how meager and unsatisfactory it is, on the virtual lack of industrialization, if it is measured not in terms of simple historic growth rates but in relation to the enormous historic task posed to our countries by industrialization as a basic component for leaving underdevelopment behind.

Many problems concerning the process of industrial growth may be debated. There is no single path or sole model of industrialization whose virtues are universally applicable. Some of these problems require extensive treatment that goes beyond the scope of this report. They refer to the optimal size of production in relation to small domestic markets; to the correlation between heavy and light industry; to the marketing abroad of industrial products; to the selection of so-called appropriate technologies; and to the role of the public sector at present, when it is no longer possible to conceive a process of industrialization based on spontaneous market mechanisms, because of the squandering of resources, cyclical crises and the profound social traumas involved and when the objective need for conscious guidance to channel and plan industrial and economic development is evident.

It is not a matter of reproducing in our countries the industrial model of the West, since it cannot be repeated under the present historic conditions; it cannot ensure stable, long-term development; and it has subjected the world to periodic crises. In the United States, the most developed capitalist country, industry manages to grow only marginally by producing for war, ignoring the social welfare of ever larger portions of the population, squandering the natural resources that are the patrimony of all mankind, contaminating the environment and turning man into a simple instrument of capital.

Our countries do not need industries that consume foreign exchange and produce weak currencies. They do not need industries that mostly produce goods that neither ensure economic and technological reproduction nor create a base for self-sustainment. They do not need industries whose growth increases the debt and debt servicing, unemployment, social marginalization, the deterioration of the standard of living, foreign dependence and internal socio-economic disproportions.

Nor do our countries need an export industry that, in order to function, requires large imports because it is limited to carrying out the simplest labor-intensive phases of an international productive process that is controlled by transnational corporations. They do not need industries that provide cheap input for transnational private capital or for closed domestic oligarchies.

INDUSTRIALIZATION IN THE UNDERDEVELOPED COUNTRIES

- The Third World only generates a little under 9 per cent of the world industrial product. If present trends are maintained, the underdeveloped countries will contribute only 13.5 per cent of that production in the year 2000.
- The underdeveloped countries' industrial production is concentrated in those branches with the least complex industrial technologies. They produce only
  - 6.6 per cent of the world's spinning machines,
  - 8 per cent of its electric motors,
  - 3 per cent of its lathes and
  - 0.06 per cent of its metal-cutting machines.
- Industry in the Third World is strongly dominated by transnational corporations, which in 1977 controlled
  - 76.5 per cent of the world's production of manufactured goods,
  - 80.0 per cent of its production of metallurgic and non-metallic products and
  - 90.6 per cent of its production of commercial and passenger vehicles.
- Some 61.4 per cent of the underdeveloped countries' industrial production was concentrated in only five Third World countries in 1980.

Industrialization does not always mean development. Statistical industrial growth and increases in exports of manufactured goods do not always mean that the path of development has been followed.

There is even the danger of following a path that, while seemingly leading toward the goal of socio-economic development, really takes us farther away from it. A very instructive lesson of the past few years is that underdevelopment may also present a façade of industrial exports without losing any of the essential characteristics of underdevelopment.

An even greater cause for concern is the fact that the incorrect formulation of our demands regarding industrialization may help to confuse the Third World's legitimate interest in development with the transnational corporations' pillaging, deforming activities in the industrial sectors of the underdeveloped countries.

The so-called transfer of technology

The problem of the transfer of technology occupies an important place in the industrialization of the underdeveloped world.

The so-called transfer of technology really constitutes the process by means of which the underdeveloped countries rent or purchase the technology they need for developing a process of industrialization that, thus far, has actually proved to be dependent and divorced, in most cases, from their development needs. Technology, turned into one more merchandise and monopolized to a great extent by a small group of powerful countries, has become an element which is nearly impossible for the underdeveloped countries to control and reproduce.

The technology market is characterized, *inter alia*, by its highly monopolistic nature, by the weak bargaining power of the recipient country and by the absence of legal bases for the development of the negotiations. These same characteristics largely explain why the underdeveloped countries are faced with significant problems in acquiring foreign technology.

In view of the foregoing, it is possible to understand some of the characteristics of the process of the transfer — actually, the sale — of technologies by the developed capitalist countries to the underdeveloped countries.

Above all, the great share of the United States in total expenditures made within the capitalist world for research and development R & D is noteworthy. Thus, both because of their number and because of their expansion throughout the world, US transnational corporations have had considerable influence in attaching strings to the technologies that are imported by the underdeveloped countries.

Moreover, UNCTAD studies have shown the existence of 14 restrictions imposed on the underdeveloped countries' exports when they use imported technologies. These include general export restrictions, the absolute prohibition of exports, prohibitions on the exports to certain countries, permission for exporting only to certain countries, restrictions on the export volumes, controls on the prices of exports and exports permitted only through certain companies, and many others.

129

As may be observed, the restrictions introduced by technology suppliers to the recipient countries are not only serious, but several prohibitions also affect trade among the underdeveloped countries themselves.

It should also be kept in mind that the technologies that the large international monopolies transfer are not usually the most up-to-date — but actually are often the most obsolete. In fact, according to a study made by the Inter-American Development Bank, 70 per cent of the technologies that Latin America imported from the developed capitalist countries at the beginning of the present decade were obsolete.

In addition to all this, we should add that, notwithstanding the enormous scientific and technological gap that separates the developed capitalist from the underdeveloped countries, the former have managed to impose an unfair system of international norms aimed at preserving their control over scientific and technological know-how, which enables them to limit its use by charging sums that are prohibitive for the Third World countries' economies.

The underdeveloped countries' payments for technology in 1982 amounted to nearly $35 billion — more than a third of the increase in their external debts during that year.

In fact, far from enabling the underdeveloped countries to reach their development goals, their imports of technologies, add to the factors that reinforce the situation of foreign domination from which most of the Third World countries suffer and which contributes to the reproduction of backwardness and underdevelopment. The underdeveloped countries' participation in the world technology market has certainly consolidated their subordinate, dependent position in the system of international economic relations.

Current international scientific and technological relations, designed as part of the present unjust international economic order, have stimulated the growing emigration of professionals and technicians from the underdeveloped to the developed capitalist countries. This international movement of skilled personnel from the underdeveloped countries should not be viewed as a normal migratory process. In fact, it is a case of an actual "brain drain," or inverse transfer of technology, abetted and sponsored by developed market-economy countries.

The extent of this alarming drain of skilled personnel is shown by the fact that an average of a little over 4 000 specialists emigrated to the United States each year in the 1962-66 period, while an average of a little more than 13 000 — that is, three times as many — emigrated there annually in the next 15 years.

This constant drain is even more serious when we note the specialties of the professionals who emigrated. Most are related to specialties that are most important and necessary for a country's socio-economic development: engineers, doctors and natural scientists. These three specialties account for around one third of all the specialists who have emigrated to the United States.

Asia, Latin America and the Caribbean have suffered the most from this drain of skilled personnel, which hinders the socio-economic development of these countries and also constitutes a subtle form of decapitalization. UNCTAD has estimated that the technological contribution of the skilled personnel that emigrated from the Third World to three developed capitalist countries — United States, Canada and Great Britain — in 1960-1972 amounted to $51 billion in terms of capital. On the basis of the $46 billion figure — the total amount of development assistance provided by these three countries to the underdeveloped world in the same period – the "brain drain" alone has accounted for a net loss of almost $5 billion for our countries in 12 years.

Industrialization and transnational industrial redeployment

The realities observed in the past ten years call for a joint analysis of the activities of the transnational corporations, the growth in industrial exports recorded in a small number of countries and the demand of the Program for a New International Economic Order, which refers to a process of relocation or industrial deployment.

Growing doubts and questions have been raised concerning redeployment ever since this topic became known in the Second General Conference of UNIDO, held in Lima in 1975. When the Heads of State or Government met in Havana for the Sixth Summit Conference of Non-Aligned Countries in 1979, they touched on some sentitive points in this regard:

The Heads of State or Government emphasized the role of redeployment of industries as a form of international industrial co-operation including resource transfers aimed at establishing productive capacities in developing countries with a view to increasing their share in the total world industrial production based on their natural resources, development objectives and other socio-economic considerations. They further stressed that *redeployment should not be used solely as a pretext for either obtaining access to the abundant and cheap labour in developing countries, or for the transfer of obsolete and polluting industries. Redeployment should be carried out in accordance with overall national objectives, priorities and aspirations of developing countries and should not be associated with the expansion of transnational corporations in developing countries.* It should be seen as part of a process designed to promote the transfer of technology to developing countries. The consultation mechanism at present under way in UNIDO should be strengthened and all countries must participate in order to achieve the redeployment of industrial capacities on a dynamic basis to developing countries and the creation of new industrial capacities in these countries.[3]

Nevertheless, the statements of the Heads of State or Government, revealing their concern over the malformations the transnational corporations introduce in industrial growth, have not changed the negative trend which they sought to halt. The industrial redeployment designed by the transnationals has continued its harmful course, in spite of all warnings and even though few are unaware of their negative characteristics and their deepest motivations.

Generally speaking, industrial redeployment calls for a transfer of industries from developed countries to the Third World. The Lima target of achieving 25 per cent of world industrial production by the year 2000 is presented as the measuring stick for the success or failure of such an effort.

Transfer or relocation is expressed in imprecise terms, with the emphasis placed on the transfer itself, as if that simple process of geographic displacement were sufficient to ensure the industrial development of the underdeveloped world. Emphasis is placed on fulfillment of the quantitative goal by means of relocation, without bringing to light the essential characteristics of the industries the Third World needs so they may act as a dynamic factor promoting true development and not lead to new forms of dependence and exploitation.

An important aspect to keep in mind when reflecting on industrial redeployment is whether it really constitutes a demand that, upheld by the Third World, has meant obtaining concessions from the developed countries or whether, on the contrary, it is a process that has been under way since before the Lima Conference, in response to the transnational corporations' logical tendencies of seeking to maximize their profits.

It is clear – and many analyses bring this out – that the present transnationals have modified their old methods of operation in the underdeveloped world and that, in reponse to these changes, transformations are being brought about in the international division of labor.

The main objective no longer consists of maintaining an agricultural-mining periphery that supplies raw materials, foodstuffs, minerals, etc., or receives banana-republic-style latifundist investments. Even though this has not been completely abandoned, the accent is now being placed on other activities that restate the old capitalist international division of labor in new ways.

A glance at the history of capital exports from the developed capitalist countries shows that, ever since its first manifestations and continuing up to around the 1930's, this process was aimed at controlling and exploiting primary activities, with profit its essential motivation and the control of natural resources its direct characteristic. Later – especially in Latin America – foreign capital sought to benefit from protected national markets, which were initiated in the 1930's and given a great boost following World War II in the context of policies of replacing imports and boosting national industries. The protected markets and industries were taken over and domestic industrial bases acquired, although the main aim was to produce for the domestic market so as to reap the benefits of protectionist policies.

These two forms are still maintained, but their importance is diminishing compared to that of the new current that arose in the 1960's, in which the transnational corporations are the main protagonists. *This new form consists of introducing the headquarters-subsidiary system to take advantage of the existence of a cheap, abundant work force in the Third World for the production of industrial goods for export.*

This headquarters-subsidiary system and the "captive" or intracorporation trade that accompanies it maintains the unalterable aim of maximizing profits, taking advantage of the low wages and longer and more intensive work shifts in underdeveloped countries in which productivity similar to that of the developed capitalist countries can be obtained in generally simple, partial operations and in which benefit can also be drawn from fiscal or other facilities granted by the recipient governments.

In concrete terms, these industrial-export transnationals usually pay wages of less than $0.25 an hour (from an eighth to a fifth of those in the developed capitalist countries) for at least 48 hours' work a week, 50 weeks a year, with very few holidays, in places where organized opposition by labor is weak.

The industries created by this means function with high dependence on imported components, making parts of a product whose manufacture the transnational corporation has split up geographically, though it retains a centralized control over the whole process and the launching of the final product.

With this industrial redeployment in the Third World, drawn by the fact that unemployment and poverty keep wages low there, the imperialist powers and their transnational corporations have found a kind of external industrial reserve army, which they still have the technological possibility of exploiting and which, as in past stages of capitalist history, fulfills its role as a mechanism of plunder encouraging the accumulation of capital.

Therefore, it is absurd to think that the transnational corporations can solve the serious problem of unemployment in the underdeveloped world, since they take advantage of unemployment as a factor for keeping wages low – and, if wages were not low, they would have no incentive for redeployment.

Moreover, while generating foreign exchange income from exports, transnational investments generate even larger outflow through profit remittances, imported supplies, payments for technology and interest. Strictly speaking, the underdeveloped countries pay four times for the capital they receive: 1) for imports when the capital enters in the form of equipment, machinery or component parts; 2) for profits remitted to the country in which the transnational has its headquarters; 3) for technology; and 4) for amortization and debt servicing. It is no coincidence that the countries which have received the most redeployment are generally the most indebted ones. The mythological nature of the "contribution to development" made by imperialist transnational capital very clearly points up the colossal debts and trade and financial imbalances of the countries that have received the largest doses of redeployment.

Industrial redeployment contains dangerous possibilities that may be developed even more if the false advantages claimed by transnational propaganda are believed. It is suggested that industrialization by means of transnational redeployment will pull the Third World out of its age-old backwardness and transform its agrarian profile into an urban industrial one by introducing efficient industries that develop competitive exports of manufactured goods without having to go through the complex process of a nascent industry with unknown markets. The transnational seemingly provides everything and acts as a factor of integration in the national economy.

Actually, the transnational subsidiaries can neither become integrated with nor contribute to the integration of our countries' economies, for they are integrated with their parent companies and with other subsidiaries of the conglomerate, constituting a system that is alien, in the best of cases, or contrary, in most cases, to national interests.

At present, a process of industrial redeployment to the Third World is taking place, but its meaning and effects have little to do with the true interests of our countries' development in the framework of the establishment of a genuine New International Economic Order. The ones who promote it, carry it out and benefit from it are the conglomerates of transnational monopoly capital.

The industrialization of the Third World must not be the sorry by-product left by the transnationals in exchange for the brutal exploitation of the underdeveloped countries' labor resources, the depletion of their natural resources and the pollution of their territories.

7
Transnational corporations

For a little over two decades, the phenomenon of the transnational corporations has been drawing international attention as there has been an alarming increase in the influence of these corporations on world economic relations. In effect, transnationals produce and distribute an increasingly important share of all the goods in the world capitalist system and generate the biggest share of international capital flow which they control by means of a vast international financial network. This means that these international monopolies are the principal agents in the world capitalist process of accumulation and exploitation. This has naturally had great social and political effects for Third World countries.

The spectacular growth, proliferation and influences of the transnationals on the international economy is revealed by the fact that in the early '70s, 10 thousand such entities with 30 thousand subsidiaries were operating around the world.[1] By the end of the decade, estimates made by the UN Centre on Transnational Corporations put the figure at 11 thousand corporations with 82 thousand subsidiaries abroad.

The immense economic power of these modern international monopolies is also evidenced by the fact that in 1981 the ten biggest US transnationals had sales of almost $500 billion, a figure that easily surpasses the aggregate Gross Domestic Product of a large group of countries.

Notwithstanding the ground lost to European and Japanese corporations, US transnationals still rank among the largest in the world.

According to the table *infra,* of the ten largest transnationals in the world, 8 are US corporations. They accounted for 76 per cent of the group's total sales and 75 per cent of the group's total profits.

The proliferation of overseas subsidiaries of the transnationals has gone hand in hand with a spectacular growth of direct capital investment, which substantially increased the cumulative share of capital in the recipient countries during the '70s. Whereas in 1971 cumulative direct investment abroad amounted to $158 billion, by 1975 this figure was $259 billion and, according to recent estimates, the figure was $450 billion in 1980.[2] These figures assume an annual average growth rate of more than 12 per cent during the decade, a growth rate even larger than that of the developed capitalist economies taken as a whole during that same period.

THE WORLD'S TEN LARGEST TRANSNATIONAL CORPORATIONS BY VOLUME OF SALES IN 1981
(Millions of dollars)

	Country	Sales	Net Profits
Exxon	United States	108 108	5 667.5
Royal Dutch/Shell Group	Netherlands-Great Britain	82 292	3 642.1
Mobil	United States	64 488	2 433.0
General Motors	United States	62 698	333.4
Texaco	United States	57 628	2 310.0
British Petroleum	Great Britain	52 200	2 063.3
Standard Oil of California	United States	44 224	2 380.0
Ford Motors	United States	38 247	−1 060.1
Standard Oil of Indiana	United States	29 947	1 922.0
International Business Machines	United States	29 070	3 308.0
TOTAL		568 902	22 999.2

SOURCE : *Fortune* magazine, May and August, 1982.

The only official figures available for 1980 are those on the United States. During that year, cumulative US investment abroad amounted to $213.5 billion, i.e., 48 per cent of the world total. On the other hand, the expansion of Japanese transnationals during the '70s has been explosive. Their direct investments abroad increased from $4.4 billion in 1971 to $31 billion in 1979, implying an unprecedented 28 per cent average annual growth for that period. This allowed the Japanese transnationals to increase their share in world cumulative direct investment from 2.8 per cent in 1971 to some 8 per cent in 1979.

World output, defined as production subject to foreign control or decision-making and estimated on the basis of sales by the transnationals' overseas subsidiaries (intrafirm sales not included), has been put at $830 billion in 1976.[3] By comparing this figure with the total volume of exports by all capitalist countries for that same year, which amounted to $911 billion,[4] the growing role played by the transnationals in world production and trade can be better observed.

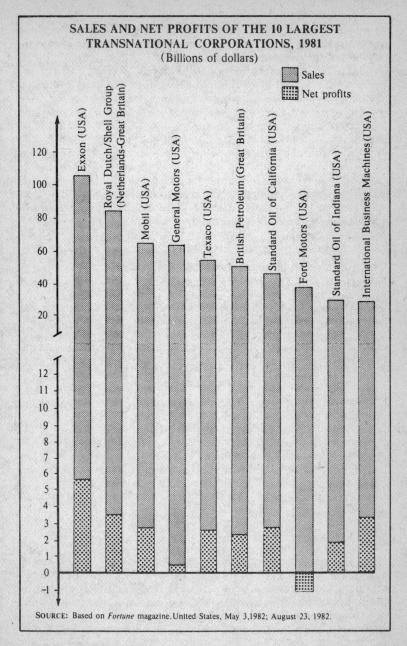

SALES AND NET PROFITS OF THE 10 LARGEST TRANSNATIONAL CORPORATIONS, 1981
(Billions of dollars)

Sales

Net profits

Exxon (USA)

Royal Dutch/Shell Group (Netherlands-Great Britain)

Mobil (USA)

General Motors (USA)

Texaco (USA)

British Petroleum (Great Britain)

Standard Oil of California (USA)

Ford Motors (USA)

Standard Oil of Indiana (USA)

International Business Machines (USA)

120
100
80
60
40
20

12
11
10
9
8
7
6
5
4
3
2
1
0
−1

SOURCE: Based on *Fortune* magazine, United States, May 3, 1982; August 23, 1982.

We have already referred to the enormous number of transnationals and the extraordinary control they have over world trade in the main commodities of the underdeveloped countries.

Equally important is the transnationals' monopoly control over technology and its "transfer" to the Third World, which in general term increases our countries' historical dependence on the capitalist metropolises. The growing role played by transnational banks on international monetary and financial relations should also be stressed. Estimates show that, by 1975, liquid assets of the transnational banks had come very close to total world reserves. This means that these banks can, at relatively short notice and at their will, transfer enormous financial reserves whose sheer magnitude can contribute not only to increase the already serious monetary imbalances, but also to neutralize effective defensive actions by various governments in view of the existing monetary instability. This also considerably compounds the underdeveloped countries' distressing situation of growing indebtedness.

The actual effects of the transnationals' direct investments in Third World countries

Direct capital investments are one of the basic mechanisms for the transnationals' incessant world-wide expansion.

CUMULATIVE DIRECT INVESTMENT
(Billions of dollars)

	1967	1971	1975
Total	105	158	259
Geographic distribution (%)			
In developed capitalist countries	69	72	74
In underdeveloped countries	31	28	26
	100	100	100

SOURCE : Based on UN. *Transnational Corporations in World Development. A Re-examination.* Table III,33.

But the share of the various groups of investment recipient countries in this growth is becoming ever-more differentiated. The above table shows that the underdeveloped countries' share in the world's total cumulative direct investments is decreasing. This very fact seriously challenges the role liberal economic theory has historically assigned to direct investments in financing the underdeveloped countries' development.

We have already mentioned how direct foreign investments distort the economy of underdeveloped countries. But the dramatic dimension of the true role played by direct investments in underdeveloped countries is fully revealed when comparing the net flows of direct investments to those countries with the inflow of repatriated profits from the Third World to the investor countries.

DIRECT FOREIGN INVESTMENT FLOW TO UNDERDEVELOPED COUNTRIES AND PROFITS ON DIRECT INVESTMENTS REPATRIATED TO INVESTOR COUNTRIES

(Accrued sums 1970-1980, millions of dollars)

	Net flow of direct investments in underdeveloped countries	Profits on direct investments repatriated to investor countries
Total of underdeveloped countries	62 615	139 703
Latin America	33 437	38 642
Africa	10 341	23 916
Middle East	57[a]	48 619
Southern and Southeast Asia	18 048	27 260
Oceania	732	1 266

[a] This low figure is due to disinvestments in the Middle East during that period.

SOURCE: Based on UNCTAD. *Handbook of International Trade and Development Statistics. Supplement 1981*, pp. 264-265.

As can be noted in the above table, for every new dollar invested in all the underdeveloped countries during that period, transnationals repatriated approximately $2.2 to their home countries. In the specific case of US transnationals, on which more information is available, during 1970-1979 they invested $11 446 million and repatriated profits amounting to $48 663 million, which means no less than a $4.25 return from the Third World for every new dollar invested.

If 1980 were included, the aforementioned figure would be even higher. During that year the transnationals carried out a large scale disinvestment amounting to −$3 454 million, mainly in the Middle East countries' oil sector. During that year the profits repatriated by US transnationals amounted to $7 325 million. This makes a grand total of almost $56 billion extracted from the underdeveloped countries from 1970 to 1980. On the other hand, the net flow of direct investments to the Third World, considering the aforementioned disinvestments, was almost 8 billion dollars.

The ratio of repatriated profits in 1970-1980 to net flow of direct investment for that same period amounts to more than $7 repatriated for every net dollar of direct investment during that period.

UNITED STATES 1970-1980
NET FLOW OF DIRECT INVESTMENTS, TOTAL PROFITS, REPATRIATED AND REINVESTED, BY SELECTED REGIONS
(Millions of dollars)

Investment recipient areas	A	B	C	D	E	F
All areas	44 009	122 705	97 283	219 988	56	18.4
Developed capitalist countries	35 399	63 482	71 850	135 332	47	16.6
Underdeveloped countries	7 992	55 988	23 338	79 326	71	24.1
Others	618	3 235	2 095	5 330	61	15.1

A: Net flow of direct investments.
B: Profits repatriated to the United States.
C: Reinvested profits.
D: Total profits.
E: Percentage of total profits repatriated to the United States.
F: Profits rate on cumulative investments in 1981 (per cent).

SOURCE : *Survey of Current Business.* August 1980 and 1981.

The above table also shows that underdeveloped countries receive only 18 per cent of the total flow of direct investments as compared to 80 per cent in the developed capitalist countries. Yet, underdeveloped countries contributed 36 per cent of the total world profits earned by US transnationals, accounting for 46 per cent of all profits repatriated to the US. This means that 71 per cent of the profits made in the underdeveloped countries were repatriated and only the remainder was reinvested. On the other hand, only 47 per cent of the profits earned in the developed capitalist countries was repatriated.

It must be added that the profit rate declared by US transnationals in the underdeveloped world in 1981 was 24.1 per cent; this easily surpasses both the rates attained in the developed capitalist countries (16.6 per cent) and the world rate (18.4 per cent).

The aforementioned figures lead to several conclusions. In the first place, as a result of a clear-cut profit repatriation strategy by US transnationals, the underdeveloped countries are the greatest contributors to that country's balance of payments. Secondly, as a consequence of the above, US transnationals can strengthen their hold and expand in the developed capitalist countries. And lastly, according to the high profit rate the transnationals attain in underdeveloped countries and the aforementioned profit repatriation policy, the effect of direct investments in those countries is a net transfer of resources to the United States and, therefore, *a continuous decapitalization of the underdeveloped countries*, which are in no small measure financing the "development" of those very same developed capitalist countries.

If to this is added the fact that the current flow of direct foreign investments in underdeveloped countries implies only a minimal outflow of capital from the investor country and that an important part of the total is covered by local resources raised in the recipient country, the picture of exploitation becomes complete.

And yet – in spite of their importance as a direct mechanism of capitalist exploitation – direct investments by transnationals are not, and have not been for more than a decade, the main component of the mass of private capital exported to the underdeveloped countries. *Direct investments have been displaced by the export of loan capital which – according to OECD data – made up almost 90 per cent of the financial flow to the underdeveloped world in 1980.* In this structural transformation in the flow of private capital towards the Third World, the transnational banks play the key role. These banks have significantly expanded their international operations, especially during the last decade.

This expansion of the transnational banks has been conditioned, among other factors, by the decline in profit rates in the main capitalist countries and the contraction in world trade and production, stemming from the deep crisis facing capitalist economy. This has decisively influenced the shift of capital flows from the productive sphere to international financial circulation.

Transnationals and development

The claims made about the supposedly positive contribution transnationals may make toward the development of the Third World countries are not new. In recent years, these claims have been linked into a conceptual matrix making up a veritable "transnational ideology" generously put at the service of the Third World needs.

As explained above, the underdeveloped countries are offered a transnationalized development model, which would turn them into "export platforms" of manufactured products for the world market.

This form of industrialization of the Third World – advanced and commanded by the transnationals – was already in operation in 1975 with varying degrees of intensity in 17 countries in Asia, 13 in Africa, and 21 in Latin America.

The industries established in the underdeveloped countries on this basis are far from meeting the basic requirements of a true economic development process in those countries. They do meet the requirements of capital which consistently invests in those branches and those countries that offer the greatest profitability and security. The very nature of the subsidiary, which is organically linked to the parent corporation and the other subsidiaries of the transnational network, has an objective tendency towards isolation from the rest of the economy of the host country, inasmuch as it depends mainly on imported inputs and subsequent re-export within the corporation. This is, of course, by definition, contradictory to the concept of development and the integrating effect it presupposes.

On the other hand, while it is true that transnationals increase employment and income levels to a certain degree, it is also true that this is because capital requires a labor force to increase its profitability. Thence, the inevitable rise in employment associated with foreign capital. But this phenomenon is highly localized since the multiplier effect of production aimed at the world market is extremely limited in its capacity to create new jobs in other sectors due to the scarce or non-existent integration into the rest of the national economy characteristic of transnational capital investment. It cannot be denied that this increased employment and income constitutes a kind of hypertrophic economic growth which is, furthermore, unstable because at any given moment the corporations can be transferred to other places in accordance with the interests of the transnational parent; but even if it were to remain stable, this could never be considered a sign of independent economic development.

THE TRANSNATIONAL CORPORATIONS:

- Totalled more than 11 000 and had approximately 82 000 foreign subsidiaries by the end of the '70s;
- Their production was estimated at $830 billion in 1976;
- Their captive trade accounted for 30-40 per cent of world trade;
- By the end of the '70s they controlled close to 40 per cent of the industrial production and approximately 50 per cent of the foreign trade of the underdeveloped countries;
- Their price manipulation causes the underdeveloped countries to lose between $50 and $100 billion a year;
- They are the principal instruments of capitalist accumulation and exploitation throughout the world.

Many incentives are offered by the governments of recipient countries to attract transnational capital. Among them one could mention the broad support for production, great facilities for foreign capital investments, unlimited facilities for the repatriation of profits, tax exemptions and other advantages. However, the labor force of the underdeveloped countries, cheap and practically unlimited, along with the abundant natural resources of the Third World are basic incentives for transnational investments.

ILO reports have shown that in 1975 the average hourly wage in a sampling of underdeveloped countries belonging to the new category of "newly-industrialized countries" (NIC's)was of almost 40 US cents, while the average hourly wage in the United States for similar tasks was over $4. This overexploitation of the labor force is reinforced, on the one hand, by the absolute extension of the work week in these countries, which, according to some studies, usually fluctuates between 48 and 52 hours, with a required minimum of 50 weeks of work per year. On the other, there is a lack of conditions for on-the-job protection and social security, along with restrictive labor legislation and the repression of the trade unions, which, of course, hampers any attempt at strikes or making demands.

Another basic ingredient in the "transnational ideology" is the claim relative to the benefits that the underdeveloped countries can derive from the technology that the transnationals can transfer to them. As a matter of fact, in the majority of cases, the transnationals base their dominant position on some technological know-how or other that they neither share nor wish to share. This know-how has not been developed to meet the national development needs of the backward countries, but rather for the global profits of the transnational and, therefore, it is superimposed on and in contradiction with national needs.

There is no effort to adapt to the host country's environment nor is there any incentive toward scientific and technological development because research and the choice of technologies is carried out in the transnational's home country. So-called technological transfer is reduced to a very fragmentary apprenticeship to employ technologies that are alien to the host country's national realities and therefore precluding all possibility of adapting or producing them.

Therefore, results are almost nil because, as has been pointed out, modern technology makes it possible to fragment more complex production processes into a number of more elementary phases. This, of course, makes it possible to carry out the greater part of the process with unskilled labor whose training requirements are reduced to a few specific operations.

However, in such vast international operations the transnationals are obliged to divulge a certain amount of technological know-how. But then the strategy is to limit and control the process. Restrictive trade measures taking the form of technological contracts that forbid the export of products manufactured with a given technology are one of the mechanisms that the transnationals use to implement this strategy.

The features of the alleged transfer of technology attempting to copy the consumerist pattern of the parent country in the midst of the underdeveloped country's unemployment, social inequality and extreme poverty, are clearly inadequate for the needs of backward countries. Far from being directed toward solving social problems, they contribute to the individual consumption of the higher-income minority.

The transnationals and the threat to national sovereignty

There is no doubt that the growing activities of the transnationals in the territories of the underdeveloped countries constitute a real threat to the national sovereignty of these countries inasmuch as the penetration they are subjected to dangerously increases the degree of their dependence on the developed capitalist countries. It has been estimated that – as was summarized above – toward the end of the '70s transnationals controlled close to 40 per cent of the industrial production and approximately 50 per cent of the foreign trade of the underdeveloped countries.

The control over technology, production and sales that the transnationals have within the economies of the underdeveloped countries can be explained to a large extent by the growing role played by intracorporation operations among the transnationals' economic relations as a whole. Thus, a growing share of imports sometimes vital to the Third World are carried out not by national corporations but rather through the subsidiaries of the transnationals. It is a well-known fact that almost 80 per cent of US technology is marketed by the transnationals to their subsidiaries as a property of the latter and not to the underdeveloped countries.

On the other hand, over one third of the Third World's total exports go, not to the open world market, but are channeled by the subsidiaries to the parent company on the latter's conditions. The losses suffered by the underdeveloped countries as a result of these intracorporation operations is extremely high. As we have already indicated, the underdeveloped countries' losses due to exports at reduced prices alone have been estimated at between $50 and 100 billion. The statistics that show the growth in production and foreign trade of the underdeveloped countries reflect to a large extent the increased exploitation of these countries by the transnationals of the developed capitalist countries.

But the threat to the national sovereignty of the underdeveloped countries where the transnationals operate becomes even clearer when we delve into the historical dossiers of these modern monopolies to review a few facts and actions whose generality and frequency serve as a summary:

- The transnationals do not comply with the legislation of the countries where they operate, e.g., in the field of foreign investments and in their tax, trade, labor and price policies.
- The transnationals intervene directly or indirectly in the internal affairs of the countries where they operate.
- The transnationals demand that their own government put political or economic pressure on the host government in favor of their private interests.

- The transnationals refuse to accept the exclusive jurisdiction of the domestic laws of the host country as regard compensation in the case of nationalization.
- The transnationals obstruct efforts by the underdeveloped countries to effectively control their natural resources.

These and many other facts have been denounced for almost a decade by the international community in varied fora and especially by the Movement of the Non-Aligned Countries. Yet the search for solutions capable of counteracting these dangers has scarcely advanced.

The so-called code of conduct

One of the most sought after solutions in recent years to counteract the negative effects of transnational activity on the underdeveloped countries is the establishment and implementation of an international code of conduct to regulate the activities of the transnationals.

Indeed, these proposals have already been embodied in United Nations General Assembly resolutions regarding the program for the establishment of a New International Economic Order and in the Charter of Economic Rights and Duties of States.[5]

Without a doubt, this demand has been defended by an absolute majority of underdeveloped countries as an indispensable component in the establishment of the New International Economic Order. And yet, after more than five years of uninterrupted negotiations within the framework of the United Nations, efforts to establish the code of conduct have not yet born practical fruit.

Within the Non-Aligned Countries this distressing stagnation has been reflected in the communiqués issued by numerous meetings held at the highest level. Thus, the Final Communiqué (economic section) of the Ministerial Meeting of the Coordinating Bureau held in Havana in May 1982, states:

> The Bureau expressed its deep concern over the extremely slow and limited progress of work concerning the formulation of a Code of Conduct to regulate the activities of transnational corporations particularly those concerning issues of interest for developing countries, on which developed countries were holding up the progress. The Bureau urged the non-aligned and other developing countries to take every step to accelerate these negotiations including, if necessary, through the convening of a United Nations Conference in 1983 for which adequate preparations should be ensured.

It was just in May 1982 that the inter-governmental working group set up to draft the Code by the UN Comission on Transnational Corporations made up of representatives of 48 countries concluded the drafting of the document containing the code. And even so, the work was done in truly precarious conditions because, as the very working group charged with the drafting recognized, "it did not come to an agreement in the wording of all the provisions. In some cases there were different formulations of a certain provision and in others the provisions appeared with different alternate wordings."[6]

This, of course, reflects the deep contradictions existing within the working group itself which is basically polarized between the positions maintained by the representatives of the developed capitalist countries and the Group of 77.

But even were the enormous difficulties implicit in achieving a single formulation for the code overcome, a formulation acceptable both to the representatives of the transnationals and to those who suffer them, there are no concrete proposals regarding the mechanisms and procedures through which this code, heretofore debated by a small group of countries, could come into general force.

These difficulties in themselves cast serious doubt on the practical and immediate viability of such a code of conduct.

In assessing the efforts carried out to formulate a code of conduct regulating the activities of transnationals, it must be recognized, first of all, that they have made it possible to gain a deep understanding of these corporations, of their quantitative and qualitative impact on the international economy and have revealed the enormous difficulties that governments face in coping with the problems created by these corporations' presence and activities for their development plans and policies. Secondly, these efforts have been a unifying factor among the underdeveloped countries inasmuch as the implementation of the code has been a demand that has received the support of all in one way or another. From the political point of view, the efforts to implement the code have meant an open denunciation of the transnationals and, therefore, of imperialism.

It must, indeed, be recognized that the transnationals are not an element exogenous to the capitalist system, but rather the contrary. They represent the most perfect synthesis, the most developed expression of monopoly capitalism in this phase of its general crisis. Therefore, transnational corporations are the international vectors of all the laws that govern the capitalist mode of production in its present imperialist stage, all its contradictions, and they are the most efficient instrument available to imperialism for developing and intensifying the subordination of labor to capital throughout the world.

In general terms, a code of conduct applied to the transnationals implies legal regulation of their activities in order to reduce the negative consequences that such activities produce in the underdeveloped countries fundamentally. We would have to ask ourselves, *can internationally negotiated legal regulations direct the transnationals toward objectives other than those that constitute their very raison d'être, i.e., maximizing profits?* Is it possible to direct the activities of the transnationals toward cooperation and mutual aid instead of toward international domination and exploitation?

The answer is obviously, no! Otherwise, we would have to admit that a simple legal instrument – even if it were monolithically signed by the entire underdeveloped world – could transform the very essence of imperialism, i.e., the system of production relations that is consubstantial to it and of which the transnationals are the present bearers.

No code of conduct could possibly refute the historically proven thesis that capitalism, in its development, generated underdevelopment. In this light, even the most perfect code could never force transnationals to channel their direct investments toward those branches that contribute to the economic progress of the underdeveloped countries unless they were highly profitable branches.

From the political point of view, the code would not offer any protection that the country receiving the foreign investments could not give itself. If an underdeveloped country with a firmly established, independent government, which defends national interests, needs that code, it could pass it itself, without any need for it to be negotiated internationally.

So, the heart of the problem lies in the measures that a given country wishes and is able to take at a given moment, in the political orientation and the nature of its economic development, and thus, in the resolute attitude of its leaders to struggle for the adoption of fundamental measures to meet the interests of its people.

Only on these bases would it be possible to obtain something in the practical field in relation to the so-called code of conduct.

8

The so-called energy crisis

In 1973, OPEC member countries' unilateral increase of oil prices undoubtedly worsened the profound crisis of neo-colonialism.

The imposition of better terms of trade for a fundamental raw material opened up new vistas in the struggle for Third World economic independence, and revealed the possibility of counteracting international monopolies. Thus, the rise in oil prices marked the beginning of a new stage in the history of international economic relations.

Much has been written in an attempt to explain the complex energy-related phenomena the world economy has had to face ever since. Few subjects, moreover, have been so controversial. However, there is an objective interpretation to these facts, which indeed are not historical chance.

First and foremost it must be recalled that capitalist development during the post-war period was influenced, among other factors, by the use of a technology characterized by high consumption of cheap oil, which notwithstanding yielded increasing profits to the transnational oil corporations – mainly US – as a result of the low prices paid to Third World countries suppliers of hydrocarbon. In 1976 the developed capitalist countries consumed 57.3 per cent of world energy while only producing 36.6 per cent. In 1950, oil accounted for 27 per cent of world energy demands, while in 1973 it had already reached 48 per cent.[1]

The Organization of Petroleum Exporting Countries was founded in 1960 with the objective, among others, of coordinating the petroleum policy of its members and defending their interests vis-à-vis the great international monopolies. By the end of the '60s, parallel to the worsening of commercial and financial relations between the Third World and the developed capitalist countries, OPEC member states demanded a larger share in the revenues accruing from their resources, and gradually raised oil prices by 40 per cent to 45 per cent from 1970 to 1973.

However, OPEC's defense of the exporting countries' interests through the rise in prices fixed for transnationals met with a serious obstacle owing to the deterioration of its real income due to the accelerated inflationary process which started in the early '70s. In view of this situation, as of 1973, OPEC once again raised oil prices in order to expand its appropriation of oil revenues.

AVERAGE EXPORT PRICE OF ONE BARREL OF OIL		
	Dollars	*Average Annual Fluctuation* (%)
1973	3.22	40.6
1974	10.49	225.8
1975	11.05	5.3
1976	11.74	6.2
1977	12.83	9.3
1978	12.84	0.1
1979	19.02	48.1
1980	30.90	62.5
1981	35.20	13.9
1982	33.80	−4.0

SOURCE : Based on IMF. *World Economic Outlook 1981*. Washington, 1981, p. 124; OECD. *Economic Outlook*, no. 32, December 1982, p. 141.

Of course, this vindicatory action by the oil-exporting countries was possible due to several factors worth listing. On the one hand, the rise in oil prices came at the time of increasingly favorable changes in the international correlation of forces, growing Third World unity in the defense of its economic interests, and solidarity of the socialist countries, all of which favored the actions undertaken by OPEC. On the other hand, from the economic viewpoint, oil has unique features. It is indeed an indispensable and universally consumed resource due to the charateristics of modern technological development, while it is supplied by a relatively small group of underdeveloped countries capable of controlling an important share of the world market supply.

WORLD PRODUCTION OF CRUDE OIL (Share – per cent)								
	1973	*1974*	*1975*	*1976*	*1977*	*1978*	*1979*	*1980*	*1981*
OPEC member countries	53.5	52.7	49.2	51.5	50.4	47.8	47.4	43.4	40.7
Developed capitalist countries	23.9	22.7	22.8	21.0	21.3	22.5	22.6	23.8	24.3

SOURCE : Based on IMF. *World Economic Outlook, 1981*; Washington, 1981, p. 146.

As shown by various surveys made, the boom experienced by the capitalist economy in the early '70s gave rise to increased energy demands, which also encouraged higher prices.

The situation caused by the rise in oil prices, especially as of 1973-1974, contributed to the widespread notion that the world was facing a huge energy crisis. The term "energy crisis" is accurate only insofar as it includes not only oil but also other energy sources and their interrelationships. However, it should be made clear that such a crisis is not to be interpreted as an imminent danger of exhaustion of world hydrocarbon resources, which, according to scientific studies conducted in various countries, can still be counted on for a reasonable period of time if rationally used. *Rather, it is a crisis of the irrational consumption patterns set by the monopolies, and an expression of the present world economic order's inefficiency in maintaining the supply structure of primary energy resources.*

On the other hand, the thesis currently in fashion among certain circles of the OECD countries, which states that the 1973-1974 oil price increase was the motivating factor of the economic crisis that broke out in 1974-1975 and the main booster of the inflationary spiral which became both outstanding and uncontrollable in the '70s, is also unacceptable. Undoubtedly, the rise of oil prices had a measure of influence upon the evolution of that crisis, upon inflation and the subsequent course of world economy, but in no way originated those phenomena.

The developed capitalist countries were not the ones to suffer most from the oil price increase since they transferred a large share of its cost to the Third World by raising the price of their exports to these countries, but the oil-importing underdeveloped countries, which in addition to the burden stemming from fuel purchases, were forced to devote a substantial part of their export revenues to pay for their oil. The negative impact of oil prices on the economies of the non-oil producing countries of the Third World alone compelled them to increase oil imports from a value of $8 billion to more than three times that figure in 1973-1974.[2]

DEFICIT OF THE OIL ACCOUNT WITHIN THE TOTAL CURRENT ACCOUNT OF THE UNDERDEVELOPED OIL- IMPORTING COUNTRIES

(Billions of dollars)

	1973	1974	1975	1978	1979	1980	1981
Current account balance	−8.9	−31.7	−36.5	−29.5	−48.2	−69.8	−81.9
Oil account balance	−5.2	−17.1	−17.9	−26.0	−40.9	−66.5	−77.5
Per cent	58.4	53.9	49.0	88.1	84.9	95.3	94.6

SOURCE : Based on IMF. *World Economic Outlook, 1981,* Washington, 1981, p. 122.

On the other hand, the oil account deficit played an increasingly prominent role in the deterioration of the Third World's financial situation.

Consequently, the purchase of fuel, that in 1973 absorbed 8.6 per cent of the export revenues of the oil-importing countries, went up to 26.3 per cent in 1980.

Thus, as pointed out previously, a new type of unequal exchange was created for underdeveloped oil-importing countries. In effect, the underdeveloped non-oil countries had to meet the simultaneous drop in export prices of their basic products, rise in oil prices and rapid increase in the price of manufactured goods imported from the developed capitalist world. To this were added the expenditures which the underdeveloped non-oil countries have had to incur to promote the substitution of imported energy by new, renewable energy sources.

The financial requirements of the underdeveloped countries to pay for oil imports were met during this period by a rise in exports and loan arrangements which in turn influenced the spiralling external debt of the Third World.

Moreover, as of 1973, OPEC member countries began to accumulate considerable financial resources. And yet the use of those resources did not contribute, as was hoped, to meet the basic financial needs for the development and strengthening of the economies of oil-importing underdeveloped countries taken as a whole.

Between 1974 and 1980, OPEC's financial contribution in the form of official bilateral or multilateral development assistance to the Third World averaged $4.8 billion a year.

DISTRIBUTION OF OPEC FINANCIAL SURPLUS (Billions of dollars)		
	1974-80	*Per cent*
Invested in developed capitalist countries and in the Euromarket	328	84.5
Invested in multilateral funds and in the World Bank	8	2.1
Invested in underdeveloped countries	52	13.4
TOTAL	388	100.0

SOURCE : Based on IMF. *World Economic Outlook, 1981.* Washington, 1981, p. 128.

Since 1976, a relative decrease in official development assistance (ODA) granted by OPEC came about as a result of the crisis and financial imbalances of some of these countries' economies. This has also been affected by the interrelationship with the developed capitalist countries' economy through the investments of the oil surpluses allocated to those areas.

Actually, over three fourths of OPEC's financial surplus were recycled to developed capitalist countries. In general, this was the trend for 1981 and 1982. The OECD estimates that OPEC countries in 1981 invested $13.3 billion in the US, and during the first half of 1982 they had already invested $11.5 billion in that country.[3]

Most of the countries with large financial surpluses channelled these resources to the world financial markets and the economies of the most developed capitalist countries seeking high profits in the most profitable spheres. Thus, economic relations between OPEC countries and the rest of the Third World have been ever-more difficult in recent years. This is why it is vital to adopt an adequate and effective strategy which involves working together for the solution of the economic problems the Third World faces at present.

Logically, the oil price increase also had an impact on the developed capitalist countries. However, it cannot be compared to the impact this measure had on the economies of the Third World. In the developed capitalist countries, the deficit on oil account imports was largely outweighed by other revenues in the balance of payments. Therefore, while the negative balance resulting from oil imports reached $818 billion in 1973-79, the positive balance on the export of manufactured goods, reached $828 billion in the same period.[4]

In addition, developed capitalist countries received and recycled $219 billion from the OPEC countries between 1974 and 1979, which helped compensate for the trade imbalance resulting from the rise in oil price.[5]

On the other hand, in the most developed capitalist countries, the rise in the prices of hydrocarbons and their by-products generated a set of measures for saving and preserving energy and transforming existing patterns of technological development, to reduce energy consumption to a minimum. Thus, the oil consumption rate as compared to the GDP in the OECD countries decreased almost 25 per cent[6] from 1973 to 1981, contributing also to lessen the negative impact of the rise in energy prices.

UNITED STATES: IMPORTED INFLATION AND INTERNALLY GENERATED INFLATION

(Percentage rate of annual fluctuation)

	1973	1974	1975	1978	1979	1980
Imported inflation	0.1	0.1	−0.5	−0.3	1.6	−0.2
Domestic inflation	7.5	11.0	7.5	8.2	6.9	9.8
TOTAL	7.6	12.0	7.0	7.9	8.5	9.6

SOURCE: Based on Bank for International Settlements. *51st Annual Report*. Basle, 1981, p. 15.

In that period, emphasis was made on the stimulating effect that the oil price increase had on inflation. However, imported inflation – including that originating from oil – has proved to be only a small share of that which is internally generated in the major developed capitalist countries.

The process of oil price increases coincided with the transnational corporations' interests since they were in a position to obtain substantial benefits through marketing control. Costlier energy areas became profitable, and investment diversification aimed at controlling the development of new energy sources could be achieved, making them energy transnationals.

According to specialized Western sources, from 1973 to 1980, five of the major energy transnationals showed an annual average profit increase of $882 million dollars.[7] It must be stressed that in 1980 alone, the international oil cartel, made up by seven transnational corporations, had $24 billion profits.[8]

The international oil cartel has obtained great profits from the oil price increase through speculation with fuel stocks and the proportionally faster price increases of by-products. In effect, since the nationalization of oil by OPEC countries, monopolies rid themselves of the more risky aspects of the business while keeping control over technology and trade, which offer the greatest benefit with minimal inconvenience.

Since 1980 there have been some significant changes in the international oil market. Although the average annual oil price for 1981 was even higher than that of 1980, significant consumption reductions were already being observed by then, reaching almost 8 per cent in 1979-1981.[9] This decrease in demand led to a decrease in oil prices for the first time since 1973.

In the face of this situation, OPEC reacted by reducing output, from 30.9 million barrels per day in 1979 to 22.5 in 1981, and it is estimated that it was down to 18 million barrels in 1982.[10]

Despite this reduction in hydrocarbon supply, for the first time since 1974, the annual average oil price decreased some 4 per cent in 1982. The main factors conditioning this situation do not seem, nevertheless, to be merely circumstantial.

While these developments have been influenced by events such as the Iran-Iraq war or the international monetary and financial disorder, the future of the market would seem to be determined by factors that are even more far-reaching. Thus, it is impossible to ignore the profound technological change and other measures being taken by developed capitalist countries which are reflected in the reduction of oil consumption per GDP unit.

The impact of the capitalist economic crisis during these years and the ensuing reduction in oil demand cannot be overlooked either. Finally, we must consider growth in oil production in other non-OPEC underdeveloped countries, which has increased from 4.4 million barrels a day in 1973 to 9.0 million in 1981,[11] thus lowering the degree of OPEC control over market and prices.

Considering all the above, a period of relative stabilization of hydrocarbon prices seems to be approaching, the consequences of which for world economy have not yet been adequately assessed.

OIL CONSUMPTION RATE PER GDP UNIT
(1975 = 100)

1973	107.9	1978	98.7
1974	101.8	1979	95.7
1976	101.5	1980	87.2
1977	99.8	1981	81.2

SOURCE : Based on OECD. *Economic Outlook,* No. 31, July, 1982, p. 136.

The possibilities of the underdeveloped countries' economic progress are limited by the amount of energy required. The rate of increase in energy consumption needed to guarantee development is tied up with the historical limitations the market-economy developed countries have imposed on the scientific-technological progress of the Third World.

The difficulties of the underdeveloped oil-importing countries are exacerbated in that they are not in a position to economize on a large scale or adopt large-scale conservation measures without endangering their own economic development projects, based on a high oil-consuming technology.

While it is true that the days of cheap fuel are past, in order to reduce the gap between developed and underdeveloped countries, the latter must increase their demand for energy. In the short run, the increase will have to be basically covered by oil, but this does not preclude achieving maximum use of available energy sources such as water and coal or the use of nuclear energy to solve the growing short-term demand for electricity. Attention should also be given to alternate renewable energy sources — other than water – such as wind, tidal, solar and other forms of energy. Despite the important role which they will play in the long run, however, these must not be overestimated now when they can only be palliatives and not solutions to the so-called energy crisis.

Nuclear energy, which, on the other hand, is the most accesible basic solution for countries with insufficient energy resources, usually has to be deferred in the underdeveloped countries due to their relatively small electrical systems compared to the reactors' commercial capacities, the lack of skilled personnel in this field, and the high financing requirements of nuclear power programs. International cooperation is, therefore, indispensable for training technicians, for specialization and training in

155

nuclear energy science and technology. Another important area for cooperation could be the development of smaller-scale nuclear reactors that could compete with conventional power plants so that nuclear power plants could be introduced sooner; or perhaps regional solutions – with larger reactors – could be found for those countries.

There is an evident need to have concerted actions by Third World oil exporting and importing countries, in order to surmount the great obstacle to economic development that obtaining energy on the international market will mean for most of them in the coming years.

9
Cooperation among underdeveloped countries

During the First Summit Conference of Non-Aligned Countries in 1961, the first ideas regarding economic and technological cooperation among underdeveloped countries emerged within the Movement. These ideas were further expanded and reiterated in various meetings.

The program for the New International Economic Order included the very significant element of cooperation among Third World countries. At that time proposals for such cooperation became more coherent and a process aimed at promoting it began. Even though this process has not yet yielded very significant and concrete results, it has served to further studies on the issue, explore untapped possibilities and draw attention to its importance and the need for it.

In some market-economy developed countries, skeptical or openly unfavorable opinions on cooperation among developing countries are frequently expressed. The scanty achievements obtained, or the alledged violation of comparative advantages derived from relations with developed countries are brought to the fore in order to further their argument that such cooperation is effective and costly. Nor is it uncommon to find recommendations that appear to be of a technological nature advocating closer links with the developed economies and the abandonment of cooperation among underdeveloped countries portrayed as an unrealizable dream or a mere propagandistic slogan.

Another means of distorting cooperation among underdeveloped countries is to brand the collective self-reliance stipulated in the documents of the Non-Aligned Countries and of the Group of 77 as an attempt to establish an impossible autarchic system within the Third World, thereby cutting itself off and turning its back on relations and cooperation with the rest of the world.

Actually, cooperation among underdeveloped countries is neither an absurd attempt at autarchy nor a utopian formula; on the contrary, it is based on our countries' concrete needs, on lessons derived from a wealth of historical experience and on concrete cooperation possibilities through the use of common resources and the best utilization of our diversity, in order to contribute to development within the framework of a more balanced world economy.

There are several reasons why cooperation among Third World countries is necessary. The first and more general reason is the fact that it is *a fighting instrument against neo-colonial dependence stemming from old historical links with former metropolises, embodied in relations of deep subordination in production, trade, finance, technology, and intellectual and cultural fields.* If anything shows with absolute clarity the historical path our countries have followed, it is the noxious effect of dependence on market-economy developed countries.

This link, forged by the common history of many Third World countries, has brought about results which may be summarized as underdevelopment, backwardness, poverty and the gradually widening gap between them. These negative effects have been constant in the history of colonialism and neo-colonialism and have become even more serious as the present economic crisis, which was not generated by our countries, weighs upon our weaker economies with a multiple impact and transfers to the Third World a good portion of the cost of domestic adjustment and of economic policy decisions adopted in the West.

The current profound international economic crisis and, with an even greater force, the history of colonial and neo-colonial relations, point out the need to develop other links, to sever dependence, diversifying Third World economic relations and exploiting our existing potentials whose benefits neo-colonial subjugation has prevented us from reaping.

For a long time, the idea has been put forward that the economic growth of underdeveloped countries is a variable depending on the growth of the so-called developed capitalist centers. The growth of such centers has been extremely sluggish in recent years, and it is even forecast that for the rest of the century an annual rate of over 3 per cent is not to be expected, due to their tendency toward chronic stagnation. It is therefore unquestionable that, even by adopting the passive attitude of waiting for the basic incentives for economic growth to come from abroad, the future of the Third World – in need of at least 7 per cent growth rates – looms bleak if it continues abiding by the present neo-colonial pattern of external economic relations.

Another reason is the fact that, due to their narrow and unfavorable nature, these relations have become increasingly more restrictive, to the extent of rejecting and excluding our countries.

Intensified protectionism in developed capitalist countries' markets is a specific factor which discriminates and blocks our exports, at a time when their expansion constitutes an important element for development and even for simple economic reproduction. Under these circumstances, it becomes imperative to find other markets, some of which we ourselves can provide, as part of the possibilities for trade within the Third World. This would not be an isolationist attitude on the part of the underdeveloped countries, but a logical reaction to the protectionist isolationism practiced with growing vigor by the market-economy developed countries.

Obviously, cooperation among developing countries will advance, not for abstract technical reasons, but because of its capability to offer economic and other types of benefits to the Third World, so as to render its foreign relations more flexible and provide effective support to national development processes.

In this regard, *the Third World's great economic diversity and the varied endowment of its material and human resources and development levels indicate important possibilities for efficient economic complementation on which to base the obtention of concrete benefits.*

The Third World, as a whole and at regional levels, has oil-exporting or potentially oil-exporting economies; economies that produce food and important mineral or agricultural raw materials; economies with a given degree of industrialization already producing equipment and machinery with a considerable level of technological sophistication; countries which already have enough highly qualified experts, technicians and doctors who can lend their services to other underdeveloped countries. There is enough human and material potential to make cooperation among our countries a powerful dynamic factor contributing to our autonomous and integral development. Such cooperation can be a positive element in developing relations in production, technology and trade in keeping with our realities and development level, thus substituting frequent imports and impositions of products, technologies and consumption patterns of a transnational origin conceived for unrestrained Western consumerism, and aimed at satisfying the whims of small elites while strongly burdening the balance of payments and establishing links of costly dependence.

Likewise, cooperation among underdeveloped countries, defined as an effort towards collective self-reliance, does not imply that former colonial powers and countries acting as hosts of transnationals are relieved of their commitment to economic collaboration with the Third World. Neither does it exclude the contribution of socialist countries in sundry ways, whose increase, according to the possibilities of those countries, would provide effective support to the underdeveloped world's efforts towards economic development and social progress.

Collective self-reliance does not mean the creation of a self-contained system nor the creation of an economic bloc, but rather the broadening of international economic cooperation to develop yet untapped possibilities and the increase of our countries' bargaining power in terms of development and the implementation of the New International Economic Order. This cooperation does not attempt to waive or replace any of the legitimate claims on economic cooperation raised by our countries in basic documents such as the Declaration and the Program of Action for the establishment of the New International Economic Order and the Charter of

Economic Rights Duties of States. Far from it, it aims at strengthening our joint stands to raise these claims with greater soundness and endorsement.

This effort of internal cooperation for the strengthening of the Third World should avoid reproducing within itself some negative phenomena which characterize relations between underdeveloped and developed capitalist countries.

Firstly, it is obvious that cooperation among our countries cannot become a mechanism for transnationals, acting through their Third World subsidiaries, to control most of the benefits of a broadened market, of best access conditions, or in practice, to govern relations according to their own interests. The transnationals' capacity and ability to profit from and become the main beneficiaries, and also the major causes for the failure of regional or sub-regional economic integration schemes implemented in the Third World, particularly in Latin America, are well known. Operating from within and on the basis of their superior financial and technological capabilities, as well as on the possibilities offered by the vast international dimension of their activities, these corporations have played major roles in reaping greater benefits and in designing frustrated integrationist schemes. They have benefited most from tariff reductions, fiscal and other facilities, in actual practice turning those schemes into broadened economic advantages for their enjoyment and integrating them into their transnational domination systems.

Thus, *cooperation among underdeveloped countries must be based on the coordination of internal efforts and include, as an important component, actual and effective forms of control over transnational activities*, coupled with full sovereignty over our natural resources and economic activities, to prevent the so-called South-South cooperation from becoming another mechanism aimed at increasing the profits of such conglomerates.

Another concomitant factor in the failure of several regional or sub-regional economic integration attempts has been the unequal distribution of benefits among the participants, to the logical displeasure of the relatively less developed countries which has even made them discard integration schemes. This experience clearly shows that *cooperation among underdeveloped countries must recognize the heterogeneity of the Third World in regards to underdevelopment levels, with a view to preventing a few countries with a certain level of industrialization and exporting capability from reaping most of the benefits.*

Cooperation would have very little meaning if it were to be limited to making it a sort of preferential zone for some Third World countries with larger economic capabilities to use their capital and their export goods in keeping with the traditional principles our countries have had to endure, ignoring the inferior situation of the most backward countries.

It is also indispensable to prevent the reproduction of other negative phenomena inherent to relations with market-economy developed countries, such as unequal trade.

Cooperation among underdeveloped countries cannot be used as a pretext for not carrying out the domestic structural transformations which, based on each country's efforts, constitute the main prerequisites for a genuine development process. Cooperation among our countries may operate as a significant complement for the decisive domestic efforts aimed at development and the eradication of colonial dependence, but never as a formula which, operating from without, could condone the non-implementation of the indispensable transformations.

Turning cooperation among underdeveloped countries into an important economic and political factor is not an easy task; neither can it be achieved in a short time. There are powerful interests which consider as disturbing and dangerous this cooperation effort to sever the links of neo-colonial dependence. It is not surprising that those interests fight cooperation among underdeveloped countries by means of practical obstacles and theroretical arguments that define it as ideological Utopia.

But there are significant objective obstacles which hinder this cooperation as well. The first is the set of historical ties of economic and cultural nature which relate most Third World countries with economic, technological and linguistic systems headed by the developed capitalist countries.

The lack of horizontal relations and communications among our countries, which were and still are to some extent private domains where relations are only vertically established with the metropolis, constitutes an obvious historical fact. From this stems the lack of infrastructures for communications, trade, financial relations and the great lack of mutual understanding which constitutes a very important element that partially explains why our countries have not taken advantage of favorable cooperation opportunities.

These objective facts show that the so-called South-South cooperation cannot be established in one stroke as a single and complete system, but that it should gradually make its way and create its own infrastructure as the relations of cooperation develop. Little ground can be gained on the basis of great formulas designed for a Third World of abstract generalizations deprived of sound foundations; rather it is necessary to establish concrete relations of cooperation wherever possible, preferably based on sub-regional and regional actions.

The above does not imply giving up broader and feasible initiatives, such as the Generalized System of Preferences among underdeveloped countries or other steps, but rather emphasizes the need to acknowledge that cooperation relations among our countries should be expanded, since their present dimension is small and the obstacles they meet powerful.

Trade relations among underdeveloped countries

In the context of the relations established in the past few years among Third World countries, trade links occupy an outstanding position.

As a result of the existing international economic situation, Third World countries have been modifying their traditional trade schemes and have developed new trade interrelations with other equally underdeveloped countries. These trends have gained remarkable momentum, particulary in the past ten years.

TRADE TRENDS AMONG UNDERDEVELOPED COUNTRIES
(Billions of dollars)

	1960	1965	1970	1975	1979	1981
Total exports	27.40	35.92	55.02	211.22	416.61	539.0
Total trade among underdeveloped countries	6.10	7.51	11.17	49.37	103.07	142.0
Percentage of total trade	22.3	20.9	20.3	23.4	24.7	26.3

SOURCE : Based on UNCTAD. *Informe sobre el comercio y el desarrollo, 1981*, New York, 1982, p. 51; GATT. *El comercio internacional, 1981-1982*, Geneva, 1982. Chart A3 of the Appendix.

Indeed, exports between underdeveloped countries increased at a 26.0 per cent annual average rate from 1970 to 1981, while their total exports increased at an average 23.1 per cent rate in the same period of time. This means that in the last decade the so-called South-South trade has had a higher rate of exports than the Third World, although these figures on total trade value were affected by the considerable upsurge of oil prices at that time and inflation's distorting effects.

Trade among underdeveloped countries, despite the progress made, nevertheless, represented only 26.3 per cent of total exports in 1981.

On the other hand, the percentage of intraregional trade has also diminished in the last ten years. Total exports decreased from 16.4 per cent in 1970 to 12.9 per cent in 1979. At the same time, interregional trade increased from 5.9 per cent to 11.8 per cent respectively in this same period.[1]

Different factors have influenced the process of expansion in South-South trade relations. Among these it is important to signify – aside from the aforesaid on oil prices influencing statistics as well as real trade among Third World countries – the relative contraction of markets in developed capitalist countries due to the negative effects of the economic crisis and the increasingly protectionist policies implemented by them.

The expansion of domestic markets in some of these countries with relatively high rates of economic growth obtained in the 1970's has also influenced this trade increase among underdeveloped countries.

162

In the same way, the diversification of exports by the Third World countries exerted its influence and revealed a change in their overall composition of commodities.

COMPOSITION OF UNDERDEVELOPED COUNTRIES'
EXPORTS
(Percentage)

	1965	1979
Food	28.2	12.4
Raw materials	25.5	10.5
Fuel	31.4	56.6
Manufactured goods	13.8	15.3
Machinery and transport equipment	1.1	5.2

SOURCE : Based on United Nations. *Monthly Bulletin of Statistics,* May 1981.

Finally, it must be pointed out that the underdeveloped countries' adoption of tariff measures as incentives contributed in some measure to the expansion of trade observed among them in the last few years.

Similar changing characteristics are present in the composition of commodities in South-South trade.

SHARE OF TRADE AMONG UNDERDEVELOPED COUNTRIES
IN THEIR TOTAL EXPORTS BY GROUPS OF COMMODITIES
(Percentage)

	1960	1965	1970	1975	1979
Food	18.2	17.4	15.4	22.8	27.0
Agricultural raw materials	17.4	14.8	21.5	26.3	27.6
Minerals	3.7	5.6	6.4	8.1	12.0
Fuels	29.7	23.6	21.1	20.8	20.6
Iron and steel	40.9	64.4	47.0	51.5	52.4
Non-ferrous metals	6.0	6.2	6.3	17.0	21.0
Manufactured goods	42.7	38.0	34.5	36.3	35.0
All products	22.3	20.9	20.3	23.3	24.7

SOURCE : Based on UNCTAD. *Informe sobre el comercio y el desarrollo, 1981,* New York, 1982, p. 52.

In general, there is an increase in the products that are traded within the Third World. This undoubtedly shows, despite the continuing enormous difficulties, the existence of a potentially expanding market and of future perspectives.

In the products traded among underdeveloped countries, fuels occupy a prominent place. According to UNCTAD statistics, in 1979 fuels represented about 47.2 per cent of the value of South-South trade and they were the determining commodities of interregional trade.

It is also important to analyze South-South trade in more detail, excluding fuels.

PRODUCT STRUCTURE OF TRADE AMONG UNDERDEVELOPED
COUNTRIES IN PERCENTAGE OF TOTAL EXPORTS
(Excluding fuels)

	1960	1965	1970	1975	1979
Food	45.5	48.6	40.1	39.4	32.4
Agricultural raw materials	24.7	17.9	15.1	10.1	10.9
Manufactured goods	12.0	17.1	24.4	35.8	44.4
Machinery and transport equipment	0.9	1.7	3.9	8.4	12.1
All other products	17.8	16.4	20.4	14.7	12.2

SOURCE : Based on UNCTAD. *Informe sobre el comercio y el desarrollo, 1981,* New York, 1982, p. 52.

In this case a notable increase of manufactured goods and especially of machinery and equipment is observed. At the same time, there is a decrease of food, agricultural raw materials and other products. This shows the widening of the market of products with a higher aggregate value, which clearly favors trade expansion on the part of underdeveloped countries.

However, according to UNCTAD, when interpreting this development it must be borne in mind that the bulk of the expansion of exports of manufactured goods from developing countries has been the work of a small group of countries, and that most developing countries have practically not participated in this expansion.[2]

In fact, the expansion of manufacturing exports by a group of Third World countries is related to the process of industrial redeployment promoted and controlled by transnational corporations, which certainly have little to do in their essence with genuine processes of economic development. It is not possible to ignore the degree of control exerted by these transnational corporations on the marketing of the commodities mostly exported by underdeveloped countries. Thus, trade among our peoples is actually subjected to a process of interference which distorts its potentialities and conceals their true beneficiaries.

Geographic orientation of trade among underdeveloped countries also presents features which should be pointed out.

GEOGRAPHIC ORIENTATION OF TRADE AMONG
UNDERDEVELOPED COUNTRIES IN 1981
(Percentage)

	Central and South America	South and East Asia	West Asia	Africa
Origin/Destination				
Central and South America	79.6	4.4	6.9	9.1
South and East Asia	7.9	66.5	16.3	9.3
West Asia	21.6	52.5	18.2	7.7
Africa	51.8	12.7	7.8	27.7

SOURCE : Based on GATT. *El comercio internacional, 1981-1982,* Geneva, 1982, Chart A25 of the Appendix.

These data emphasize the importance of intraregional trade for Latin America, followed by South and East Asia, regions where the most relevant economic integration and cooperation agreements of the Third World have been signed.

However, despite its relative importance, the underdeveloped countries' interregional trade, according to GATT estimates, represented only 22.5 per cent and 21.8 per cent of the total trade of Latin America and South and East Asia, respectively, in 1981.[3]

The results of trade among underdeveloped countries, especially in the 1970's, indicated the need of creating an adequate institutional framework for the development of these relations. The first obstacle faced in this area referred to tariff barriers and non-tariff barriers in underdeveloped countries, as incentives to their industrial and agricultural development, against rivalry in commodities exported by developed capitalist countries.

However, since the early 1960's, the different types of economic integration carried out especially in Latin America promoted tariff reductions as a mechanism to stimulate trade in the region.

Thus, up to 1979 some 50 countries had applied mutual trade preferences as members of different integration groupings such as the Latin American Free Trade Association (LAFTA) – which since 1980 became the Latin American Integration Association (ALADI) – the Andean Group, the Central American Common Market (CACM) and the Caribbean Community (CARICOM).[4]

The extension of this policy in 1979 led some 90 countries to apply or negotiate the implementation of trade preferences in South-South trade.[5]

On the basis of the experiences obtained from trade cooperation schemes in effect on different levels, the Group of 77 launched the initiative of establishing a global system of trade preferences (GSTP) at the Mexico Conference in 1976.

Afterwards, the Ministerial Meeting of the Group of 77, which took place in Arusha in 1979, began its negotiations.

However, the negotiating process has faced serious difficulties so far on the concrete forms of implementing this generalized system of preferences, taking into account the possibilities of including other measures to promote trade, global or product-by-product discussion and the existence of a preferential system already in force in the different regional integration agreements.

Recently, other institutional trade arrangements have also been attempted. An example of these possibilities is offered by the Energy Cooperation Program for Central American and Caribbean Countries promoted by Mexico and Venezuela. Through this agreement, promoting countries commit themselves to guarantee the supply of up to 160 thousand barrels daily, granting credits to beneficiary countries on 30 per cent of the costs of oil imports, on a five-year term and a 4 per cent interest rate, subjet to modifications for up to 20 years, and a 2 per cent interest rate if the credits are allocated to top priority economic development projects.

As stated by ECLA, this mechanism may contribute to solving problems similar to those in other countries equally affected by the imports of hydrocarbons, but its importance stems, above all, from its value as an example to explore new forms of cooperation in other sectors and among other countries.[6]

The creation and operation of the Latin American Economic System (SELA) as a mechanism to promote cooperation among underdeveloped countries based on flexible principles is also a positive element. Among these mechanisms it is important to mention the creation of the Action Committees for economic and other activities, in which member countries participate according to their possibilities and interests. Equally important, and even more important in the future, will be the use of SELA as a forum for the coordination of positions and to increase bargaining power.

The search for new mechanisms of trade cooperation among underdeveloped countries has led to the creation of multinational trading enterprises. These enterprises have emerged as a result of the need to face the mechanisms of trade exploitation used by transnational corporations, which end up taking over a substantial part of the producers' profits.

It is important to take into consideration Latin America's experience with the Empresa Multinacional de Comercialización de Fertilizantes (MULTIFERT), established in 1979; the Naviera Multinacional del Caribe (NAMUCAR), established in 1976; and the Comercializadora Multinacional del Banano (COMUNBANA), which began in 1977. However, these enterprises have faced difficulties that underline the obstacles that could hinder work in this field.

Monetary-financial relations among underdeveloped countries

During the 1970's, monetary-financial cooperation played a major role among underdeveloped countries, as trade and other relations among them increased.

Development of cooperation in this field implied the establishment of regional and sub-regional payment arrangements in the form of clearing houses, payment unions and reserve centers (often within trade integration plans), and the creation of multinational institutions for the financing of development and of national development funds for foreign assistance.[7]

The type of cooperation in force in the form of clearing houses, obviously demonstrated its usefulness by reducing the volume of foreign exchange actually transferred among associated countries. According to UNCTAD data, there were 7 agreements of this type involving 49 Third World countries by 1979.

GEOGRAPHIC ORIENTATION OF OFFICIAL DEVELOPMENT ASSISTANCE GRANTED BY OPEC (Percentage)		
	1979	*1980*
Bilateral assistance	100.0	100.0
Arab countries	84.2	80.1
Non-Arab African countries	2.7	3.6
Non-Arab Asian countries	2.9	10.7
Europe	0.5	4.4
Latin America	0.6	0.3
Unspecified	9.1	0.9
Multilateral assistance from OPEC		
Arab member countries	100.0	100.0
Arab countries	48.5	44.5
Non-Arab African countries	28.4	39.6
Non-Arab Asian countries	9.5	6.4
Europe	3.0	3.0
Latin America	6.4	2.3
Oceania	0.4	0.4
Unspecified	3.8	3.8

SOURCE : Based on OECD. *Development Co-Operation Review 1981,* Paris 1981, p. 113.

However, the most relevant and important field in which these links have developed has been that of development financing.

OPEC-originated financial flows represented 21.3 per cent of the official development aid offered to the Third World between 1974 and 1980. On the other hand, this aid was offered with a concessionary element, that reached 89.1 per cent in 1980, practically similar to the rate of capitalist developed countries that same year.[8]

However, the volume of financial resources from OPEC did not meet the expectations of the Third World in this field, since they only represented approximately 13 per cent of the surplus capital obtained between 1974 and 1980. These resources were concentrated in a very restricted economic area and did not significantly benefit the countries most highly affected by the increase in oil prices.

Economic cooperation among underdeveloped countries has also been attempted in other spheres, on an experimental basis, and with more modest results.

There is no doubt that it is in the field of trade and in the monetary-financial sphere where the most progress has been attained in these relations. However, so far, considering the important ties established during the past decade, there remain numerous obstacles that have prevented the South-South cooperation from playing a more important role in the international economic relations of the Third World.

Developed capitalist countries, which see in this type of cooperation a threat to their mechanisms of colonial and neo-colonial domination, have opposed this cooperation, often covertly. This form of cooperation has been distorted and misguided by transnational corporations, persisting in the appropriate handling of their profit-seeking objectives, which have nothing to do with the legitimate interests of our peoples.

Among other things, there has not been adequate communications and concertation of efforts among the underdeveloped countries themselves to carry forward new mechanisms of cooperation which, in the long run, would equally benefit all.

A fair and objective analysis of our realities indicates, however, the great progress that can still be made in the field of the so-called South-South cooperation.

Without disregarding our limitations and casting aside the projects that may idealize these potentialities, much can be done to solve the very serious problems affecting our peoples. The problem of food and agricultural development; cooperation in the spheres of health, education and culture; industrial complementation; and the rendering of assistance and technical services are some of the spheres in which, in addition to what has already been achieved and can be achieved in the trade and monetary-financial spheres, we have a right to place real hopes for cooperation and mutual assistance to the benefit of our peoples.

10
The quality of life in the underdeveloped world

The deep economic crisis the contemporary world is experiencing is exacerbated in the underdeveloped countries as a result of the poor overall development of the productive forces and the malformation of their economic structures. It is a crisis that directly worsens the dramatic situation peoples in those countries face, heightening the terrible scarcities that shape the quality of life in the Third World. Hunger, poverty, disease, ignorance, unemployment, lack of opportunity, insecurity, inequality, hopelessness are the terms that could well define the living conditions of a great part of the present population of our planet.

The economic and social injustice implied in the gap between the living conditions of the highest strata in developed capitalist societies and the humble and exploited masses the world over, in the underdeveloped world in particular, is an affront to the collective conscience of mankind. It is an imperative need of our times to be aware of these realities, because of what a situation affecting three quarters of mankind entails in terms of human suffering and the squandering of life and intelligence.

The cold eloquence of these figures, indices and statistical data is in itself terrifying enough. But beyond them lies the tragic situation of hunger, abject poverty and neglect that is individualized hundreds of millions of times over. This is the expression of the enormous abyss separating the underdeveloped from the developed countries today and, furthermore, of the evident inequalities still existing within the overwhelming majority of Third World countries, not fully reflected in the overall statistical indicators.

Population

In the first century AD, world population was 200-300 million. Sixteen centuries elapsed before reaching a population of 500 million, in 1650. The population annual growth rate was then 0.3 per cent; at that same pace, world population would double every 250 years. In the next 200 years it

POPULATION GROWTH

(Projections for the year 2000 by region and selected countries)

	1975 (millions)	2000	Per cent of growth in the year 2000	Average per cent of annual growth	Per cent of world population in the year 2000
World total	4 090	6 351	55	1.8	100
Developed countries	1 131	1 323	17	0.6	21
Underdeveloped countries and China	2 959	5 028	70	2.1	79
Africa	399	814	104	2.9	13
Asia and Oceania	2 274	3 630	60	1.9	57
Latin America	325	637	96	2.7	10
USSR and Eastern Europe	384	460	20	0.7	7
North America, Western Europe, Japan, Australia and New Zealand	708	809	14	0.5	13
People's Republic of China	935	1 329	42	1.4	21
India	618	1 021	65	2.0	16
Indonesia	135	226	68	2.1	4
Bangladesh	79	159	100	2.8	2
Pakistan	71	149	111	3.0	2
Nigeria	63	135	114	3.0	2
Brazil	109	226	108	2.9	4
Mexico	60	131	119	3.1	2
United States	214	248	16	0.6	4
USSR	254	309	21	0.8	5

SOURCE : Based on *The Global 2000 Report to the President,* Vol. 1, p. 9.

grew by 500 million, and by one billion a century later. In 1925, world population reached the 2 billion mark. By 1962 it was 3 billion and, with a 2.1 per cent annual growth rate, it doubled in 33 years. In 1975 it reached 4 billion. World population, amounting to 1.6 billion in 1900, almost tripled during the first 80 years of this century; and it will take just 20 years more for there to be an additional 2 billion, to surpass the 6 billion mark by the beginning of the 21st century. During the last two decades of the 20th century, world population will grow more than it did throughout the whole of history up until 1900.[1]

But these figures are more impressive in the case of Third World countries.

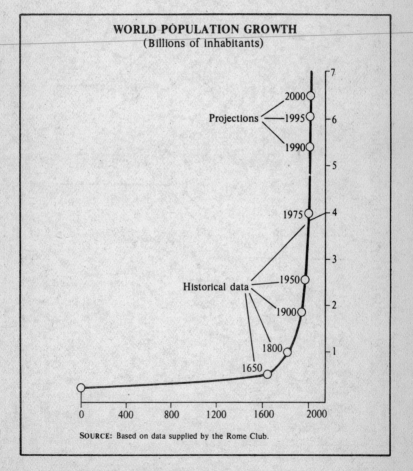

WORLD POPULATION GROWTH
(Billions of inhabitants)

SOURCE: Based on data supplied by the Rome Club.

171

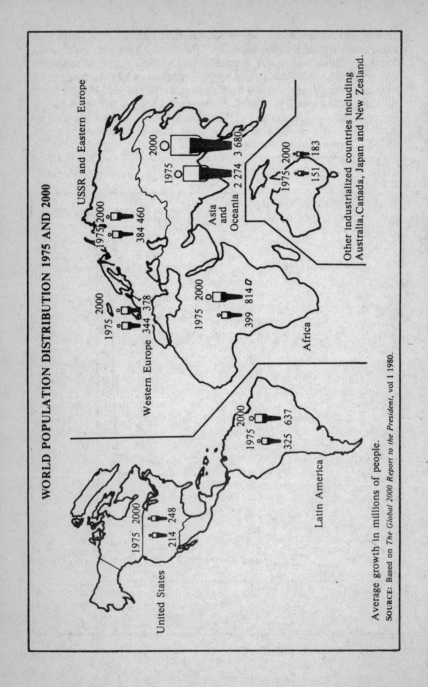

WORLD POPULATION DISTRIBUTION 1975 AND 2000

USSR and Eastern Europe

2000

1975

United States

1975 2000

214 248

Western Europe 344 378

1975 2000

384 460

Asia and Oceania 2 274 3 680

Africa

1975 2000

399 814

Latin America

1975 2000

325 637

Other industrialized countries including
Australia, Canada, Japan and New Zealand.

1975 2000

151 183

Average growth in millions of people.

SOURCE: Based on *The Global 2000 Report to the President*, vol 1 1980.

In 1980, three out of every four inhabitants of our planet lived in the underdeveloped world. In view of its present growth trend, from 1990 onwards, there will be 95 million additional inhabitants in the underdeveloped countries every year. That is, every eight years its growth will equal the present population in India and double that of Latin America in 1981.

While the population in the developed regions will grow at a 0.6 per cent average rate until the year 2000, in the underdeveloped world as a whole it will grow at a rate of 2.1 per cent, i.e., three times faster. A detailed breakdown of this rate shows that on the African continent the population will increase 2.9 per cent annually; in Latin America, 2.7 per cent; 2.1 per cent in Southern Asia and 1.4 per cent in the underdeveloped countries of Eastern Asia.

In other words, these growth rates mean that the population of the underdeveloped world will increase by 70 per cent during this quarter of the century while that of the developed countries will do so only by 17 per cent. *More than 90 per cent of the total population growth in the period up to the year 2000 will occur in the underdeveloped countries.*

Hence, at the end of the century, 79 per cent of the world population will live in the least developed part of the world. Four out of every five citizens of the planet will live in an underdeveloped country. The population of Africa will more than double during the last 25 years of the century, from 399 million in 1975 to 814 million in the year 2000. That of Latin America will also grow by 96 per cent, almost twice the 325 million it had in 1975. The population in some of the most populous countries of the underdeveloped world will more than double, as in Bangladesh, Pakistan, Nigeria, Mexico or Brazil.

Until recently, the year 2000 seemed an indicator of a distant future of unforeseeable events. Even today, the year 2000 is referred to at times as a remote date, a distant milestone in the path of mankind. Some do not fully realize that the year 2000, which has served as the basis for generally catastrophic forecasts for the future, is almost within reach. It is just around the corner. Two thirds of the world population in the year 2000 are already living in today's world; the infant population born each day in our countries will comprise the overwhelming majority of the adults by that time; the children who in the year 2000 will be under 15 – a population used for so many statistical figures – will be born just two years from now.

Whatever efforts are made today to protect them, to prevent their death and illnesses, to provide them with food, housing, medicine, clothing and education, will shape the basic human qualities of that decisive percentage of the future population of the planet. And yet, in view of the present trends, what sort of world will we hand over to those children? What sort of life lies ahead for those 5 billion mouths that have to be fed in the countries of our underdeveloped world, those 5 billion bodies that have to be clothed, shod and sheltered, those 5 billion minds that will strive for

173

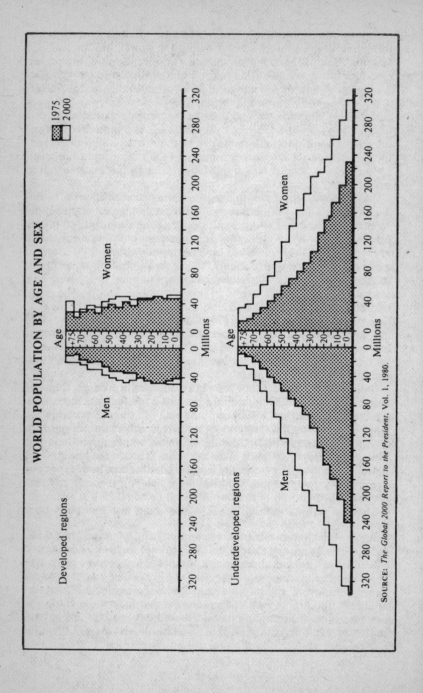

WORLD POPULATION BY AGE AND SEX

SOURCE: *The Global 2000 Report to the President*, Vol. 1, 1980.

knowledge, those 5 billion human beings who will struggle for a decent life, worthy at least of the human condition? What will their quality of life be like?

It must not be forgotten, however, that the population phenomenon, its growth and impact on the evolution of world economy – and very especially in the critical situation of the underdeveloped countries – cannot be seriously and rigorously analized if, together with the eloquent figures that have been indicated, the social and economic factors that are the basis and the main cause of that growth are not taken into account. The peoples of the underdeveloped countries are not poorer or hungrier, nor do they suffer from disease, nor are they illiterate, as a result of their high birth rates. The uncontrollable growth of the population does not respond solely to biological factors; it is, above all, precisely the product of the social, economic, and cultural conditions to which our peoples have been subjected throughout centuries of oppression and exploitation. It is evident that peoples' development in itself leads to a reduction in birth rates. One could speak about birth control, family planning, population policy on a moral, ethical and truly human basis if the first action is aimed precisely at solving the causes that give rise to the problem.

Income

Statistics on income show the notorious inequality in today's world between the richest and poorest countries. According to estimates based on World Bank data, the per caput Gross National Product of a select group of 19 developed capitalist countries amounted, in 1980, to $6 658 at 1975 constant values, while 63 of the so-called middle income countries showed an average of $903, and an additional 33 of the so-called low income countries averaged $168. Hence, according to this indicator, the gap currently separating the average inhabitant in the more developed countries from the average dweller in some of the poorest countries is reflected in a per caput Gross National Product that is 40 times higher.

A study concluded five years ago in the United States showed that in the year 2000 the world per caput Gross National Product will have increased by some 53 per cent, reaching the figure of $2 311 at 1975 constant values. In the developed countries as a whole, the average per caput Gross National Product will amount to almost $8 500, while in the underdeveloped countries it will remain under $590. This means that, as a whole, for both groups of countries, the value of per caput gross production, which in 1975 was 11 times lower for the underdeveloped world, will be 14 times lower by the year 2000, thereby increasing the inferiority gap. Our countries will be poorer as compared to the more developed nations.

While in the last 25 years of the century the developed countries will increase their per caput Gross National Product by some $4 160 at 1975 constant values – an increase of more than 96 per cent – this increase will barely reach $205 in the case of the underdeveloped countries, that is, 54 per cent. Each one-dollar increase in the per caput Gross National Product of the underdeveloped countries as a whole will mean a $20 increase in the developed nations.[2]

Concomitantly, if the differences in per caput income levels between the developed capitalist countries and the Third World have been notable in recent years, the uneven per caput income distribution within the underdeveloped countries themselves is even sharper.

Indeed, according to World Bank data relating to a sample of 23 underdeveloped countries, it can be noted how 20 per cent of the population of

---

Let us ask ourselves the following question: at their growth rates during the 70's, how long will it take the peoples of the underdeveloped countries, and particulary those of the poorest nations, to reach the *present* per capita income of the major developed capitalist coun tries?

The mathematical answer is more than significant.

TRENDS IN THE GAP
BETWEEN UNDERDEVELOPED AND DEVELOPED COUNTRIES

*Year in which the same
GDP/inhabitant level
would be attained.*

Countries	GDP/Inhabitant dollars - 1980	All underdeveloped countries	Less developed countries
United States	9 890	Year 2407	Year 6007
Federal Republic of Germany	11 096	2463	6508
France	9 289	2379	5757
Japan	9 097	2370	5677
Great Britain	5 620	2208	4233

SOURCE : Prepared on the basis of UNCTAD. *Handbook of International Trade and Development Statistics, 1981.*

In other words, *at their current growth rates, the poorest countries would need two to four thousand years – or more in some cases – to bridge the gap separating them from the present level of the most developed capitalist countries.*

the lowest income levels only receives 1.9-10.4 per cent of total income. Meanwhile, the 10 per cent with the highest income levels gets 27.5-50.2 per cent of total income. Under such circumstances, it is not surprising that in 1980, 800 million people in the underdeveloped countries received an annual per caput income of less than $150. This means that around 24 per cent of the Third World population had a daily income of $0.41 that year.

The uneven income distribution observed in most countries still subject to unjust and discriminatory social relations indicates the need for deep essential changes in their domestic, political and social structures which will guarantee the broad majorities' access to the benefits of development policies.

Hunger

Over 500 million human beings go hungry in the world today, almost all of them in our underdeveloped countries. According to FAO estimates, in 1975 chronic malnutrition affected 22 per cent of the population in Africa, 27 per cent in the Far East, 13 per cent in Latin America, and 11 per cent in the Near East. Hunger and undernourishment are permanent conditions of life for more than one fifth of the population of the underdeveloped world, some 15 per cent of the world population.

According to recent FAO data, 40 million people – half of whom are children – die every year from hunger and malnutrition. If we were to decide to keep a minute of silence for every person who died in 1982 owing to hunger-related causes we would not be able to celebrate the advent of the 21st century because we would still have to remain silent. And this reality pales when compared to the present tragedy of a world that has come to accept hunger as a day-to-day endemic phenomenon.

UNICEF estimates that over 100 million children under the age of five – 20 per cent of the world population in that age-group – suffer from protein-calorie malnutrition. At least 10 million of them suffer from serious malnutrition, not including the overwhelming majority of children affected by diseases caused by various types of deficiency.

In 1975, in 80 underdeveloped countries, over 10 per cent of the population suffered from undernourishment. In 49 of them, this figure was over 15 per cent. Twenty to 25 per cent of the children, 20 to 40 per cent of adult women and 10 per cent of the men suffered from nutritional anemia.

According to recent data from the Pan American Health Office, one million children die every year in Latin America as a result of hunger and malnutrition. Hunger is the direct cause or main factor associated with 38 per cent of deaths in children under the age of one, and 70 per cent in children from ages 1-4 in that region of the underdeveloped world, which is the least critical in terms of food.

It is estimated that currently in the developed countries, the average per caput calorie intake amounts to 3 400 daily units, while in the underdeveloped world it fluctuates from 2 000 to 2 400 and much less than 2 000 in the poorest nations. In 1979, the daily per caput calorie intake was 7 per cent under the minimum vital requirements in African countries as a whole. In the poorest countries the deficit was estimated at over 17 per cent. Indeed, this indicator – which has generally experienced a slight overall statistical improvement in recent years – has worsened by more than 5 per cent in the poorest countries as compared to 1970. In many underdeveloped nations, the ratio between calorie intake and calorie requirements deteriorated in 1963-1975.

AVERAGE CALORIE INTAKE
(1974-76 Average)

	Calories per capita	Average requirements (percentage)
World	2 535	107
Developed countries	3 315	129
Underdeveloped countries	2 180	95
Africa	2 180	93
Far East	2 025	91
Latin America	2 525	106
Near East	2 560	104

SOURCE: Based on FAO. *Agricultura. Horizonte 2000*, p. 3.

Qualitative analyses show that cereals account for 60 per cent of the calorie sources in the underdeveloped world. The situation is more serious in Africa where per caput food availability has dropped in recent years and where, as a whole, 21 per cent of the calories come from roots and tubers – over 50 per cent in some countries – with an ensuing critically low level of protein intake.

The average inhabitant of any underdeveloped country today consumes one third fewer calories than one from a developed nation does, and has a per caput protein supply equivalent to just 58 per cent of the latter's. In the underdeveloped countries, per caput animal protein intake is almost 80 per cent lower, and that of fats 3.5 times lower than in the developed countries.

In comparative terms, during the mid '70s, per caput food supplies rose 3.2 times more in the developed than in the underdeveloped countries. During the first five years of the past decade, it increased 2.9 times, thus showing that the food abyss separating the two groups of countries far from closing is growing wider.

This situation is particularly distressing because it is increasingly obvious that the problem is not production or the physical inability to ensure an adequate food supply to the growing world population. Indeed, contrary to some tendentious statements on this question, there is no inverse correlation between the growth rate in food production and the growth rate of the population. In any case, the correlation between these two elements is not mathematical but social. The conditions for production and reproduction of material life determine the form and proportion in which food is distributed, both among nations as well as among social groups in every country.

In other words, *sufficient food is produced in the world. However, there are people who go hungry and there are people who starve to death.*

It is obvious that an important part of the solution to this acute problem lies in guaranteeing sufficient food sources. Everyone agrees with that. But the solution does not depend only on the search for technical or scientific answers to increase food production and productivity, or on the incorporation of new lands to food production; rather, it is inextricably linked to the solution of the main structural problems of the economies of most underdeveloped countries and to the present international economic order, thus preventing equitable food distribution, both domestically among the various population and income groups, as well as internationally.

For instance, in Latin America – the Third World region with the best relative food situation – the United Nations Economic Commission for Latin America (ECLA) verified that during 1971-1974 the poorest 20 per cent of the population – representing only 3 per cent of the total income – consumed an energy-deficient diet ranging from 550 to 700 calories below the required level. In turn, 50 per cent of the Latin American population – representing 14 per cent of income – barely reached the minimum calorie intake. On the other hand, 5 per cent of the population – accounting for 31 per cent of the income – consumed 1 700 to 2 300 calories above average requirements.

FAO considers that just by supplying some 230 kilograms of cereals a year per person, the minimun daily calorie requirement of an average human being would be adequately met. The world produces some 1.3 billion tons of cereals per year, making it possible to supply the required 230 kilograms to more than 5 billion people, that is, a figure almost 20 per cent larger than the present world population. Various recent studies have reached the conclusion that the Earth's present cereal production capacity can be increased many times over. Taken as a whole, the total world food output currently is above the calorie and protein requirements of every inhabitant on the planet.

Consequently, the causes of the currently dramatic problem of hunger lie elsewhere. Global statistics do not reveal its true dimension since all too often they do not take into account the differentials between the various income sectors of the population of a given country or region. Hunger is a phenomenon intimately associated with poverty, with the marked income imbalances in most of our countries, with the lack of opportunities, with ignorance, inequalities and injustice.

An eloquent example of food inequality between the various regions of the world today is the fact that while tens of millions of people literally starve to death in the poorest countries every year, health statistics from the developed capitalist countries reveal the continuous growth – among the highest income population strata – in the incidence of illnesses deriving at least partially from an excessive food intake or unbalanced diets. This is a result of excess consumption of energy sources of which huge portions of the population in the underdeveloped world are deprived.

While in some developed capitalist countries there are huge food surpluses and the world frequently witnesses deliberate cutbacks in production or the absurd destruction of sizeable amounts of food in the interest of price and market competition, FAO considers that the underdeveloped countries' food reserves have reached the most critical level ever recalled.

This inequality is notably compounded by the relatively faster rise in food prices in Third World countries as compared to developed nations. While in the latter, prices rose at a 10 per cent average annual rate in 1972-1980, in the poorest nations it averaged over 16 per cent during that same period.

The FAO Director-General recently referred to this situation as a "terrible paradox":

> Though there is sufficient food for everyone, 500 million people are still suffering from hunger and disease and even die because they are too poor to buy the food that is already there. In some countries mountains of food are stockpiled, while in others hunger and poverty persist. The obese are seeking new cures and the malnourished are offered no remedies. Many pets are pampered while hungry children are forgotten. Is this not a strange phenomenon that historians and economists of future times will undoubtedly consider mysterious and inexplicable?[2]

Almost all recent projections coincide in stating that by the beginning of the new century there will be more hungry and undernourished people in the world than there are today.

FAO, for example, estimates that 10 years from now 150 million human beings will join those who are currently suffering from hunger and malnutrition. For its part, the World Bank estimates that the number of undernourished will rise from 400 to 600 million in the mid-'70s to the impressive amount of 1.3 billion in the year 2000. That is, the number of hungry people in the world will more than double. UNICEF foresees that in the year 2000 one out of every five children in the world will be malnourished. According to one such projection, hundreds of millions of human beings in the underdeveloped world will starve to death before the year 2000.

As regards food, the gap between underdeveloped and developed countries will also widen. While in 1974-1976, in the developed countries, per caput calorie intake was already 29 per cent above the minimum daily requirement, it will continue to rise sharply toward the year 2000. In other words, the average inhabitant of the developed world will have at that time well over one third more than the calorie resources required. However, the average inhabitant in the underdeveloped world as a whole will have fewer calories per capita. In 1974-1976, this calorie intake was already 5 per cent below minimum requirements for the normal development of the human being's vital faculties.

A regional projection of food data shows that, among other alarming indicators, in the final quarter of the century the estimated per caput calorie intake will in fact drop by 4 per cent in Northern Africa and the Middle East and by a disastrous 13 per cent in sub-Saharan Africa, as compared to current levels. In the latter, the prospect of an overall per caput calorie intake of 23 per cent below minimum daily requirements is envisaged by the year 2000, with even more dramatic figures in some individual countries.

Projections in per caput cereal consumption are equally somber. While in 1975 in the developed world individual annual consumption averaged 180 per cent more cereals – including those transformed into meat, milk and eggs – than in the underdeveloped countries, this difference will increase to 237 per cent in the year 2000.

Health

Squalor, disease and lack of health care are other basic aspects – together with hunger – characterizing the dramatic social situation in the underdeveloped countries. The analysis of some indicators and figures is revealing.

While in the developed countries life expectancy at birth ranges from 72 to 74 years, in the underdeveloped world this rate does not surpass 55 years. This means that the average inhabitant in a developed country may hope to live at least 17 years more than the inhabitant in an underdeveloped country. These 17 years are precisely those separating us from the 21st century. Billions of human beings who could have continued living until that date will nevertheless die before the year 2000, many of them due to the lack of adequate health care.

In some Third World regions, life expectancy is even shorter. In the countries in Central and Western Africa, for example, life expectancy fluctuates from 42 to 44 years.

This difference is not confined solely to the possibility of a longer life but is also reflected in the premature aging and relative deterioration of in-

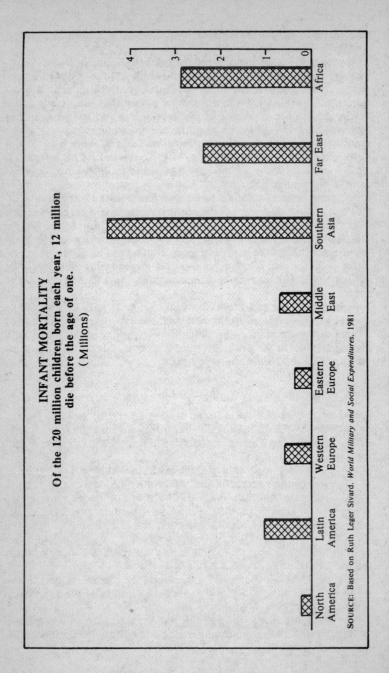

INFANT MORTALITY

Of the 120 million children born each year, 12 million die before the age of one.

(Millions)

North America | Latin America | Western Europe | Eastern Europe | Middle East | Southern Asia | Far East | Africa

SOURCE: Based on Ruth Leger Sivard. *World Military and Social Expenditures*, 1981

dividual health. While in the developed countries full maturity is attained at the age of 45, in other nations this is the most it can be hoped to live.

According to World Health Organization data, infant mortality – fluctuating from 10 to 20 deaths per 1000 live births in the developed countries as a whole in 1981 – amounted, in the group of the poorest countries, to a figure at least ten times higher. UNICEF has stated this reality graphically and dramatically: of the 122 million children born in 1980 – declared by the international community as International Year of the Child – 12 million (one out of ten) died before the end of 1981, 95 per cent of them in underdeveloped countries. UNICEF itself points out that two years later, i.e., in 1982, the number of children who died before the age of one surpassed the figure of 14.5 million.

According to WHO figures, in the poorest countries, some 200 children out of every 1000 live births die before the age of one, 100 die before the age of five and only 500 reach the age of 40. UNICEF estimated at 17 million the number of children under 5 who died during the past year.

During their first year of life, 9 out of 10 children in the poorest countries are never given the most elementary health services, much less are they vaccinated against the most common childhood diseases. Malnutrition, squalor and infectious and parasitic diseases – factors closely associated with poverty and social and economic backwardness – are the leading cause of child deaths in the underdeveloped countries.

In a report published at the beginning of 1982, the Executive Director of UNICEF summarized the overall situation of children in the underdeveloped world as follows:

> The life of a child, far from being invaluable, was worth less than $100 in 1981. If judiciously spent in favor of every single one of the 500 million poorest children of the world and their mothers, this sum would have covered basic health assistance, elementary education, care during pregnancy and dietary improvement, and would have ensured hygienic conditions and water supply for them. In short, it would have covered basic vital needs. In practice, it turned out to be too high a price for the world community. That is why, in 1981, every two seconds a child paid that price with his life. Barely 10 per cent of these children were vaccinated against the six most common and dangerous childhoood diseases. No more than $5 per child would have been needed to vaccinate all Third World children. Not doing so takes 5 million lives every year.
>
> The year 1981 has been another year of 'silent emergency': 40 thousand children have died silently every day; 100 million children have silently gone to bed hungry every night; 10 million children have silently become physically or mentally deficient; 200 million children between the ages of 6 and 11 have witnessed in silence how others attended school; in short, one fifth of the world population has struggled silently for mere survival.[3]

HEALTH AND RELATED SOCIO-ECONOMIC INDICATORS

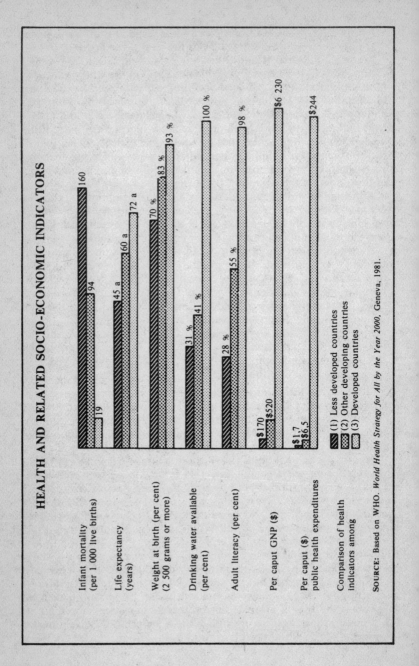

Infant mortality
(per 1 000 live births)
160
94
19

Life expectancy
(years)
45 a
60 a
72 a

Weight at birth (per cent)
(2 500 grams or more)
70 %
83 %
93 %

Drinking water available
(per cent)
31 %
41 %
100 %

Adult literacy (per cent)
28 %
55 %
98 %

Per caput GNP ($)
$170
$520
$6 230

Per caput ($)
public health expenditures
$1.7
$6.5
$244

Comparison of health
indicators among

(1) Less developed countries
(2) Other developing countries
(3) Developed countries

SOURCE: Based on WHO. *World Health Strategy for All by the Year 2000*, Geneva, 1981.

Hunger and malnutrition are directly responsible for the so-called deficiency diseases. Endemic goiter, for example, caused by iodine insufficiency, affects an estimated 200 million people.

Between 180 and 250 million human beings suffer from schistosomiasis in the underdeveloped world, particularly in 70 countries where this disease is endemic. An additional 650 million people suffer from ascariasis, and 20 million from onchocercosis or river blindness which affects up to 20 per cent of adults in some regions in Africa.

Malaria kills one million children a year in the African continent. Eight hundred and fifty million people live in areas where the fight against malaria has been only partial, and an additional 250 million in areas where nothing has been done in fighting this disease. Nevertheless, it is estimated that the world cost of malaria campaigns would amount to $2 billion per annum.

Every day, 35 thousand children under the age of five die victim to diarrheic diseases, almost all of them in the underdeveloped countries. In Latin America alone, these diseases caused some 200 thousand deaths a year.

In 1982, the discovery of the causal agent of tuberculosis reached its centennial. This disease, more than any other, is deeply associated with socio-economic factors, among which malnutrition, overcrowding, deplorable living conditions, squalor, debility from related diseases, ignorance and lack of medical care are paramount. According to WHO data, every year 3 million people die from tuberculosis, 4 to 5 million new serious cases occur, and a similar figure suffer from milder forms. These cases occur mainly among the large impoverished masses of the underdeveloped world and among the poorest, disadvantaged and exploited individuals in the more developed societies. This terrible disease nevertheless, could be prevented for a few pennies' worth; and, when it does occur, it can be cured. One hundred years after Robert Koch's brilliant discovery, tuberculosis continues to be a terrible scourge for mankind.

The balance of these and many other statistical illustrations that could be mentioned leads to a distressing conclusion: diseases defeated by science, which could be prevented and eradicated through adequate measures and at times minimal resources, are still the leading cause of death today in the underdeveloped world. UNICEF estimates that 90 per cent of the lives of small children who die in underdeveloped countries could be saved through the implementation of adequate programs of vaccination, nutrition, perinatal care, drinking water supply, environmental improvement, and nutrition and health education for mothers.

Maternal malnutrition and health problems result in the birth of 21 million underweight babies in the underdeveloped countries. According to a WHO study, 43 to 47 per cent of all perinatal deaths in 7 countries occur in cases of underweight babies.

Twenty-five million women experience serious complications during pregnancy and delivery every year. Maternal mortality rates are 20 to 100 times higher in the underdeveloped than in the developed countries. In absolute figures, UNICEF estimates that 500 000 women die in Africa and Asia every year due to pregnancy and delivery–related causes, two thirds of them victims of malnutrition and anemia.

One hundred and twenty million children in the underdeveloped countries suffer from some kind of physical or mental handicap, over 100 million of them lacking all the means or services for rehabilitation. In 1978, ten per cent of the population in Africa – over 40 million people – suffered from various forms of disability.

Polio, a disease eradicated in the most developed countries, continues to take a toll of tens of thousands of victims every year among children in the underdeveloped countries, where still no vaccination programs are being launched. Vaccines, worth only a few pennies, could prevent the occurrence of new cases, thus saving thousands of people every year from joining the huge mass of the handicapped.

According to data published by WHO, every year there are 250 000 new cases of blind children in the world, one hundred thousand of them due to lack of vitamin A. The latter could be prevented by simply adding a handful of vegetables to their daily diet, or merely by administering, every six months, a vitamin A pill costing a few pennies.

The struggle against contagious ophthalmopathologies could save 7 million people from blindness in the Middle East during the coming two or three decades. WHO recognizes that the most important factor in preventing blindness is the improvement of living conditions, diet, drinking water supply and environmental conditions. Without adequate measures, by the year 2000 in the world there will be twice the number of blind people existing today.

UNICEF states that most of the ailments of handicapped children in underdeveloped countries could have been prevented through sufficient nutrition, adequate obstetric practices and better programs against infectious perinatal diseases. Moreover, with early diagnosis and appropriate treatment, many of these aliments would not have led to disability. In 9 out of 10 cases, these ailments could have been prevented or kept from becoming permanently incapacitating.

In this regard, WHO has confirmed the decisive effect of poverty – with its offshoots of malnutrition, infectious diseases and other environmental problems – on ailments leading to mental disability and handicap. According to WHO publications, 25 to 30 per cent of the children living in poor neighborhoods in the big cities of underdeveloped countries who go to a general health–care center suffer from some kind of mental deficiency. This ratio ranges from 15 to 18 per cent in rural areas.

However, in the light of these figures, what are health care realities like in the underdeveloped world now? In the developed world, there is 1 doctor for every 520 inhabitants. In the underdeveloped countries, this rate fluctuates from 1 for every 2 700 in countries with the highest relative development, to 1 for every 17 000 in the poorest nations. In some rural areas of the latter, there is only 1 doctor for every 200 000 inhabitants.

As a whole, the same amount of people in a developed country has 6 times more doctors, 5 times more pharmacists, and 12 times more nurses than in an underdeveloped country. In the latter, 1.5 billion – over two thirds of mankind – lack all possible access to medical care, among them 400 million children under the age of six.

A total of 120 000 doctors from the underdeveloped countries are working in five developed countries alone – the United States, England, Canada, Federal Republic of Germany and Australia. Meanwhile, the population in the underdeveloped countries has an overall average of 10 to 14 hospital beds for every 10 000 inhabitants, as compared to 95 in the developed world.

The comparative figures for per caput public health expenditures are equally illustrative. According to 1980 estimates, developed countries spent – statistically speaking – a per capita of $244 from their annual budget on health care, while per caput public expenditures in the poorest nations was $1.7 a year, i.e., 144 times less. In percentages of GNP, figures are 3.9 per cent for developed countries as compared to 1 per cent for the poorest nations.

The health situation in the underdeveloped world is revealed to be all the more serious when factors such as the true quality of, and access to, medical services or the mere possibility of purchasing medicines – in the case of the largest segment of the population who lack sufficient income to afford the cost of these services – are included in the analysis.

According to the data published in the WHO official magazine, in 1978 the world market for pharmaceuticals amounted to $70 billion. Eighty-five per cent is located in the industrialized world and 65 per cent in OECD countries. The share of the underdeveloped world – three quarters of the world population – accounts for only 15 per cent. Eighty–eight per cent of the production of pharmaceuticals takes place in industrialized countries, and only 12 per cent in underdeveloped nations. In this item alone, the trade deficit that year amounted to $2 billion. Whereas in the underdeveloped world per caput expenditure on drugs is less than $1, in the developed countries it is more than $70 per capita.

The population's access to drugs and biological products is essential to health. The bleak reality is that this fundamental item, far from becoming more accesible, has been turned into a source of exploitation and economic plunder of Third World countries.

In general terms, given the present technological and scientific development, the transnational pharmaceutical industry of the market–economy developed countries obtained gigantic profits through the marketing of products with very low production costs. This accounts for the fact that manyof these products cannot be purchased by those who need them and have furthermore become an important foreign exchange drain for underdeveloped nations. WHO issued a list of some 200 drugs deemed essential for countries of the underdeveloped world. They were products that would adequately meet the basic requirements of these countries, thus enabling them to avoid huge occasional expenditures on unnecessary drugs. Many of these drugs and vaccines, moreover, could be produced in the Third World countries at a very low cost.

Some health projections indicate that – in line with present trends – by the year 2000 infant mortality rates in developed countries will reach 10 for every 1000 live births, whereas in the underdeveloped world, with great difficulty, it will remain at 50; that is, it will continue to be at least 5 times higher. As regards life expectancy at birth, more optimistic forecasts put it at approximately 65 years in the underdeveloped countries as a whole and from 75 to 80 in the developed world. Nevertheless, even in that case, the poorest one third of mankind cannot expect to live over 50. These basic indicators show that if these conditions and tendencies continue, there would be relatively little change in the health situation at the beginning of the 21st century.

As long as health fails to be considered as a fundamental right of man and a duty of the community; as long as the responsibility of the State and of society in regards to health-care fails to be recognized; as long as inequalities in the distribution of health resources, both internationally and domestically, fail to disappear; as long as poverty, hunger, ignorance and squalor fail to be directly fought against, little will be achieved in improving human health in the underdeveloped world.

Education

Underdevelopment is, among other things, lack of learning and lack of the possibility to learn. It is not only how many cannot read or write. It is also how many cannot learn to read or write, or pass on to higher levels of education, due to the lack of teachers, schools and the minimum conditions beyond those most elementary for subsistence. That is why the dramatic educational and cultural problems of the underdeveloped world cannot be isolated from its overall socio–economic situation.

UNESCO estimates that in 1980 there were 814 million illiterate adults in the world, most of them in the underdeveloped countries. In this respect, the progress attained by mankind in the 20 years that have elapsed since the early 1960's – a period of sudden upsurge in science and knowledge – brought with it an increase of 100 million people who cannot read or write. Should these trends continue, by the turn of the 21st century, the world will have nearly one billion illiterates, that is, over 15 per cent of the estimated world population by that time.

According to UNESCO data, 48 per cent of the adult population in the underdeveloped countries is illiterate. Ten underdeveloped countries alone account for 425 million illiterates. In 23 of the poorest countries, over 70 per cent of their adult population cannot read or write.

A characteristic of illiteracy is that it is greater in rural than in urban areas, and among women than among men. The World Health Organization estimates that women account for 66 per cent of the illiterate population.

It is not by chance, however, that the geographic and social distribution of illiteracy is almost the same as that of poverty. Illiterates are, as a rule, also the poorest, the most poorly fed, the least healthy, the most disadvantaged and exploited. The illiteracy figures reveal the frustrated development of human capacites and potential; the limitations on the individual as a human being and as part of a community; exploitation and ignorance as to a better future; the dramatic social effects of underdevelopment; loss of national identity; social and economic backwardness.

According to UNESCO and UNICEF data, over 200 million children in the underdeveloped world lack schools or the means and possibilities to attend school. Less than half the children born every year will have the possibility of learning to read and write. Less than 4 out of every 10 children attending school in the underdeveloped countries as a whole finish elementary education. About 15 to 20 per cent of primary school pupils are repeaters, and drop-out levels are extremely high.

The rationale behind these data and the cause of these indices is the situation of poverty that forces them to drop out of school, the distances that have to be covered to get to school and the deplorable material conditions of many of the schools. It should be borne in mind that no less than 14 per cent of the children between 10 and 14 years of age in the underdeveloped countries have no other alternative in their lives than to join the active labor force to help support themselves and their families. One out of every 4 children in the underdeveloped world enters economically active life without an education.

In the data of the World Bank's *Report on World Development in 1980*, it is noted that – in spite of the huge demographic differences – for every secondary-level student in an underdeveloped country, there are almost 4 in the developed capitalist countries. In the underdeveloped world, only 4 per cent of the population between 20 and 24 years of age is enrolled in university education, while in the developed countries it is 36 per cent. To add to an already gloomy situation, there is the number of university graduates that are lost every year in the underdeveloped countries due to the brain drain of the major capitalist powers.

With a population three times that of the developed countries, the underdeveloped world had 732 000 teachers less in 1977. Another factor to be borne in mind is the insufficient training of teaching staff and the lack of ways and means to remedy this insufficiency in many underdeveloped countries, which has its effect on the limited and poor quality teaching provided.

In the developed countries, in 1978, there were 22 scientists and engineers for every ten thousand inhabitants. In the underdeveloped countries as a whole, this same ratio was barely 1.2. UNESCO estimates that during that same year developed countries accounted for 95.6 per cent of all expenditures in scientific research.

According to UNESCO estimates, in 1977 the world invested in education an average of $126 per inhabitant. But, while in the developed countries the indicator was $314 per inhabitant, in the underdeveloped countries it was less than $24, i.e.,13 times less resources per capita for education.

It is imperative to stress another aspect that hampers efforts in the pursuit of education and cultural development in our countries. Imperialist mass media are continuously, sometimes subtly and sometimes openly, carrying out a process of ideological and cultural penetration aimed at eroding our national identities, creating habits and patterns of conduct foreign to the needs and possibilities of the peoples of the Third World, belittling and deforming our people's cultures in their own eyes. This, of course, has no bearing on the flow of ideas or on the legitimate exchange of the products of their cultures among peoples. These very mass media are working to create a consumerist image devoid of all rationality and are trying to impose mesmerizing illusions on our peoples as absolute truths. An enormous percentage of the television programs broadcast today in the Third World come from developed capitalist countries. The transnational press agencies manipulate the news coming out of our countries and present it to their own convenience; or they transmit foreign news to our countries from an intentionally slanted view point. Thus, they use the press and radio to flood the underdeveloped countries with a product designed to distort reality. This endeavor to dominate our minds was clearly exposed and denounced in a forum of the Ministers of Culture of the Latin American countries recently convened by UNESCO.

Employment

While poverty is the very basis of the present social situation in the underdeveloped world and is directly related to the serious problem of low income for large segments of our countries' population, it is in turn closely linked to the employment situation there.

The phenomenon of unemployment and underemployment is another facet of the present social situation of the underdeveloped countries. It cannot be seen as a mere quantitative issue, i.e., as a simple non-use or inability of these economies to use the entire labor force, but as a qualitative result of the irrational and unjust nature of the existing system of economic relations. From it stems the paradox that productive human capacity is not fully used in a world where there is so much poverty and where the most basic needs of millions of human beings are not being met.

In the early 1980's, the world's economically active population was estimated at approximately 1.8 billion, of which some 1.2 billion – 67 per cent – lived in the underdeveloped countries. In comparison with the demographic growth rate, the economically active population in the underdeveloped countries increases by 1.7 per cent, whereas in the developed countries it increases by only 1.1 per cent.

The huge economic, scientific and technological gap between underdeveloped and developed countries is evidenced in the different structures of the economically active population. In 1980, according to World Bank data, in the underdeveloped countries, 71 per cent was employed in agriculture, 14 per cent in industry, and 15 per cent in services, while the figures for developed countries were 6, 38 and 56 per cent respectively. The obvious malformation of the occupational structure in the underdeveloped countries is one of the elements which are at the root of the serious unemployment and underemployment situation in these countries.

According to the most recent ILO estimates, the total amount of unemployed and underemployed in the underdeveloped world is already over 500 million, accounting for approximately 50 per cent of the region's economically active population. According to available data from a sample of underdeveloped countries, their average unemployment rate has been over 10 per cent since the early 1970's. In addition, the overall socio-economic situation in the underdeveloped countries produces huge masses of underemployed, which constitute a substantial waste of the labor force in these countries.

The phenomenon of unemployment and underemployment in the underdeveloped countries is aggravated by the growing migration of large rural masses to urban areas, due to extremely poor living conditions and to the lack of employment in rural areas. This they paradoxically attempt to solve by crowding into the slums where living conditions are not so different, thus also swelling the vast army of urban unemployed. The global analysis of the unemployment and underemployment figures in the underdeveloped countries masks the different evolution of these phenomena in the two main sections of the population in each country. Overt unemployment is higher in urban areas. On the other hand, productive activities in rural areas tend more to produce covert unemployment, or underemployment.

The low income of the Third World countries' population and the high percentage of households depending on only one income are one of the main reasons why child labor is higher in the underdeveloped world than elsewhere. According to ILO data, of the 52 million children under 15 that were part of the labor force in 1979, almost 51 million, that is 98 per cent, lived in the underdeveloped countries. Needless to say, very often it is these children who have the menial and lowest paid jobs. A consequence of the serious economic situation of the capitalist countries has been that employers tend to replace male labor by child and female labor as a way to increase profits.

As to working conditions, the duration of the working week may be an illustrative indicator. In developed countries, it goes from 35 to 40 hours, while in underdeveloped countries it ranges between 45 and 56, averaging approximately 47, 48 and 44 hours in Africa, Asia and Latin America, respectively. Thus, the working week is at present between 28 and 40 per cent higher in the underdeveloped countries than in the developed countries.

In the market-economy developed countries themselves, unemployment has presently reached the highest figures of the post-war. In OECD countries it already amounts to over 32 million, 10 per cent of the total labor force. Many of them – the most exploited and disadvantaged of the system, lacking jobs and inmediate prospects – constitute the core of the explosive and critical situation about which their governments are so concerned. However, in the underdeveloped world hundreds of millions of workers are permanently jobless and many are temporarily employed in secondary and poorly remunerated activities. They lack subsidies and ways to cope with their situation, the root causes of which are precisely the conditions of backwardness and dependence the underdeveloped countries have been subjected to. It is necessary to struggle to find solutions for the 32 million unemployed in developed countries, but it is also essential, morally indispensable and economically decisive to find solutions for the huge unemployed masses of the underdeveloped countries.

The relationship between unemployment, underemployment and poverty has become ever-clearer. In the face of a more or less chronic world-wide recession, affecting the level of unemployment and underemployment, workers tend to accept lower wages, very often below the legally-established limits. This also has a direct impact on the increase of the number of people living in conditions of extreme poverty.

Forecasts as to likely trends in the employment situation in underdeveloped countries often coincide on its gradual worsening. Thus, for example, according to the ILO, in 1987 the economically active population will be 2 045 million, some 250 million additional workers, 85 per cent of whom will be in the underdeveloped countries. In order to absorb the demographic growth and eliminate unemployment, jobs would have to be annually increased by 3.9 per cent in the underdeveloped countries. ILO estimates that from 1980 to 2000 it would be necessary to create 880 million jobs in the underdeveloped countries.

We could not conclude this section without making a number of references to women, both as regards employment and general living conditions which are specially cruel and unequal in the underdeveloped countries.

In general, women suffer incredible exploitation and discrimination, but this becomes more acute in the Third World where they are forced to bear the brunt of poverty in the economic sphere as well as in the spheres of health and culture. One can get an idea of the extremely serious economic situation facing women in underdeveloped countries, from ILO data, which show that although women make up 35 per cent of the world labor force, they receive only one tenth of world income.

But in the developed countries there is a much greater percentage of women who have access to work. In the underdeveloped world, in countries where male unemployment and underemployment sometimes extends to more than 50 per cent of the labor force, women –including those who have some sort of skill – face insurmountable obstacles. They get the most menial and lowest paid jobs.

As a sector of Third World society, women suffer doubly all the calamities related to the living conditions that exist in our area. Because they are the ones that bear the heavy burden of the home, they are the worst hit by the lack of hospitals, medical care, schools, children's institutions, child-mother programs, hygiene, and so on. An extremely high number of women receive no attention during pregnancy. A much higher percentage than in the developed countries die during delivery without any type of care; and it is women who, in the poorest countries, must see half their children die before they are 15 years old.

Housing and other material conditions

Over one billion people – one fourth of mankind – today live in conditions of extreme poverty, with all its overcrowding, insecurity and unsanitary conditions. Around 300 million children, approximately 20 per cent of the world's infant population, are in this situation.

Although the housing problem in underdeveloped countries is directly related to demographic growth, an analysis centered only on this factor would be a partial and consequently superficial approach to the problem. It is self-evident that this problem is also closely linked to the so-called phenomenon of "explosive urbanization" in the underdeveloped world, among others.

For the first time in history, urban population growth in the underdeveloped countries is, in absolute terms, higher than that of the rural population. In 1950, there were 25 cities in these countries with over one million inhabitants and a total population of 50 million. By 1985, there will be 147 cities in the underdeveloped world with over one million inhabitants, and a population of 465 million. It has been predicted that by the year 2000, 12 of the 15 most populous cities will be in underdeveloped countries. Rural exodus will, in some cases, account for 90 per cent of the estimated urban population growth.

In the last 20 years of the century, the urban infant population in the underdeveloped world will almost double, to reach 666 million by the late 1990's. Ten cities at least in the underdeveloped countries will have over

10 million inhabitants, among them Mexico with over 30 million, and Calcutta and Bombay with almost 20 million each. By the year 2000, approximately 40 per cent of the population of the underdeveloped world will be urban.

This projected urbanization means that the underdeveloped countries will demand an increase of almost 70 per cent in their urban services to be able to keep the 1975 per caput services level, which is known to be highly insufficient in most cases.

To cope with demographic growth alone, it would be necessary to build almost 750 million new houses in the underdeveloped countries before the end of the century. UNESCO has estimated that an annual housing construction rate of 8-10 per 1 000 inhabitants would be globally required. At present, in most underdeveloped countries, the rate is 2-4 per 1 000 inhabitants, and in many countries it is under 1.

Apart from the effective proportional decrease of the rural population and potentially, agricultural production, this phenomenon of accelerated urbanization in the underdeveloped world entails other significant social problems. Firstly, the unrestrained growth of such urban concentrations produces significant sources of environmental pollution, which add to other factors that in today's world contribute to degradate the environment.

But perhaps even more serious is that a significant per cent of this urban population increase is based on the proliferation of slums, with the consequent worsening of problems resulting from the very poor and unhealthy conditions characterizing such human settlements. Overcrowding, promiscuity, lack of running water and sanitary facilities, increased violence, prostitution, drug addiction, crime and other signs of anti-social behavior, are some of the social consequences generated in most underdeveloped countries by this type of urban growth. Given its known social and economic roots, such growth, is not and cannot by any means be planned in order to ensure minimal elementary conditions of urban development.

Even now, in many large cities of the underdeveloped countries, between one fourth and two thirds of the population live in slums. The trend, unfortunately, is to an increasing proliferation of these deplorable human settlements. Most of the population in these monstruous urban conglomerates that are expected to grow even more over the next two decades, will live under the same or perhaps even worse conditions.

Another problem greatly affecting the living conditions of broad masses of the population in the underdeveloped world is the access and availability of proper water sources.

Although water covers three quarters of the planet's surface, only 0.8 per cent of the world's sources is fit for human or animal consumption. Of that minimal porcentage, only part is available or accessible, and an even smaller part is not yet polluted by human or natural forces.

It is estimated that water requirements for human consumption, agriculture and industry by the year 2000 will triple. In addition, in many areas of the world – mainly the underdeveloped world – water supply is already a problem. According to some projections, the world per caput water supply will decrease by 35 per cent as a result of demographic growth alone. The problem also relates to the increasing destruction or pollution of water sources and coastal ecosystems due to accelerated urbanization, uncontrolled industrialization and the use of pesticides and other polluting chemicals in agriculture.

At present, according to WHO estimates, about 2 billion human beings lack permanent and adequate water supply sources. WHO also estimates that in 1976, 78 per cent of the world's rural population, mostly in underdeveloped countries, lacked appropriate water supply facilities. The UN estimates that four out of every five children living in rural areas of the underdeveloped world lack suitable drinking water and sanitary conditions.

The main causes of the underdeveloped countries' morbidity and mortality rates are water-related diseases: enteric fevers, dysentery, typhoid fever, cholera, amoeba infections, schistosomiasis, and many others. WHO estimates that some 750 thousand people die each month from diseases caused by polluted water. Over 1.5 billion inhabitants of the underdeveloped world are exposed to these diseases, and hundreds of millions of new cases are registered every year.

A survey conducted under the auspices of WHO shows that a mother in East Africa consumes 12-27 per cent of her energy every day carrying water to be used at home by her family. In some African cities, a worker may spend 10 per cent of salary to purchase water.

In a world witnessing spectacular advances in science and technology, devoting colossal resources to the creation of means capable of destroying mankind, the permanence of conditions forcing tens of millions of women and children in underdeveloped countries to spend a considerable part of their time and energy merely to find and fetch this vital liquid sometimees from several kilometers away, is something shameful. With an annual $6 billion contribution on the part of the international community – less than the amount mankind devotes to military expenditures in five days, a very small share of yearly expenditures in alcoholic beverages – the objectives of the UN Water Decade would be totally fulfilled.

One thing should not be overlooked in this analysis and it is the fact that almost two billion inhabitants of the underdeveloped world depend on wood for cooking and heating. FAO estimates that the annual consumption of wood for these purposes is over 1.4 billion cubic meters and that it could rise in the year 2000 much above that figure. In fact, firewood for cooking and heating accounts for almost 90 per cent of wood consumption in the underdeveloped countries. In the poorest countries, 9 out of every 10 people depend on firewood for these vital needs.

The traditional sources of energy – firewood, manure and plant wastes – meet 50-75 per cent of the total energy needs of the underdeveloped countries, according to World Bank data. In Africa it is 90 per cent. Firewood is the most widely used. In Tanzania firewood accounts for 59 per cent of the energy spent, manure 38 per cent, plant wastes 2.5 per cent and other sources 0.5 per cent. Firewood represents 70 per cent of total consumption of energy in Africa, 34 per cent in Latin America and 30 per cent in Asia.

According to the World Bank, firewood consumption in the underdeveloped countries leads to the deforestation of 10-15 million hectares per year. Due to the destruction of forests, the obtention of firewood is already a critical problem in many regions of the underdeveloped world. FAO itself estimates that over one billion people live in areas where there is a serious firewood shortage. And current trends indicate that by the turn of the century the shortage of firewood will likely affect over two billion people, that is, about one third of mankind, for whom such a vital resource will be physically and economically further out of their reach.

THE UNDERDEVELOPED WORLD	
Hungry	+ 500 million
Life expectancy under 60	1.7 billion
Lacking medical care	1.5 billion
Living in extreme poverty	+ 1 billion
Unemployed and underemployed in the underdeveloped world	+ 500 million
Annual per capita income under $150	800 million
Illiterate adults	814 million
Children lacking schools or unable to attend	+ 200 million
Lacking permanent and adequate water sources	2 billion
Depending on firewood for their vital needs	+ 1.5 billion

The indicators examined do not fully reveal the scope of the social problems being faced by the underdeveloped world, almost at the turn of the century. No matter how illustrative figures may be, they could never show the tragic realities of life for the broad masses of the population in the underdeveloped countries.

Underdevelopment is a singularly global economic and social phenomenon. It is first and foremost, a political fact. While isolated for individual analysis, all its manifestations are integrated into a single whole. They are complementary, interrelated elements that are both active and essential in conditioning the overall phenomenon. Exploitation and dependence, poverty and hunger, insecurity and unemployment, lack of sanitation and ignorance, are in a way forms or approaches to the single reality of underdevelopment, the basis of which is but an unjust international economic order and blatant inequality in the distribution of wealth, both among nations and within nations.

A comprehensive approach is required to fight this situation and to struggle for diminishing or eradicating such inequalities. It is not, as some say, a matter of lowering fertility and birth rates separately to check or control demographic growth. Nor is it a matter of implementing effective policies for the preservation of resources and environmental conservation. The solutions are not solely or even mainly physical, but social. It is a question of improving the quality of life, not only fighting the serious shortages in every sphere, but acting on them where the development of our societies is concerned, which is not necessarily economic growth.

The trends which serve as the basis for the somber immediate outlook for the world – and for the underdeveloped countries in particular – are the most obvious expressions of the unbearable situation of injustice and inequality still prevailing today. But they are not necessarily inexorable. Mankind can, if it really wants, act to change that increasingly unjust future for one that is bright and equitable.

11

Arms build-up and development

Faced with the most severe economic crisis in the last 50 years, today's world is confronted by the most absurd arms race in all of its history, an arms race which, because of its scope, destructive power, and technological sophistication, poses the greatest danger ever known to mankind, and provides the clearest proof of the irrationality and squandering that characterize the present crisis in international relations.

As part of its policy of coercion, threats, destabilization and aggression – with the ensuing increase of international tension and the climate of cold war – the United States Government has launched the greatest peace-time arms build-up program in its history. This program, aimed above all at disrupting the strategic military balance reached during the '70s between the NATO countries and the socialist camp, is indeed the decisive factor in the gigantic upsurge of military expenditures and the arms race. The aggressive and interventionist course of President Reagan's Administration, backed by the enormous combined offensive potential of the United States armed forces and its NATO allies, is the gravest conceivable threat to peace and security of all the peoples of the world.

In strategic nuclear strike forces alone, the United States has currently more than 2000 nuclear arms delivery vehicles capable of carrying 10 000 highly destructive charges. And yet, at the end of the '70s the United States launched a comprehensive program for increased military strike capability and, particularly, strategic nuclear potential; to this end, among other actions, it is developing the Cruise missile and the MX ICBM, with ten 600-kiloton independently targetable nuclear warheads, and the B-1 strategic bombers; it is building Trident nuclear submarines carrying 24 nuclear warheads each; re-equipping 300 Minuteman-III ICBM's with highly accurate targetable 350-kiloton warheads; producing the neutron bomb; deploying 572 new medium-range nuclear delivery vehicles in Europe; organizing quickly the so-called rapid deployment forces, a globe-spanning tool for intervention; increasing and diversifying its chemical and biological weapons arsenal, aimed at volatilizing, paralyzing, sterilizing or animalizing the human being.

From the economic viewpoint, this wild arms race meant a 3.7 per cent increase, in real terms, in US military expenditures in 1980 as compared with 1979, and a 6 per cent increase in 1981. According to the Reagan plan, military expenditures will increase at an annual rate of 8 per cent between 1983 and 1987, reaching $356 billion by 1987, close to 36 per cent of total US spending for that year. The $258 billion already earmarked for military expenditures in 1983 would just be the beginning of a vast buildup which would total $1.6 trillion by 1987. According to this project, between 1977 and 1987, there would be an unprecedented 272 per cent increase in US military expenditures.

It is this policy of building up an impressive military force to try to solve the complex problems of today's world through the indiscriminate use or threat of use of force that has committed mankind to an arms build-up spiral seriously endangering peace and man's own survival.

The growing pressure brought to bear by the United States on its own allies in this direction, the ensuing increase in military expenditures and the unavoidable and proportional reaction to this policy by the socialist countries are the reasons why in today's world – in the midst of one of its greatest economic crises and at a time when billions of people can scarcely count on minimal resources for basic subsistence – gigantic sums are being earmarked for military expenditures.

WORLD MILITARY EXPENDITURES
(Millions of dollars at 1979 constant prices)

1972	416 304	1977	464 127
1973	421 045	1978	478 007
1974	435 629	1979	492 927
1975	448 421	1980	502 542
1976	456 045	1981	518 727

SOURCE : Based on SIPRI *Yearbook, 1982*, p. 140.

Estimates put world military expenditures in 1982 at a figure close to $650 billion. More than $1.7 billion a day, $74 million an hour, more than $1 million a minute!

The direct cost of the arms race has surpassed the fabulous figure of $6 trillion since World War II, which in practice equals the world's total Gross National Product in 1975. According to UN data, world military expenditures in 1980 equalled the aggregate Gross Domestic Product of Africa and Latin America for that same year and 6 per cent of the overall value of world production of goods and services.

Mankind already has the means to annihilate itself several times over. Just the blast power of the 50 000 bombs, warheads and nuclear charges deployed or stockpiled in the world amounts to 16 billion tons of TNT, more than a million times the destructive power of the bomb dropped on Hiroshima. And yet, *every day it becomes increasingly obvious that, far from guaranteeing greater security, the arms race implies greater and more immediate risks.*

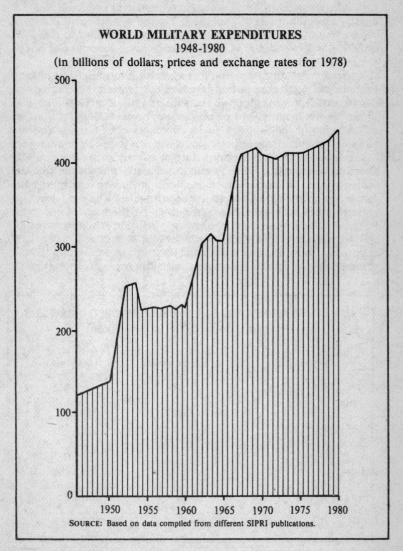

WORLD MILITARY EXPENDITURES
1948-1980
(in billions of dollars; prices and exchange rates for 1978)

SOURCE: Based on data compiled from different SIPRI publications.

Furthermore, the increase in military means of destruction, spurred on by the present US Administration, comes about in the midst of the profound crisis affecting the world capitalist economy and ignores the negative consequences traditionally stemming from military expenditures. Indeed, historically, economic militarization has not only had political impact on capitalist society but also, as greater resources have been spent for military purposes, it has had increasingly pernicious economic effects.

As a result of the momentum the war industry provided to economic activity during World War II, military expenditures began to play a relatively important role in the process of capitalist reproduction.

It soon became clear, however, that whatever favorable effects military expenditures might have had on economic development were simply circumstancial. The most objective and wide-ranging scientific studies confirmed the fact that the short-range economic benefits stemming from the militarization of the economy under conditions of idle resources were probably annulled by the negative long-range effects on economic growth.

This revealed the inflationary nature of military expenditures which stimulate purchasing power and effective demand without the countervailing increase in consumable production or productive capacity to meet future consumption requirements – a negative effect which is further aggravated since such expenditures are made on the basis of enormous budget deficits. It also exposed the inverse correlation existing between increased military expenditures, which deviates human and material resources, and growth in investments and labor productivity. It also showed that military expenditure, as compared to civilian expenditures, was much

MILITARY EXPENDITURES IN UNDERDEVELOPED COUNTRIES
(Millions of dollars at 1979 constant prices)

	Expenditures	Percentage of world total expenditures
1972	32 980	7.9
1973	37 296	8.8
1974	48 074	11.0
1975	56 034	12.4
1976	63 946	14.0
1977	63 630	13.7
1978	66 085	13.8
1979	67 838	13.7
1980	71 316	14.1
1981	81 281	15.6

SOURCE: Based on SIPRI. *Yearbook 1982*, p. 140.

less capable of generating jobs and thereby mitigating one of the most acute aspects of the crisis. Estimates have shown that just the increase in military expenditures proposed by the present US Administration, over the amount budgeted by the previous Administration, will keep 900 000 people unemployed.

In the distressing general context of the world arms race, *the increase in military expenditures in the underdeveloped world is particularly alarming, especially in view of the extremely serious economic and social problems facing these countries today.*

Calculated at 1979 constant prices, military expenditures in Third World countries amounted to $33 billion in 1972. Ten years later, in 1981, they had already reached the figure of $81.281 million, that is, two and a

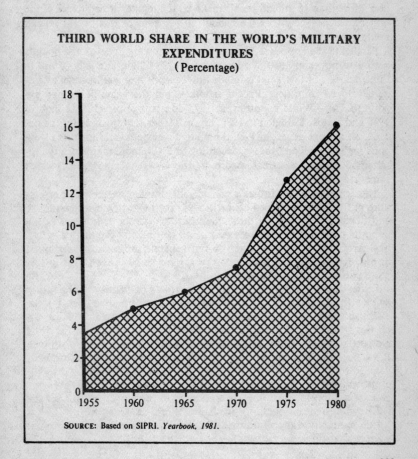

THIRD WORLD SHARE IN THE WORLD'S MILITARY EXPENDITURES
(Percentage)

SOURCE: Based on SIPRI. *Yearbook, 1981.*

half times more. Their share in total military expenditures has doubled in the last ten years and now accounts for about 16 per cent of the world total.[1]

The international climate of tension and violence generated by the aggressive policies of the imperialist powers and their regional gendarmes, the aggressions and direct or indirect pressures aimed at destabilizing or destroying revolutionary processes and defending neo-colonial interests, the regional conflicts often encouraged by those very interests: these are the major factors that have contributed to Third World involvement in the arms race.

Over 30 countries of the underdeveloped world today produce weapons. In 1979, military industrial output in these countries amounted to $5 billion. More than 15 million people make up the regular armed forces of the underdeveloped countries, i.e., about 60 per cent of total world regular military personnel.[2]

Parallel to the arms race, the *arms trade* is growing by leaps and bounds with a turnover in 1980 of approximately $26 billion annually. Close to three quarters of this total is imports of weapons and war materiel by underdeveloped countries.[3] Recent estimates put the value of weapon exports to Third World countries, at 1975 constant prices, at $3 billion in 1970 and almost $9 billion in 1980, i.e., a 200 per cent increase for the decade. At current prices, in 1980 the underdeveloped world imported weapons for $19.5 billion,[4] that is, according to FAO, more than twice the total amount spent on cereal imports by the lowest-income countries that same year.

The arms trade constitutes a considerable burden on the weak economies of the underdeveloped countries. It is the most sterile, unproductive and unequal exchange for those countries. The arms trade deprives the importing country of resources that could be used for productive activities. Arms imports expenditures do not generate increased consumption or production, or future production to pay for its costs, nor do they promote public health, education or culture.

Under such conditions, the economic effects of military expenditures are for the underdeveloped countries even more negative than for the more advanced countries as a whole. According to recent studies, increases in military expenditures, expressed as a percentage of the Gross Domestic Product, are inversely correlated with the economic growth rate. It has been established that for each dollar spent on arms in the underdeveloped countries, domestic investment is reduced by 25 cents. Arms imports worsen the balance of payments deficits of the underdeveloped countries. In 1978, arms imports accounted for almost 50 per cent of the deficit in current accounts for the Third World as a whole.

Can humanity really afford the luxury of the colossal squandering of resources that the arms race implies?

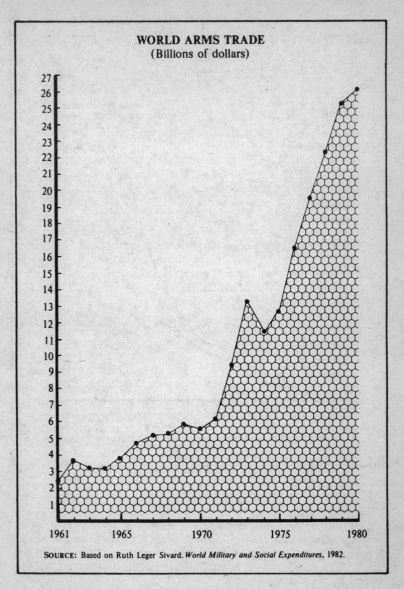

WORLD ARMS TRADE
(Billions of dollars)

SOURCE: Based on Ruth Leger Sivard. *World Military and Social Expenditures*, 1982.

In 1980, 100 million people were directly or indirectly involved in military activities of no effective economic use to society. This figure is at present three times the total number of teachers and doctors throughout

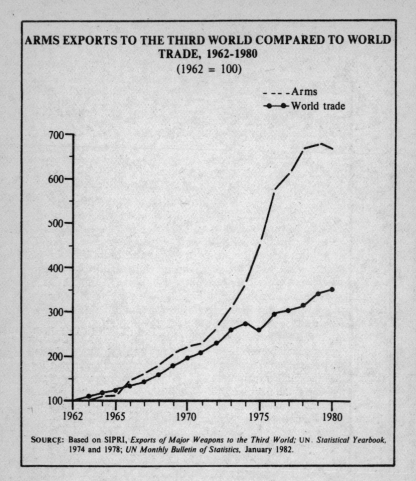

ARMS EXPORTS TO THE THIRD WORLD COMPARED TO WORLD TRADE, 1962-1980

(1962 = 100)

- - - - Arms
—●— World trade

SOURCE: Based on SIPRI, *Exports of Major Weapons to the Third World;* UN. *Statistical Yearbook,* 1974 and 1978; *UN Monthly Bulletin of Statistics,* January 1982.

the world. In the late '70s, half a million scientists and engineers were de-∙ voting their creative potential to military and weapons development research, with a total world investment of more than $50 billion per year.

The amount used in military expenditures in a single day could finance the annual cost of a program for the total eradication of malaria. Five hours of the world's military expenditures equals the total yearly UNICEF budget for child-care programs.

Throughout the world, military activities consume an enormous amount and variety of non-renewable resources and raw materials reserves. The US military demand alone for metals such as aluminun, copper, lead and zinc fluctuates between 11 per cent and 14 per cent of total world demand. World military consumption of liquid hydrocarbons is more than double the annual consumption of Africa.

Training costs of US military personnel amounts to twice the education budget of 300 million school-age children in southern Asia. Public health expenditures throughout the world amount to only 60 per cent of military expenditures.

The cost of a modern bomber prototype equals the salaries of 250 000 teachers for one year, or the construction and equipment cost of 75 hospitals with 100 beds each. The price of a Trident nuclear submarine equals the annual cost of sending 16 million children to school in underdeveloped countries, or the cost of building 400 000 homes for 2 million people. The money spent on a modern tank could pay for the construction of 1 000 classrooms for 30 000 children in Third World countries.

In the countries of Asia, Africa and Latin America, 5.9 per cent of the Gross National Product is invested in weapons and military expenditures, whereas 1 per cent is allotted to public health and 2.8 per cent to education. The average military expenditures of the poorest countries – whose per caput income is below $200 a year – nearly equals their total investment in agriculture. A mere 1 per cent of the military expenditures of the developed countries could solve the existing deficit in international financial assistance for increasing food production and establishing emergency reserves.

In the underdeveloped countries as a whole there is one soldier for every 250 inhabitants and one doctor for every 3 700. According to recent estimates, the world is now spending an average of $19 300 per year for every soldier, while public expenditures for education average a mere $380 for each school-age child. For every 100 000 inhabitants in the world there are 556 soldiers and 85 doctors. The budgets of the United States and the EEC countries earmark $45 per capita to military research and $11 for health research.[5]

If the present trends in the arms race continue in the coming twenty years, the astronomical figure of $15 trillion, at current prices, will have been spent on weapons. By the year 2000, the global arms trade will have reached $100 billion a year and the world will have more than doubled the present nuclear capability to destroy mankind.

The amounts devoted to military expenditures in the world today and the extraordinary squandering of resources that the arms race implies are the most obvious expression of the absurd madness and irresponsibility of its ideologues and advocates. *The knowledge that many of the social and economic problems that afflict and oppress the majority of the human race could be considerably mitigated by using a mere fraction of the resources devoted to military expenditures for the noble aims of progress and well-being for the peoples cannot but evoke a feeling of disbelief and indignation in all honest minds.*

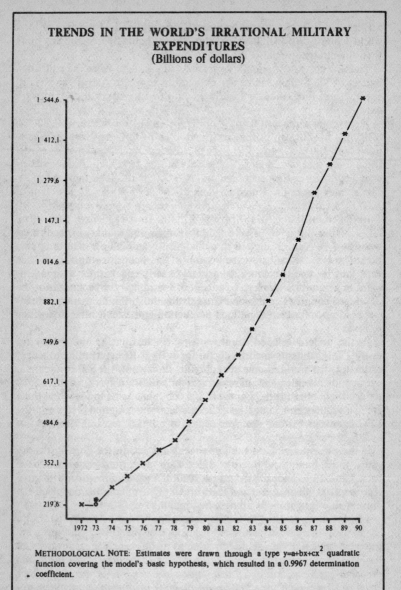

TRENDS IN THE WORLD'S IRRATIONAL MILITARY EXPENDITURES
(Billions of dollars)

METHODOLOGICAL NOTE: Estimates were drawn through a type $y=a+bx+cx^2$ quadratic function covering the model's basic hypothesis, which resulted in a 0.9967 determination coefficient.

SOURCE: Based on SIPRI *Yearbook*, several issues; OECD, *Main Economic Indicators*, December 1982.

According to an UNCTAD survey,

> the arms race means a continued and increasing detraction of scarce resources – both human and material – while the most pressing needs of many peoples remain unmet. At present, the developing countries' per caput income averages 12 - 13 times lower than in the developed countries. Some 570 million people in the developing countries are malnourished; 800 million adults are illiterate; 250 million children do not attend school; 1.5 billion have little or no access to medical care. In addition, there is little chance that the situation may improve significantly by the end of the century. Even in the most developed countries economically, there are millions of people whose standard of living is below the official poverty line. Giant resources are needed to solve such global problems as food, energy, raw material and environment.[6]

Moreover, what sense does it make to speak of strategic nuclear balance, of military security, of participation in the political life of the community to the hungry, the dispossessed, the sick, the ignorant, to those who have been deprived of opportunity or even of hope? Let us not forget that world peace – the peoples' main concern – will not be attained unless a solution is found to the dramatic situation of billions of human beings whose lives are reduced, in the best of cases, to the daily struggle for mere survival.

Along with the danger posed by the arms race, there looms the tragic reality of genocide by omission that mankind perpetrates day by day in dooming millions of human beings to death merely by devoting such huge resources to developing alternate means to kill them.

Military expenditures, wars and weapons are phenomena promoted and developed by the capitalist system and the imperialist policy of aggression and intimidation. The struggle against such irrational and dangerous expressions of that policy is today one of the most urgent actions facing all mankind and, particularly, the peoples of the underdeveloped world, who are among those most directly affected by war and the arms race.

In economic terms alone, the possibilities that disarmament could open for the development of our peoples are clearly positive. All projections indicate that at the present pace, the arms race would have violently negative effects on general economic well-being throughout the world, with almost no exception. In the underdeveloped countries as a whole, it would worsen the already desperate situation of the enormous masses of the dispossessed and the exploited. On the other hand, the United Nations has estimated that disarmament could bring about a 3.7 per cent increase in the world Gross National Product up to the year 2000, among many other social and economic benefits.

Helping to transform this Utopia into reality is our unavoidable duty to future generations.

The absurd rationale which would seek to ensure greater security by launching this gigantic arms program, and the commensurate reaction it would entail, have paradoxically led the world to the moment of greatest peril, least security and most fragile stability in all its history, and has forced mankind to face the actual possibility of its total and final destruction. The arms race mankind faces today is, in point of fact, the most immediate and direct threat to its very survival. Stopping and reversing it is today, beyond the shadow of a doubt, the most decisive contribution to the cause of peace, the most essential and definitive goal the world has before it.

Epilogue

These facts and realities are irrefutable. Everyone must be aware that such complex and difficult problems do not have easy solutions. Our aspirations and demands clash with the lack of understanding; selfishness; colossal interests; and enormous technological, economic, military and political power of imperialism and its neo-colonialist forms and with the rigid, inexorable laws that govern that system, which has imposed brutally exploiting, unequal, asphyxiating and unjust economic relations on the Third World – relations that are even worse and more sophisticated than those of the colonial system, whose eradication following World War II gave rise to so many hopes.

We have no alternative but to struggle for recognition of our demands. We constitute the vast majority of mankind, and our rights and interests cannot continue to be trampled underfoot forever.

All the peoples in the world, without exception, are threatened, first of all, by a devastating nuclear war that could even mean the end of mankind.

If a real climate of peace and security for all States, both large and small, is not created and if the absurd arms race – which is spiraling dizzily, faster than in any other time in history – is not halted, not only will the danger of world war become a terrible reality, but it will not even be possible to dream of having the resources that are needed to meet the Third World's needs as set forth in this report. The task will be impossible if military spending is not reduced drastically.

When anyone wonders where the enormous resources that the underdeveloped countries will need in the next 20 years are going to come from, the answer is there: from the $650 billion that are spent for military purposes each year; from the fabulous figure of $15 trillion that, according to a conservative estimate, will be used in the next 20 years for such unproductive and absurd expenditures if the present growth rate continues. A third of that amount would be more than enough for our needs.

The present conditions of the world economy and its gloomy prospects should be cause for deep reflection by the rulers and the clearest thinkers

In the developed countries. The storm that is hanging over our heads will seriously affect the nations of the world. The economic backwardness, lack of financial means, severe contraction of foreign trade, hunger, unemployment and absence of even the most basic living conditions in the Third World cannot, in the long run, be beneficial to any of the developed capitalist countries. To the contrary, the positive outcome of our situation would have a favorable influence on the upsurge in world trade and would alleviate the unemployment, under-utilization of installed capacities and stagnation of their economies. It is an obvious truth that, if our economies expanded, this would help reduce the tense crisis situation that has been generated in those countries. The continuation of the exploitation that is ruining the Third World would inexorably end in ruin for all.

Broadly, the main efforts of the Movement of Non-Aligned Countries and all the other Third World countries may be summed up in the following aims:

● *To struggle tirelessly for peace, improved international relations, a halt to the arms race and a drastic reduction in military spending and to demand that a considerable part of those funds be dedicated to developing the Third World.*

● *To struggle without respite for an end to the unequal trade that depresses our real export income, shifts the cost of the inflation generated in the developed capitalist countries onto our economies and ruins our peoples; for the effective functioning of the existing commodities agreements and the signing of others; and for fulfillment of the demands on commodities contained in the Action Program for the establishment of a New International Economic Order.*

● *To struggle against protectionism, that multiplies the tariff and non-tariff barriers and hinders our export commodities' and manufactured goods' access to markets, reduces our products' competitiveness and acts as a powerful mechanism of pressure and coercion against the underdeveloped countries.*

● The enormous resources that, historically, have been taken from the Third World through unequal trade, unjust interest on debts, profits on foreign private investments, the brain drain and other forms of exploitation are much greater than the external debts contracted by the underdeveloped countries.

To struggle for the cancellation of the external debts of the large number of countries which have no real possibilities of paying them and drastically lighten the burden of debt servicing for those that, under new conditions, may be able to fulfill their commitments.

● In order to achieve an equilibrium in the underdeveloped countries' balances of payments, a massive flow of resources is needed, not only to

212

cover their deficits but also to compensate for the drop in their export earnings and to expedite development.

To struggle for emergency measures to halt or compensate for the drop in the underdeveloped countries' export earnings and other measures of direct assistance to bring about sound balances of payments – which, as has been seen thus far, cannot be achieved through more indebtedness or reductions of imports.

• *To struggle to establish a new, equitable, stable and universal international financial and monetary system whose credit and voting options reflect the needs of the various groups and categories of countries rather than the economic power of some of its members; that is capable of acting in a genuinely multilateral sense rather than in response to the pressures exerted by transnational banks or a group of capitalist powers; and that, in short, can respond in the long run in keeping with the magnitude and structural character of the underdeveloped countries' balances of payments.*

• The existence of large numbers of hungry and undernourished people in the world constitutes an affront to all mankind. A stable, permanent solution must be found for this serious problem.

To struggle, with international support, to draw up plans so that each country can meet its own needs for basic foodstuffs as much as possible: to create an awareness of the inevitable need – if we wish to end rural unaeremployment, unemployment and hunger – for profound socio-economic and structural changes, such as agrarian reforms, that will make it possible to adopt higher forms of agricultural production; and, also with international cooperation, to promote programs against erosion, desertification, deforestation and other forms of soil deterioration, also protecting the main sources of water in each country and creating new reserves through dams and other means.

An immediate solution should be found for the acute deficit in foodstuffs in certain regions of the world, by means of a considerable flow from the large world excesses, transferred in the form of donations, soft credits and sales at special prices.

It is vitally necessary to create world reserves of foodstuffs and, at the same time, to struggle against the deliberate reduction of the production of foodstuffs and their absurd destruction for commercial reasons in certain developed countries, as this is both inhuman and selfish.

• The so-called industrial redeployment, which seeks maximum profits for the transnationals by using a cheap work force, simple technologies and systems of intra-subsidiary trade, cannot meet the underdeveloped countries' legitimate needs for industrialization. Our development cannot be based on this new form of dependence, which seeks to turn us into exporters of simple manufactured goods and swindles us out of the production of equipment and capital assets.

To struggle for industrialization that responds to our interests, can be integrated with the rest of the economy and paves the way for development, and to keep the transnational corporations and foreign private investments from controlling it and from carrying out a deforming process of industrialization in the Third World.

• Our States' staunchness in the defense of their sovereignty constitutes the best code of conduct against the uncontrolled actions of the transnational corporations, which seek to impose a transnationalized model of apparent development on our countries.

To struggle in each of our countries for the adoption of measures to control and limit the activities of the transnational corporations, fully exercising our right to sovereignty over our resources, including the right to nationalize them, and keeping those corporations from applying models of investment, technology, profit remittances and consumption that are alien to the realities and needs of the underdeveloped countries.

• *To struggle resolutely for a stable and definitive solution to the Third World's energy needs, keeping in mind, in addition to oil, the joint use of other renewable sources of energy and the international economic cooperation that is absolutely necessary for their development.*

• The tragic situation of the underdeveloped world – which is aggravated by the effects of the current deep economic crisis – creates obligation for all the developed countries, and especially those that, over the centuries, have grown rich through their pitiless exploitation of the Third World.

To struggle to ensure – along with the absolutely necessary flow of substantial resources derived from the reduction of military spending and other sources – a contribution of financial, technological and human resources that will help solve the complex problems already analyzed. Many countries (including a group of underdeveloped ones) that do not have the required financial means could participate by contributing other resources, in line with their possibilities – for example, by sending doctors, engineers, planners, teachers and other technicians, either free of charge or under favorable payment conditions.

• We must make the best possible use of our vast possibilities, which include technical assistance, training and diverse forms of cooperation in the fields of health, education, agriculture, construction and other aspects of vital interest to our countries.

To struggle consistently for a solid, coherent movement of cooperation among the underdeveloped countries that should not subordinate the weaker economies to the stronger ones but rather act as an effective instrument of struggle in our collective self-defense against economic attack, in the coordination of positions for international negotiations and in the best possible joint utilization of all our resources and experiences.

• The experience we have gained in the years that have passed since the launching of the Declaration and Action Program for the establishment of a New International Economic Order enables us to clearly see its unquestionable virtues, its present limitations and its possibilities for development. Nevertheless, not a single one of its demands has been achieved thus far, nor has a real process of negotiations even been initiated, due to the negative attitude taken by the main developed capitalist countries.

To struggle to rescue and apply the most positive aspects of our demands for a New International Economic Order fighting those who attempt to water them down, and to continue calling for a process of global negotiations that would serve as a real forum for the discussion of and search for solutions to our most pressing problems.

• The transformation of international economic relations is a prerequisite for, but not a guarantee of our countries' progress.

To struggle to make all the Third World states aware of the need to promote indispensable internal structural changes and measures aimed at raising the people's standard of living, which are an inseparable part of any real process of development – especially those related to income redistribution, job creation, health, housing and education.

• Health is an essential right of all men and a responsibility of society as a whole. The data in this report show the severity of the tragic health conditions that adversely affect the vast masses of the people in the Third World. It is clear to all that the solution for this and other serious problems lies in the elimination of underdevelopment, but a lot can be done right now.

To struggle urgently to tackle the present critical situation of health in the Third World through the massive mobilization of national and international financial and human resources required. It is absolutely necessary to promote mother and child care programs, the control of communicable diseases, environmental protection, distribution of foodstuffs for children, water supply and the like. In addition, there is a crying need to extend health services, train the required technical personnel and guarantee the essential basic medicines which such conditions demand.

• The incredible backwardness of general and technical education – which is absolutely necessary for any process of real development and for the use of the great scientific and technical advances that man has made in all fields – is one of the most serious negative consequences of the Third World's underdevelopment.

To struggle firmly, with the required international assistance, to develop programs to combat illiteracy; to provide schooling for all children; to raise the levels of teaching; to train technicians and skilled personnel on a mass scale; to give our people access to a university education; and to develop the rich, age-old potentials of our peoples' cultures, combating all forms of dependence and cultural colonialism and the deformation of our cultures.

● The United Nations, through its specialized agencies – the FAO, UNESCO, WHO, UNICEF, the UNDP, UNCTAD, UNIDO, economic commissions and other regional entities – has often, in its thorough, in-depth work, reflected the extreme seriousness of the problems we have been analyzing. These studies have actually been the permanent denunciation of so much injustice, selfishness, insensitivity and lack of interest; they have also issued a permanent call to the conscience and responsibility of all mankind in the face of the incredible drama reflected by the facts set forth in this report. There is no possible substitute for this world organization, which includes all States.

To struggle to increase the prestige, authority and role of the United Nations and its specialized agencies; to give them our solid support as a majority in the struggle for peace and security for all peoples, for a fair international order and for a solution to the tragic problem of underdevelopment that adversely affects the vast majority of countries. The existence of such an organization as the United Nations, with growing solidity, influence and power, is increasingly indispensable for the future of the world.

● Lastly, the unity of all the Third World countries is absolutely necessary. The problems set forth here are common to us all, regardless of political concepts, systems of government, philosophical convictions and religious beliefs. The approach to these vital questions affecting us and the solutions we seek can and should be shared. We should also rise above the local controversies that sometimes turn us into enemies because of old disputes or intrigues, ambitions or the machinations of imperialism. Generally speaking, all are the product of the system of domination and colonial control that subjugated us for centuries. The aboliton of wars between Third World countries should be a basic law of our States and an integral part of our struggle for universal peace.

To struggle tenaciously to promote the closest possible unity in the Movement of Non-Aligned Countries and with all other Third World states. We must not allow anybody or anything to divide us. We must use political formulas and negotiations to solve those problems which make some of our countries occasionally oppose each other. Let us form an indestructible battle line of peoples to demand recognition of our noble aspirations, our legitimate interests and our inalienable right to survive, both as Third World countries and as an inseparable part of mankind.

We have never been characterized by resigned submission or defeatism in the face of difficulties. We have confronted complex, difficult situations in the last few years with unity, firmness and determination. Together we have striven and struggled and together we have scored victories. In this same spirit and with this same determination, we must be ready to wage the most colossal, legitimate, worthy and necessary battle for our peoples' lives and future.

Notes

1 INTRODUCTION

[1] UN. *Informe mundial económico, 1981-82.* Retranslated from the Spanish.

[2] OECD. *Economic Outlook,* No. 32, December 1982.

[3] UNCTAD. *Handbook of International Trade and Development Statistics,* 1972. Fuels not included.

[4] *Ibid.,* 1980.

[5] FAO data.

2 THE ECONOMIC CRISIS AND ITS IMPACT ON THE UNDERDEVELOPED WORLD

[1] IMF data. *World Economic Outlook,* Washington, June 1981, p. 111.

[2] *Ibid.,* p. 112.

[3] UN. *World Economic Survey 1981-82,* New York, 1982.

[4] ECLA. "Balance preliminar de la economía latinoamericana durante 1981". Document L. 260/Rev. 1, p. 5.

[5] "Survey of Economic and Social Conditions in Africa 1980-81". Document E/ECA/CM. 8/17, p. 4.

[6] UN. *World Economic Survey 1980-81,* New York, 1981, p. 71.

[7] UN. *World Economic Survey 1981-82,* New York 1982, pp. 3-7 and 14-17.

[8] OECD. *Economic Outlook,* No. 32, December 1982, p. 5.

[9] *National Institute Economic Review,* No. 4/82, London, p. 30.

[10] OECD. Estimate of December 1982.

[11] UN. *World Economic Survey 1981-82,* New York, 1982, p. 7. Retranslated from the Spanish.

3 COMMODITIES AND OTHER TRADE PROBLEMS

[1] Data taken or estimated from GATT. *El comercio internacional 1980-81.*

[2] FAO. *Situación y perspectivas de los productos básicos 1981-82,* pp. 111, 112, 113, 114, 119, 120 and 121. Retranslated from the Spanish.

[3] ECLA. *Las relaciones económicas externas de América Latina en los años ochenta,* p. 57.

[4] UNCTAD. "La transformación de productos primarios antes de su exportación". TD/229/Sup. 1. Manila, 1979.

217

[5] Article published in the magazine *CERES*, September-October 1981, p. 25. Retranslated from the Spanish.

[6] UNCTAD. "Relación existente entre los precios de exportación y los precios de venta al consumidor de algunos productos básicos y exportados por los países en desarrollo". TD/184/Sup. 3. 1976.

[7] UNCTAD. "Dimensiones del poder de las empresas transnacionales". TD/B/Cl/219. 1981, p. 55.

[8] *Ibid.*, p. 61.

[9] *Ibid.*, p. 60. Retranslated from the Spanish.

[10] *Ibid.*, p. 92. Retranslated from the Spanish.

[11] UNCTAD. "Sistema de comercialización y distribución del banano". TD/B/Cl/162.

[12] UNCTAD. "Dimensiones del poder de las empresas transnacionales". p. 17.

[13] *Ibid.*, par. 72. Retranslated from the Spanish.

[14] "Evaluación de los resultados de las Negociaciones Comerciales Multilaterales". TD/B/778. Add. 1. February 26, 1980.

[15] ECLA. *Las relaciones económicas externas de América Latina en los años ochenta*, p. 22. Retranslated from the Spanish.

[16] *Ibid.*, p. 19.

4 MONETARY AND FINANCIAL QUESTIONS

[1] Estimated on UNCTAD data. *Handbook of International Trade and Development Statistics*. Supplement 1980, pp. 250-253.

[2] Estimated on UN data. *World Economic Survey 1981-82*, pp. 9 and 56.

[3] Estimated on World Bank data. *Informe sobre el desarrollo mundial, 1982* and IADB. *Informe anual 1981*.

[4] World Bank. *Informe sobre el desarrollo mundial 1981*, Washington, 1981, p. 69.

[5] UNCTAD. *Trade and Development Report 1981*, New York, 1981, pp. 3 and 13-14.

[6] UN. *World Economic Survey 1981-82*, p. 66.

[7] IMF. op. cit., p. 135.

5 AGRICULTURE AND FOOD

[1] FAO. *Agricultura. Horizonte 2000*, Rome, 1981.

[2] FAO. *CERES* magazine, January-February 1982.

[3] Mesarovic, Mihailo and Eduard Pestel. *La humanidad en la encrucijada*. Report to the Club of Rome, Fondo de Cultura Económica, Mexico, 1975.

[4] FAO. *CERES* magazine, May-June 1981, p. 24.

[5] *UNESCO Courier*, May 1980.

[6] FAO. *CERES* magazine, September-October 1982.

[7] FAO. *CERES* magazine, July-August 1981.

6 INDUSTRIALIZATION AND ECONOMIC DEVELOPMENT

[1] UNIDO. *La industria mundial desde 1960. Progresos y perspectivas*, 1979, pp. 81-82. Retranslated from the Spanish.

[2] *Ibid.*, p. 80. Retranslated from the Spanish.

[3] Sixth Summit Conference of the Non-Aligned Countries. *Declaración económica*. Par. 58. Havana, 1979. Italics added.

7 TRANSNATIONAL CORPORATIONS

[1] UN. *Transnational Corporations in World Development. A Re-examination*, Table II-8.

[2] *Ibid.*, Table II-32.

[3] *Ibid.*, p. 35, note 64.

[4] UNCTAD. *Handbook of International Trade and Development Statistics* 1979, p. 13.

[5] UN General Assembly resolutions 3201, 3202 and 3281.

[6] UN, ECOSOC, "Commission on Transnational Corporations". E/C. 10/1982/6. May 28, 1982.

8 THE SO-CALLED ENERGY CRISIS

[1] World Bank. *Informe sobre el desarrollo mundial 1979*, Washington, 1979, p. 43; 11th World Energy Conference. "Energy Problems of the Developing Countries", Munich, September 1980.

[2] *Perspectivas de la OCDE*, No. 27, Paris, July 1980, p. 143.

[3] OECD. *Economic Outlook*, No. 32, December 1982, p. 61.

[4] GATT. *El comercio internacional, 1975-80*, Geneva, 1980, p. 9.

[5] IMF. *World Economic Outlook 1981*, Washington, 1981, p. 128.

[6] OECD. *Economic Outlook*, No. 31, July 1982, p. 136.

[7] Estimated on *Fortune* magazine data, May issues 1973-1980.

[8] *Ibid.*, August 1981.

[9] UN. *World Economic Survey 1981-82*, New York, 1982, p. 50.

[10] OECD. *Economic Outlook*, No. 31, July 1982; UN. op. cit., p. 53.

[11] IMF. op. cit., p. 146.

9 COOPERATION AMONG UNDERDEVELOPED COUNTRIES

[1] UNCTAD. *Informe sobre el comercio y desarrollo 1981*, New York, 1982, p. 51.

[2] UNCTAD. op. cit., p. 52. Retranslated from the Spanish.

[3] GATT. *El comercio internacional, 1981-82*, Geneva, 1982. Inset 25A of Appendix.

[4] UNCTAD. "Cooperación económica entre países en desarrollo: consideraciones y datos complementarios relativos a las esferas de acción prioritaria". TD/244/Supp. 1. Manila, May 1979, p. 14.

[5] *Ibid.*

[6] ECLA. "Integración y cooperación regionales en los años 80". *Estudios e informes de la CEPAL*. No. 8, Santiago, Chile, 1982, p. 100. Retranslated from the Spanish.

[7] UNCTAD. *Informe sobre el comercio y el desarrollo 1981*, p. 53.

[8] OECD. *Development Co-Operation Review 1981*, Paris, 1981, p. 79.

10 THE QUALITY OF LIFE IN THE UNDERDEVELOPED WORLD

[1] FAO and UNESCO data and reports to the Club of Rome.

[2] Speech by Edouard Saouma, Director-General of FAO, on the occasion of 2nd World Food Day, Rome, October 16, 1982. Retranslated from the Spanish.

[3] *El estado mundial de la infancia 1981-1982*. Report by James P. Grant, UNICEF Executive-Director, New York, 1982. Retranslated from the Spanish.

11 ARMS BUILD-UP AND DEVELOPMENT

[1] *SIPRI Yearbook 1982*, London, 1982, p. 140.

[2] Ruth Leger Sivard. *World Military and Social Expenditures 1982*, p. 26.

[3] *Ibid.*, p. 9.

[4] *Ibid.*, p. 26.

[5] *Ibid.*, p. 22.

Principal sources

MOVEMENT OF NON-ALIGNED COUNTRIES

Sixth Summit Conference of Non-Aligned Countries: *Declaración Económica*, Havana, 1979.

UNITED NATIONS

Informe económico mundial 1980-81. Department of Economic and Social Affairs of the Secretariat, New York, 1981.

Informe económico mundial 1981-82. Department of Economic and Social Affairs of the Secretariat, New York, 1982.

"Transnational Corporations in World Development. A Re-examination". ECOSOC. Commission on Transnational Corporations. E/C.10/1982/6. May 28, 1982.

Statistical Yearbook 1979-80, New York, 1980.

"La croissance de l'industrie mondiale", 1969 and 1970.

Yearbook of Industrial Statistics, 1977, 1979 and 1980.

Ibid., 1979.

Ibid., 1980.

Monthly Bulletin of Statistics, 1980 and 1981.

"Estudio de la relación entre desarme y desarrollo". Report by the Secretary-General. Document A/36/356. October 5, 1981.

FOOD AND AGRICULTURE ORGANIZATION (FAO)

Agricultura: horizonte 2000, Rome, 1981.

Speech by Edouard Saouma, Director-General of the FAO, on the occasion of the 2nd World Food Day, Rome, October 16, 1982.

Situación y perspectivas de los productos básicos 1981-82, Rome, 1982.

El estado mundial de la agricultura y la alimentación. 1980, Rome, 1981.

Ibid., 1981. Rome, 1982.

Ibid., Rome, 1979.

Magnitud de las necesidades, Rome, 1981.

Carta encuesta alimentaria mundial, Rome, 1977.

Plan indicativo mundial provisional para el desarrollo agrícola, Rome, 1970.

La agricultura hacia el año 2000: problemas y opciones de América Latina, Rome, February 1981.

La agricultura hacia el año 2000. C 79/24. July 1979.

La lucha contra el hambre, Rome, undated.

"El estado mundial de la agricultura y la alimentación en 1981". Report by Director-General of FAO to the 21st Session. Document C 81/1 and Supp. 1. August and November 1981.

CERES MAGAZINE

January-February 1980, No. 73; March-April 1980, No. 74; May-June 1980, No. 75; July-August 1980, No. 76; September-October 1980, No. 77; November-December 1980, No. 78; January-February 1981, No. 79; March-April 1981, No. 80; May-June 1981, No. 81; July-August 1981, No. 82; September-October 1981, No. 83; November-December 1981, No. 84; January-February 1982, No. 85; May-June 1982, No. 87; July-August 1982, No. 88; September-October 1982, No. 89.

UNITED NATIONS EDUCATIONAL, SCIENTIFIC AND CULTURAL ORGANIZATION (UNESCO)

Estadísticas de educación. Most recent year available. Paris, November 1981.

Anuario estadístico 1981. Paris 1981.

UNESCO COURIER

June and October 1976; March, April and July 1977; February 1978; April 1979; May and September 1980; February, April and October 1981; May and June 1980.

UNITED NATIONS CHILDREN'S FUND (UNICEF)

Estado mundial de la infancia. 1981-1982. Executive Director's Report, New York, 1982.

Annual Report 1982, New York, 1982.

The State of the World's Children, 1980, New York, 1980.

Informe general del Director Ejecutivo sobre la marcha de los trabajos. Document E/ICEF/681. April 24, 1981.

Report of the executive Board. Document E/ICEF/685. May 1981.

UNICEF News, No. 113, 1982. New York, 1982.

WORLD HEALTH ORGANIZATION (WHO)

World Health Statistics Annual. 1980, Geneva, 1980.

Sixth Report on the World Health Situation. 1973-77, Geneva, 1980.

Estrategia mundial de salud para todos en el año 2000, Geneva, 1981.

SALUD MUNDIAL MAGAZINE

February-March, May and July 1977; August-September 1980; January, February-March 1981; April 1982.

UNITED NATIONS CONFERENCE ON TRADE AND DEVELOPMENT (UNCTAD)

Handbook of International Trade and Development Statistics. 1972, New York, 1972.

Ibid., 1979. New York, 1979.

Ibid., 1980. New York, 1980.

Ibid., 1981 and Supplement. New York, 1981.

Document. UNCTAD/TDR/2 (Vol. 2).

Document TD/229/Supp. 1. "La transformación de productos primarios antes de su exportación". Manila, 1979.

Document TD/184/Supp. 3. "Relación existente entre los precios de exportación y los precios de venta al consumidor de algunos productos básicos exportados por los países en desarrollo". 1976.

Document TB/B/C. 1/219. "Dimensiones del poder de las empresas transnacionales". 1981.

Document TD/B/C.1/162. "Sistema de comercialización y distribución del banano".

Document TD/B/778/Add. 1. "Evaluación de los resultados de las negociaciones comerciales multilaterales". February 25, 1980.

Trade and Development Report 1981, New York, 1982.

"Cooperación económica entre países en desarrollo. Consideraciones y datos complementarios relativos a las esferas de acción prioritarias". Document TD/244/Supp. 1. p. 24. Manila, May 1979.

UNITED NATIONS INDUSTRIAL DEVELOPMENT ORGANIZATION (UNIDO)

La industria mundial desde 1960. Progresos y perspectivas, Vienna, 1979.

ECONOMIC COMMISSION FOR LATIN AMERICA (ECLA)

Las relaciones económicas externas de América Latina en los años ochenta, Santiago de Chile, 1981.

"Balance preliminar de la economía latinoamericana durante 1981". ECLA/L. 260/Rev. 1.

"Integración y cooperación regionales en los años 80", in *Estudios e informes de la CEPAL,* No. 8, Santiago, Chile, 1982.

ECONOMIC COMMISSION FOR AFRICA (ECA)

"Survey of Economic and Social Conditions in Africa. 1980-1981". E/ECA/CM.8/17.

GENERAL AGREEMENT ON TARIFFS AND TRADE (GATT)

International Trade 1980-81, Geneva, 1981.

El comercio internacional en 1979-80, Geneva, 1980.

INTERNATIONAL MONETARY FUND (IMF)

Informe anual 1982.

World Economic Outlook, Washington, June 1981.

International Financial Statistics, Washington, May 1978 and May 1982.

ORGANIZATION FOR ECONOMIC CO-OPERATION AND DEVELOPMENT (OECD)

Economic Outlook, No. 30, December 1981; No. 31, July 1982; No. 32, December 1982.

Concentration et politique de concurrence, 1979.

Development Co-Operation Review, Paris 1981.

Main Economic Indicators, April 1982 and December 1982.

WORLD BANK

Informe sobre el desarrollo mundial 1981, Washington, 1981.

World Development Report 1982, Washington, 1982.

Informe anual 1980, Washington, 1980.

Annual Report 1982, Washington, 1982.

INTER-AMERICAN DEVELOPMENT BANK (IDB)

Informe anual 1981.

Informe anual 1979.

STOCKHOLM INTERNATIONAL PEACE RESEARCH INSTITUTE (SIPRI)

World Armaments and Disarmament. SIPRI Yearbook 1982.

"Armaments or Disarmament". SIPRI Brochure 1982, London, 1982.

World Armaments and Disarmament. SIPRI Yearbook 1981. London, 1981.

"¿Armamentos o desarme?" SIPRI Brochure 1981, London, 1981.

CLUB OF ROME

Peccei, Aurelio. *Testimonio sobre el futuro.* Taurus, Madrid, 1981.

Meadows, Dorella *et al. Los límites del crecimiento.* Report to the Club of Rome. Fondo de Cultura Económica, Mexico, 1981.

Mesarovic, Mihailo and Eduard Pestel. *La humanidad en la encrucijada.* 2nd report to the Club of Rome. Fondo de Cultura Económica, Mexico, 1975.

Peccei, Aurelio. *La calidad humana.* Taurus, Madrid, 1977.

Timbergen, Jan *et al. Reshaping the International Order.*
A report to the Club of Rome, Dutton, New York, 1976.

US GOVERNMENT SOURCES

The Global 2000 Report to the President. A Report Prepared by the Council on Environment Quality and the Department of State. Washington, 1980.

Economic Report to the President, 1982.

Survey of Current Business, August 1980 and August 1981.

World Indices of Agricultural and Food Productions. US Department of Agriculture. Washington, July 1981.

US Exports. US Department of Commerce. Washington, September-December 1981.

OTHER SOURCES

Sivard, Ruth Leger. *World Military and Social Expenditures 1982,* World Priorities, Leesburg, 1982.

National Substitute Economic Review, National Institute of Economic and Social Research, London.

11th World Energy Conference. "Energy Problems of the Developing Countries. Round Table Discussion Papers", Munich, September 1980.

World Wheat Facts and Trends. Report One. Centro Internacional de Mejoramiento de Maíz y Trigo. Mexico, August 1981.

National Geographic. Vol. 163, No. 1. January 1983.

Sivard, Ruth Leger. *World Military and Social Expenditures 1981.* World Priorities, Leesburg, 1981.

Bank for International Settlements. *51st Annual Report,* Basle, 1981.

IMPERIALISM TITLES FROM ZED

Bade Onimode
AN INTRODUCTION TO MARXIST POLITICAL ECONOMY
Hb and Pb

Bjorn Hettne and Magnus Blomstrom
DEVELOPMENT THEORY IN TRANSITION
The Dependency Debate and Beyond: Third World Responses
Hb and Pb

Cedric Robinson
BLACK MARXISM
Hb and Pb

Dan Nabudere
THE POLITICAL ECONOMY OF IMPERIALISM
Hb and Pb

Ben Turok
REVOLUTIONARY THOUGHT IN THE 20TH CENTURY
Hb and Pb

Susantha Goonatilake
ABORTED DISCOVERY
Science and Creativity in the Third World
Hb and Pb

V. G. Kiernan
AMERICA — THE NEW IMPERIALISM
From White Settlement to World Hegemony
Hb and Pb

LATIN AMERICAN TITLES FROM ZED

George Black
GUATEMALA: THE MAKING OF A REVOLUTION
Hb and Pb

George Black
TRIUMPH OF THE PEOPLE
The Saninista Revolution in Nicaragua
Hb and Pb

George Brizan
GRENADA: ISLAND OF CONFLICT
Hb and Pb

Teofilo Cabestrero
MINISTERS OF GOD, MINISTERS OF THE PEOPLE
Testimonies of Faith From Nicaragua
Hb and Pb

Ronaldo Munck
POLITICS AND DEPENDENCY IN THE THIRD WORLD
The Case of Latin America
Hb and Pb

Roxanne Ortiz
INDIANS OF THE AMERICAS
Self-Determination and Human Rights
Hb and Pb

Tom Barry, Beth Wood and Deb Preusch
DOLLARS AND DICTATORS
A Guide to Central America
Hb and Pb

Chris Searle
WORDS UNCHAINED
Language and Revolution in
Grenada
Hb and Pb

Latin American and Caribbean
Women's Collective
SLAVES OF SLAVES
The Challenge of Latin American
Women
Hb and Pb

Michael McClintock
THE AMERICAN CONNECTION
Vol. I State Terror and Popular
Resistance in El Salvador
Vol. II State Terror and Popular
Resistance in Guatemala
Hb and Pb

Carmelo Furci
THE CHILEAN COMMUNIST
PARTY AND THE ROAD TO
SOCIALISM
Hb and Pb

Mario Hector
DEATH ROW
Hb and Pb

Maurice Bishop
NOBODY'S BACKYARD
Maurice Bishop's Speeches
1979-1983: A Memorial Volume
Hb and Pb